The Happy Critic

W9-AWO-873

THE HAPPY CRITIC

A Serious but Not Solemn Guide
to Thinking and Writing about Literature

Harvey Birenbaum
San Jose State University

Mayfield Publishing Company
Mountain View, California
London • Toronto

Copyright © 1997 by Mayfield Publishing Company

All rights reserved. No portion of this book may be reproduced in
any form or by any means without written permission of the publisher.

Library of Congress Cataloging-in-Publication Data
Birenbaum, Harvey.
    The happy critic : a serious but not solemn guide to thinking and writing about
literature / Harvey Birenbaum.
        p.   cm.
    Includes indexes.
    ISBN 1-55934-706-6
    1. Criticism.   2. Criticism—Authorship.   I. Title.
        PN81.B5415   1996   96-23360
                                                                             CIP

Manufactured in the United States of America
10 9 8 7 6 5 4 3 2 1

Mayfield Publishing Company
1280 Villa Street
Mountain View, California 94041

Sponsoring editor, Thomas V. Broadbent; production editor, Carla L. White; text
designer, Andrew Ogus; cover designer, Jean Mailander; cover art, Tamar Haber-
Schaim; art manager, Jean Mailander; manufacturing manager, Randy Hurst. The
text was set in 9/12 Meridien by Thompson Type and printed on 50# Finch
Opaque by The Maple-Vail Book Manufacturing Group.

to Rosemary Martinez
and all the students after her
for whom our work together
mattered

Nevertheless, human life was thus image-graced and image-cursed; it could comprehend itself only through images, the images were not to be banished, they had been with us since the herd beginning, they were anterior to and mightier than our thinking, they were timeless, containing past and future, they were a twofold dream-memory and they were more powerful than we. . . .

—HERMANN BROCH, *The Death of Virgil*

CONTENTS

FREE COPY FREE COPY FREE COPY FREE COPY FREE COPY FREE COPY FREE COPY

Chapter 2
Understanding *Understanding:* How Valid Is Interpretation?   42

FREE COPY FREE COPY FREE COPY FREE COPY FREE COPY FREE COPY FREE COPY

Chapter 4

How Literature Expresses Our Reality by Making Its Own   88

PART THREE
SELF AND FORM   101

Chapter 5

Being Self-ish: How Literature Depends upon Consciousness   103

Chapter 6
A Formal View: How Literature Takes Shape   128

PART FOUR
A HAPPY STYLE   173

Chapter 7
The Critical Essay as a Literary Form   175

PREFACE

The Happy Critic is for serious students of literature—not serious-solemn, of course, but seriously interested, curious (maybe even driven) to find out what it is really all about. I have worked out in these chapters assumptions and convictions about literary study that I have grown and peddled during thirty years of teaching. These assumptions also lie behind the few books that I've written before, which, for the most part, have also come out of my work in the classroom. Here I have recorded many points I often make in class, and I have explained, more fully than I usually can while teaching, what I mean by them and how they fit together. I hope that this picture of literary study will help students to clarify their own assumptions about the subject and to think out more explicitly what literature means to them.

Since the later days of my graduate studies, I have generally followed an approach to literary criticism based primarily upon what has been called the philosophy of symbolism, or symbolic theory. Since *symbolism* means too many things and these terms remain vague, I suggest *symbolistics* as a less-than-lovely name for this approach. My own slant I think of as *symbolic ontology*, drafting a philosophical term for the study of being. The most important key to understanding literature has been, for me, thinking about the kinds of reality that are created by the "symbolic forms" of literature and then seeing in turn how this symbolic reality relates to our own more obviously real being.

The authors on symbolic theory who have influenced this view are not particularly popular among critics these days. I recommend them to you: Ernst Cassirer, Susanne Langer, Kenneth Burke, Philip Wheelwright, and Northrop Frye. To anyone who likes thinking about literature and the happy activity of teaching it, I would also like to recommend the chemist-philosopher Michael Polanyi. His chief book, *Personal Knowledge,* explores the view that learning and knowing are personal activities in which we participate (entering into what we know) in a spirit that he pleasantly calls "conviviality." This is a view that I share.

I hope that, through most of the following book, I have kept these broader concepts discreetly in the background, without putting too great a stress upon them. Although much of what I have to say may not be very original, I have assembled and blended ideas that I think need to be seen together and recalled amid the present atmosphere of literary criticism. I have tried to cover many of the topics that are commonly explained in the various good anthologies and other textbooks on interpreting literature. However, I have tried to present them in contexts that should suggest a more integral view of things, a view which follows from my assumptions about the symbolic nature of all writing.

My arrangement of topics may warrant some defense, or at least apology. In particular, readers will find important subjects distributed between Chapters 5 and 6 on "self" and "form." The division may—but also should—seem arbitrary, especially when I treat tragedy under "self" and romance under "form." The discussion of poetic rhythm comes under "form," although it extends the discussion in Chapter 3 on literary language; actually, it too might have been covered under "self" as one of the ways we express and experience ourselves in language. My point is that form *is* experiential and that the literary sense of self must be known in modes of form; and, further, that in imaginative literature consciousness takes form, inevitably, in language. I offer these relationships as a basic principle of symbolism, and I offer symbolistics as a way of understanding that unity. Nevertheless, I hope it will be clear in context why I am treating each topic from the perspective I have chosen for it. Any single aspect of symbolic form, like anything else, needs to be discussed by itself. It needs to be understood, however, as part of the whole. It can most clearly be related to the whole, I suggest, from one perspective or another, in terms of that dimension of the whole: tragic form under "self," and so forth. Perhaps the arbitrary separation will itself be meaningful as well as convenient. I have most often drawn my examples from works that are commonly taught. If they are not familiar to students, they are easily accessible. Other examples will be, perhaps, enticements.

Because I have wanted this book to be relatively informal, I have kept the footnotes few most of the time, minimizing, I am afraid, my intellectual debts. Although the MLA (Modern Language Association) documentation technique has been made standard for English studies and instructors are likely to expect it, I have followed the more traditional University of Chicago Press style. In the final chapter, I provide an outline of both the MLA and Chicago styles. My own notes offer additional examples of the latter; an example of MLA form appears in the sample research paper at the end of the book.

The Index of Terms inside the front cover points students to the major discussion of each literary term, where the term itself appears in boldface.

When I was in high school, I happened to read a book called (if I am not mistaken) *An Introduction to Literature* by a professor with the engaging name of Ernest Earnest, a name that inspired confidence. I was excited to see how much could be understood about the ways in which literature works, and that excitement has lasted over forty years now. I am not aware of any book like it nowadays. That is probably because we do not have any consensus about these matters—if that is not an understatement of the case—and also because there are more than enough excellent anthologies that lay out the basics concisely amid their selected readings. Nevertheless, I hope this book can serve for readers now, in more complicated times, the function that Professor Earnest's book served for me in my young days. I hope that some readers will discover how very interesting it can be to consider the workings of literature, and what a happy pursuit that can be. If these workings seem at times all too intricate, that may be, I think, because of the marvellous intricacy with which *we* work, in all the aspects of human being. At a time when technology excites such enthusiasm, we must remember the richness of sensibility and the language that understands it. When communication and information are as inescapable as they are unprofound, we have a special need to see things sincerely, with depth, urgency, and good cheer.

I am extremely grateful to my editor, Tom Broadbent, for his enthusiasm and tolerance. Carla White saw the book through production with intelligence and discretion.

The Happy Critic

Introduction

Toward Subjective Accuracy

One of the most basic educational values in our culture is objectivity. From the earliest grades, we are taught to learn about the world as detached observers. We are taught to see ourselves as others see us. We are taught to acquire as much information as we can and to understand the relationship among facts. Everything we examine we are encouraged to comprehend as it is in itself: organisms, galaxies, wars, and ideas. In our new "Information Age," we will have everything we need, at our fingertips, on our computers.

There is a considerable body of thought, however, that argues we cannot know anything *in itself*, but only as the human mind *can know*, only, in fact, as our own minds in our own culture can know. Many philosophically-minded people believe that we cannot really *know* anything, we can only have our own ideas about what we take to be the case. Nor can we come to any kind of consensus, but only share and compare impressions. All "knowledge," in this view, is merely subjective.

It is not surprising that teachers of literature have often favored one of these approaches or the other. Needing to give grades, we require something fairly clear-cut to measure. Wanting to reassure our students, we acknowledge that there is something clearly recognizable that good students of literature

1

can learn. Eager to seem as intellectually respectable as the scientists and historians—and as self-confident about what we are doing—we like to rely on a methodology that can be described clearly in abstract terms, with results that will seem undeniably concrete. Or, tired of coaxing students to see what feels like self-evident truth, we invite all responses, focusing on the reading rather than on the poem, on the student's mind rather than the poet's. Interpretation becomes a process of exploring, not the arrival at a right place, and virtually any response becomes valid. Perhaps we most often try to play from both sides at once, pragmatically ignoring the fact that they represent irreconcilable attitudes, each set to resist the other.

This book takes a third position. It seems to me that the other two are both based on the same fallacy (or very limiting assumption) at the basis of our whole culture: what is called subject-object dualism. The two familiar views oppose each other because they are two sides of the same coin. Our usual conception of knowledge assumes essentially that we are subjective minds somehow inside an objective world. We can look either outward to the world or inward to ourselves. Yet culture itself, our very mode of knowing, is neither inside nor out. We are in our culture as it is in us. It is a world that we live, and as we live it, it is a world that we are. We know it as experience, so it is subjective; but what we experience comes to us from others. Among the various dimensions of culture, however, literature (along with the other arts) allows us to communicate experience and to transform it into a special kind of aesthetic reality. It must, therefore, have a degree of, a kind of, reliability.

If this is true about literature, it is also true about that extension of literary experience called criticism. Our knowledge about the literary realm may not be precise in an objective sense, but we can know it with a kind of fallible truthfulness, as we discover in it a recognizable sensitivity. Such knowledge is more slippery than scientifically verifiable data, but it is rich with the infinitely subtle texture of living. Such knowledge, therefore, is true to our own being as it is true to the life in the poems, the plays, and the works of fiction that embody the qualities, predicaments, and triumphs of living.

Who Is the Happy Critic?

Dealing with literature engages one's whole personality, including one's sense of what is real and what is important in life. Authors worth studying generally create their work in this spirit; if we want to deal honestly with the results, we do likewise. If we write critical essays either as mechanical exercises—objectively analyzing data—or simply as records of our private impressions, we trivialize, I believe, both literature and life. If we read well, we recognize the urgency with which authors write and know that this urgency is essential to the significance of the work. If we ourselves do not write out of a similar sense of urgency, caring about the work because it has delighted or moved us (or annoyed that it has imposed upon us unfairly), then our writing is inauthentic. We have betrayed our own response.

For the "happy critic," thinking and writing about literature is a meaningful and intense part of life. It is a natural extension of reading pleasure, extending the (relatively) passive literary experience into active, creative expression. Writing about literature can be literature too, touched perhaps with the sense of greatness to which the critic responds. Of course, composing essays involves hard work, sometimes excruciatingly hard, and we may be writing about painful subjects, but if we write as we care, we are happy in the meaningful engagement of our minds with texts that we have enjoyed reading. We are "happy" because our work is alive. We have a reasonable chance, then, of engaging a reader for our own words. In our essay, a vision may emerge that can strike someone else with our own living presence.

The "happy critic," then, takes the task of criticism as serious pleasure, a pleasure that involves one's self-awareness, one's sense of reality as a human being in the world, one's passion to know the features of life and art, one's friendly capacity to mingle with other minds. Such pleasure includes frustrations, difficulties, and uncertainties, but it comes from dealing honestly with the richness of literature. It reflects the excitement of reading with satisfaction as one grasps the nature and significance of what one has read.

This Book, Therefore

This book, as I say in the preface, is meant to help the student who has undertaken the serious study of literature—not serious-solemn, as I put it, but serious in the sense that one truly cares to find out what such study is all about. You have already found in novels and other literary works, I hope, something that speaks to you in a way that matters. Now you may want to feel more at home in the study of literature, comfortable among stylistic nuances, involutions of characterization, the tricky rhythms of verse, the strategies of stagecraft, and even the critics' various ways of being merrily obsessed with analysis. You need to write essays, but you want your essays to sound as though you care and as though you know what you are talking about.

The Happy Critic, therefore, attempts a fairly deep picture of what literary experience is like. This may not seem like such a good idea for a book that is offering itself as an introduction to an academic discipline. (Let's have a little academic discipline around here!) However, I believe that clarifying one's assumptions about what literature is and how it operates should help make literary study more happily meaningful. Perhaps you will see that some of the assumptions you've been working from have made the official study of literature harder and less interesting than it needs to be.

Of course, some students of literature will be teaching it themselves some day, and it is especially important for teachers to have their values and their intentions straight. Teachers ought to know why they are teaching, in what spirit their subject is to be taken, what *they* mean to convey about the process of studying it. If education is not just acquiring data, it is establishing and clarifying a personal relationship to the world—to our interlayered world, in fact, of nature, of culture, of other people, and of our own being. The coherent study of literature provides, in fact, a model for this larger process.

In this book, then, my main concern has been to envision both reading literature and writing about it as more than just mechanical processes: examinations of specimens, disassembly and identification of parts, extractions of meanings—or on a more sophisticated level, applications of parochial methodology. Such processes may feel safer when you are expecting a grade, and they may be easier when I am giving one. But they miss the essential relationship we have with the work. Meaning in literature depends absolutely, I insist, on the feelings it gives us, the power it has over us, the difference it makes that we have read it. The study of literature, therefore, needs to be both personal *and* valid. Good criticism expresses personal feelings, personal insight, and personal concern for others. And yet, if it is personal, it is not merely private, entirely my own opinions and my own feelings. It is also a special form of communication, one through which we can all hope our own voices will be heard and understood. It is a significant way of being personal publicly.

PART ONE
Creative Criticism

Chapter 1

Thinking about Literature

Getting Sophisticated

We study any subject to become more sophisticated about it. Literature we study not only to familiarize ourselves with good poems, novels, and other works, but also to acquire some further sophistication about how literature itself works and how it has meaning. This is sophistication not—one hopes— as overly intellectual specialization but as an ability to see things in context and in proportion, with a sense of what kind of approach is appropriate for understanding a work, as much as possible, on its own terms.[1] It should lead to a kind of trained intuition, an aware interest.

A "naive" reader thinks about a story as though it were real life, only more entertaining and agreeable (assuming it's a good story). Such a reader may prefer to read mostly about likeable, more or less familiar folks being treated fairly by life. From this viewpoint, it may seem that we should be able to talk about the characters as though they were living independently when the author came along and persuaded them into his tale.

---

1. I generally use the word "work" where many contemporary critics would say "text." When I say "text," I mean simply the words on the page; by "work" I mean the text as it comes alive to the imagination.

The sophisticated reader, on the other hand recognizes the story as an artifact crafted to achieve effects. Primary features of the story are, certainly, its characters, who are persuasive images of people, seducing us into their fictive world and the sense of their reality. We like to believe in this illusion—and we actually need to do so in order to read well. But we also know that the story as a whole is a complex imagining of pictures, events, personages, tricks, and touches—carpets to be extracted from under us and hammers to be applied delicately to our skulls. And much of this we may take in only peripherally or subliminally.

Literary criticism—which is simply the discussion of literature—pays close attention to such images and maneuvers. You are doing criticism of sorts if you just tell someone why you loved or hated a book you just read or a movie you have seen. In its more sophisticated and constructive form, however, criticism is deliberately sustained discussion meant to illuminate an art work, its make-up, and its value. Appreciation, therefore, is fundamental, in the two related meanings of the word: *appreciating*—or being glad about—*what art can do for us,* recognizing the pleasures and the revelations with due feeling (and with due annoyance at the bad stuff); and *appreciating*—or comprehending—*what art is,* understanding it *as* art, as particular achievements of skillful creativity. We know it by enjoying it; we enjoy it by recognizing its nature.

Creative Reading

We readily understand that poetry and fiction are forms of creative writing; criticism, by contrast, we know as a form of expository writing, just saying what one thinks is true. In fact, we may expect criticism to be humdrum and dreary or stuffy and pretentious, unlike delightfully imaginative writing—and all too often we may find that we're right; but criticism can be creative too, in its way, at least when you and I write it.

Compared with criticism, the poem or short story comes to us more emphatically as what it *is* than what it is *about.* For that reason, it enters our minds in an essentially *qualitative* way, through the qualities we experience directly in it, such as the sense of its form, the quality of its tone, its imaginative vision, and the particularity of its images. In Susanne Langer's term, works of art are essentially *presentational.* That is, they communicate by presenting their reality to us directly for our delectation (as do our dreams) rather than by discoursing around a subject, as I am doing at the moment.[2]

---

2. Langer contrasts presentational symbolism to the "discursive" symbolism of language. Perhaps we could speak of *discoursive* symbolism instead. It would include history, philosophy, and the sciences. Such distinctions do not need to be hard and fast: a novel, obviously, may include discourse.

How then is the critic properly creative? If creativity means, in an obvious sense, producing something that wasn't there before, we do bring forth our new essays just as the poet brings forth poems. As critics, of course, what we make allows us to reenter the world that the author has first created for us. It might be appropriate, therefore, to think of our work as being in this sense *re-creative*, keeping in mind that when we make the work over we make it also partly ours. Although we can never say enough to capture the author's vision exactly and our own perspective will never coincide fully with the author's, we can grasp a great deal of a work's substance just as truly as we can miss the boat. We should never underestimate how much we can know of what is there: Our version of a poem can be very pointedly a *version* of the poem.

However, simply producing something new is not the only thing we may mean by creativity. Our world is bombarded with new products (including new forms of "entertainment") that are exactly the opposite of creative, as original as they may be. When we strive foremost for something unheard of, we settle for freaks. When we remain aware of what is human about us, true individuality should follow. Thus, we feel creative and we write creatively when we enter into the process of composition with our personalities reasonably intact, with intelligence following our feelings, with our enthusiasm building knowledge. We enter into the text by participating in its spirit, enjoying the vitality of communication, within our times or over the ages. Then we want our writing, quite naturally, to capture that spirit in the vein of our own style, in the presence of our own minds at work, so we can picture readers participating in our own intelligent concern.

Seeing What's Happening

The first requirement of good reading is shrewd observation. We need to pay attention to exactly what we see, hear, feel, suspect, and smell. Our author is likely to be a very sharp observer to begin with, providing us with a world of detailed features and nuances that reflect a keen sensitivity to living. We recognize that the details are selected (or created) deliberately and follow patterns that the details fall into. The observant eye is the appreciative eye, taking it all in but also making connections. The more fully and vividly we see, the more we involve ourselves in the work. In our criticism we reflect upon that involvement. Similarly, we enjoy a vacation to the extent that we let ourselves be *there*, alert to an unfamiliar landscape; and to that degree we have all the more to write home about, or record in a journal, when we stop to think about what we've seen.

The "landscape" of the literary world certainly includes the countryside or cityscape, the bedroom or factory that provides the setting. Also, it includes the population, which may be the lone poet ruminating in memory or it may be a family, the crew of a ship, or a small sampling of society living in a village. The data we observe will consist of how the "natives" look and talk, but also how they feel, how they experience themselves and one another, how they experience being in their world. And, of course, it will include what exactly they are up to: what they do to themselves, what they do to one another, and what nature, gods, and history do to them as well.

We observe what is said, what is shown, what is enacted, but also what is subtly suggested or implied. These are facts of the story too, these implications. An event may very well be ambiguous, not simply because the author wants us to decide the matter for ourselves, but because that's the way things are—like the ending of Hemingway's story "The Short Happy Life of Francis Macomber," where Mrs. M. may or may not have meant to shoot her husband and may or may not have known herself what she meant to do. What we need to observe in such a case is the actual balance of uncertainty; we take the ambiguity seriously.

We need to observe, then, the images and events in a work and also the feelings that these images and events evoke. All of the particular effects the work produces add up to its **impact,** that very particular way in which it moves, delights, enlightens, or enrages us, drawing us into its world to make us care about it one way or another. We realize that its impact is the cumulative effect of all its characteristics—the way voices, ideas, styles, images, and associations all interact simultaneously and continuously. Most importantly, impact is, as the word suggests, the way it all "hits us."

One of the most important features of the work that we will want to observe is its **tone,** for it is through tone that we are allied to the author's world most meaningfully. Tone is the quality of consciousness that the author adopts. Like the tone of voice with which one speaks, it conveys attitude and feeling. It may come through a narrative voice, a lyric poet's mood, the spirit with which characters are characterized (such as pathos or ridicule) and with which places are described. Primarily (and I do mean "primarily" because I am certainly simplifying things to make my point), tone has two sets of poles: *attraction-repulsion* and *gravity-levity:*

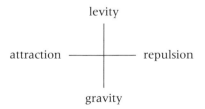

That is to say, we are made to like or dislike characters and situations to different degrees; and our attitudes are made to be more playful or more painful (or an ambiguous blend). Thus we hate and love in more comic and more tragic veins, with all sorts of possibilities among delight, despair, grief, and outrage. An essential part of observation, then, is *gauging the tone,* as we try to find words that can account accurately for what we feel when we read. Sometimes a fairly easy word may sum it up: bitter, pathetic, sentimental, satiric, hilarious. Often we can be more accurate by drawing on a wider vocabulary that pinpoints some specific mood: sardonic, meditative, morose, somber, ludicrous, titillating. Very often we will need to discuss our impressions before we feel we have got it just right. More importantly, the tone of a work lies in the particular attitude toward life that it expresses. Each story, play, or poem is a way of experiencing life and, therefore, a view of what life is all about, what it feels like, with what understanding life is most appropriately to be lived. As we read, we recreate the tone in imagination and enter into these feelings along the way.

To realize the sense of a work, we will want to observe the specific experience in some detail, but also we will want (and need) to give due weight to what is important. The experience includes a response to emphasis. The text focuses our attention (though we may disagree on exactly where and how) and we will want to focus ourselves accordingly, with a decent sense of proportion. You might very well write about a minor character like Hamlet's confidant Horatio, but I presume you would not try to pass him off as the hero. Rather, you would convey your sense of proportion in the way you talk about him as you explain his subsidiary function in the play. You would need, therefore, to give some sense of the whole as you discuss the part. This is one way to keep a short essay significant—on the principle that anywhere you strike the surface of the earth you can reach toward the center. Whether you write about a character, a scene, a moment of interaction, a metaphor, or a speech, you can discuss it in such a way that you bring out the spirit of the whole. Putting Horatio in his place, you show how full of Hamlet the whole play is, a verily Hamletized Denmark, fraught with his tragic tone.

Let us now look separately at four main aspects of criticism. The first is really a foundation for the others, bringing our observation firmly into an essay:

- **Representation** shows what is in the work as we experience it, describing what it is like, explaining what it *is* and how, in general, it goes about its business.

- **Interpretation,** or **commentary,** explains what issues we see the work reflecting upon, showing exactly what views it suggests about these issues.

- **Analysis** examines ways in which the work achieves its particular effects, demonstrating its technical features.

- **Evaluation** expresses our sense of the work's worth—its degree of importance or integrity or mastery.

In full-fledged critical studies, all or most of these aspects are likely to operate together, as in intelligent reading they should take place at least subliminally in one natural process. Critical essays, however, may very well emphasize either commentary or analysis. In the rest of this chapter, we will cover each of these four aspects in turn, our main question being: How can we see each aspect of criticism in a creative spirit so that we can want to do it and can do it therefore in a way that is meaningful and gratifying?

Representation

Your reader needs to know what you are talking about, and you need to keep the work alive as you are discussing it. What I am calling **representation** is simply description, showing fairly and clearly what the work is and what it is like. You may want to first describe the work, then go ahead and discuss it. You may start with a brief account, then add to it as you go along. Or your representation may emerge as a running thread through your discussion. This is the most flexible method, and of course the hardest to describe, since how you go about it will depend on what your case requires and what your text provides. At any rate, it is almost always helpful to represent before you discuss. What and whom are you talking about? What kind of work, what kind of action, what kind of character, what kind of world? For examples of integrating representation smoothly into a discussion, see the samples from my students starting on page 16.

In practice, representation may involve or overlap with paraphrase, summary, or explication. You may be asked to compose one of these as an exercise, like doing piano scales. **Paraphrase** "retells" the work in detail but in different words. **Summary** condenses, leaving out details but showing what is interesting and unique about it. **Explication,** which means unfolding, or working out the implications, is a technical term for a detailed literal explanation. It takes us well into both interpretation and analysis.

Addressing a Poem: An Illustration

We can clarify these distinctions by applying them to Edwin Arlington Robinson's poem "Richard Cory":

RICHARD CORY

Whenever Richard Cory went down town,
We people on the pavement looked at him:
He was a gentleman from sole to crown,
Clean favored, and imperially slim.

And he was always quietly arrayed,
And he was always human when he talked;
But still he fluttered pulses when he said,
"Good morning," and he glittered when he walked.

And he was rich—yes, richer than a king—
And admirably schooled in every grace:
In fine, we thought that he was everything
To make us wish that we were in his place.

So on we worked, and waited for the light,
And went without the meat, and cursed the bread;
And Richard Cory, one calm summer night,
Went home and put a bullet through his head.

Notice that the following paraphrase reproduces the poem's own perspective, from inside, speaking as its speaker does. The representation, on the other hand, would come from your perspective as reader, observing the piece and describing it, as you would describe anything else you have experienced. Notice also just how much detail you may need in order to account for the experience accurately. When you represent any communication, you want to be fair by getting, as well as you can, what has actually been said, which is likely to be quite specific.

Paraphrase Richard Cory drew a good deal of attention whenever he appeared in town. We saw in him a complete gentleman with ideal appearance. He was modest in his dress and in his manner, which was kindly towards others. Nevertheless, people were excited by his greeting, and he seemed to gleam as he passed among us. He was extremely wealthy and genteel. In short, he was exactly what we wished we could be. In this way, we went on with our humdrum existence, bitter about our relative poverty. Meanwhile, Richard Cory shot himself to death one peaceful night.

Representation Edwin Arlington Robinson's poem "Richard Cory" dramatizes the chasm between the common view of a public figure and that person's experience of his own life. We see how the people of a town regarded a local socialite and judged themselves according to their feelings about him. This man, Richard Cory, is described by someone who speaks for the locals, while expressing the feelings that he or she shared with the others. They had envied Cory for his wealth, but also for his gentlemanly bearing and social poise. Most of all, however, they were struck by the simple humanity with which he treated them: They seemed touched that he was not spoiled by his wealth and position. Nevertheless, his presence seemed to make them aware of what their own lives lacked and to increase their dissatisfaction. The poem ends abruptly as the speaker notes, without any logical connection or any comment, that Cory committed suicide "one calm summer night." Apparently, the townspeople were shocked at the disparity between their image of the man and the reality of his private existence. The poem tells this story in a sequence of four four-lined stanzas, in a very simple language suggestive of a fairy tale or nursery rhyme.

Explication would describe the people and summarize the events but it would also observe and explain the images of royalty (commenting on the ambiguous word "crown"), and it would explain the quality of understatement, particularly in the omission of logical connections. *Commentary* would work out implications in the poem's silence. It might discuss the process by which people judge themselves through their assumptions about others. It would conjecture about the reasons for Cory's death: Are they implied in the poem? Have people admired him for qualities that might have destroyed him? It would avoid a moralistic conclusion that money does not bring happiness. What else do we feel was true of him that should have made him happy but could not? *Analysis* would show how the techniques of the poet relate to the poem's theme. It might comment on the parallel sentence form, showing how it expresses a sense of awe and how the cumulative style changes abruptly into the direct, bald statement of Cory's death. Analysis might describe the way in which the contrast between Cory and his admirers strikes the reader, as it develops *their* sense of reality only to superimpose upon it the implied reality of *his* life. It might show how the poem develops through indirect means the portrait of the man whom we do not hear speaking for himself. *Evaluation* might raise the questions of sentimentality and sensationalism. Does Cory take his life because he is weak, merely because he is lonely—and if so, are we asked unfairly to admire his weaknesses? (We are not evaluating the character but the poem.) Does the shock ending seem superficial and melodramatic? Are the verse rhythms simplistic or is their simplicity justified?

Using Representation

Good representation provides support for commentary and analysis, and it has further virtues:

- *Representation gives us material to work with.* Seeing more fairly and more precisely what is there, we are likely to have more to say about it. Whatever we observe is data or evidence on which to build a case. The better we account for what we experience, therefore, the more raw material we have to draw upon for extended discussions.

- *It helps us think.* Describing something moves us naturally into discussing it, often imperceptibly. If you get stuck sometimes as you write, try quoting a passage related to what you have just said, then paraphrasing it, then explaining what you have shown. The process of putting experience in words has us already thinking. With our mental energy now in action, we may persuade ourselves the more easily to just keep going.

- *It engages us in the work.* As we recall the work vividly, we return to our feelings about it, so we are more likely to write out of a real sense of its effect upon us. We are therefore more likely to be interested ourselves in what we have to say and more eager to communicate our insights. Imagination and intelligence are stirred together.

- *It keeps us honest.* You may find it tempting to elaborate upon loose ideas based upon vague impressions or go off in a direction suggested by some idea about an idea. If criticism is interaction with the text, however, then that kind of procedure is something else. It is also likely to be unnecessarily hard labor and quite possibly boring. Having a vivid sense of the work reminds us of what caught us up as we first read, and that should make us more inclined to expatiate upon it. At the same time, it obliges us to talk about it with some sense of responsibility, making our writing more realistic and presumably, therefore, more convincing. As we think and as we write, we try to develop our views to fit what we take to be the case. If we give ourselves a sharp picture of what we see, we test the "fit" as we go along. Our readers then can also have a fair chance of judging our reliability, of seeing where we are coming from and understanding how we have come where we are. At the same time, we show them why the work deserves attention in the first place.

In short, good representation sees to it that we stay *grounded* as we write. It keeps the work present in our discussion, with a sense of its concrete and lively spirit. If we convey that spirit, rather than just disembodied thoughts, our writing should be clearer and it should mean more. It should also be easier to enjoy (for both writer and reader) because the discussion will move along more naturally and perhaps, therefore, more vigorously as well.

Interpretation

People sometimes think of **interpretation** as "analyzing meanings" or digging out hidden messages. Such an expectation is all too likely to set us against the text, as though it were an obstacle we need to overcome. How can we think of interpretation in a happier, more friendly spirit?

Basically, interpretation is laying out one's comprehension of the material at hand: Here is what I gather is going on, and what I take it all to be about. And along with clear observation comes comprehension (literally, "grasping together"), as we take in the situation, recognizing the movement of the

REPRESENTATION INTEGRATED IN SOME STUDENTS' ESSAYS

A Lamb in Tiger's Clothing

. . . I had never read any of Adrienne Rich's poems before I stumbled upon "Aunt Jennifer's Tigers," but I knew that the symbolic importance of the main image of the tigers would resonate through the poem. I didn't know anything about Rich, but I knew that here was a poem deserving of deeper thematic investigation.

The main image is a simple one: the speaker's Aunt Jennifer has sewn a picture of some tigers against a green background, and the speaker sees the tigers as being very brave and independent, very regal. She says in the first stanza that the tigers "do not fear the men beneath the tree" that must also be in the panel she has sewn.

It occurs to the reader after the first stanza that the tigers are representative of something about Aunt Jennifer. The title, the tigers' contrast as "bright topaz denizens" to the "world of green," and the suggestion that the animals do not fear men and pace with certainty all appear to have some import in describing not just the tigers but Jennifer herself. As early as the beginning of the second stanza, we are led to believe that the tigers are representative of Jennifer's personality, of her individuality. And since we have no other information to go on, we take the information about Jennifer on faith, that the tigers symbolize her strong will.

The second stanza is in sharp contrast to the first in that it provides a very different look at Aunt Jennifer. . . . —*Ian Oeschger*

A Woman's View

Poets often find it more effective to express a theme through a persona or speaker. Poets who are especially perceptive and sensitive can speak through characters with whom they have little or nothing in common. In his lovely poem "Wedding-wind," Philip Larkin reveals an extraordinary understanding of a woman's heart and mind, enabling him to successfully illustrate his theme of the paradoxical connection between sublime content and its ever-present companion, gnawing anxiety.

The speaker in "Wedding-wind" is a bride who is reflecting on her turbulent emotions. The setting is her husband's farm, where the couple apparently went soon after the wedding. In the first part of the poem, the woman is looking back upon the previous night, her wedding night. A strong storm is passing through and when her husband is forced to go out and close a loose stable door, she can only sit in a stupor, awaiting his return. At this point there is no clear indication of what the speaker is feeling, aside from a sense of an underlying anxiety suggested by her comment that she has waited "stupid in candlelight." She then states that when her husband returned and told her the horses were restless, she felt sad that not every living creature was as happy as she. We are given now our first sign of the intense happiness that she is actually feeling. She is happy and sad at the same time, underscoring the discordant nature of her feelings. —*Laura Walsh*

Death Is the Mirror of Life

. . . Leo Tolstoy's "The Death of Ivan Ilyich" is a powerful story about a man who thinks that his life has been perfect only to come to the horrifying realization on his deathbed that it has, in fact, been only a mockery. Ivan Ilyich, a middle-class man, emulates the upper-class ideals of right and wrong. . . . The main satisfaction he gets out of life is not love, adventure, or any such thing, but simply making his life run as smoothly, conveniently, and decorously as possible. Interruptions to this harmony, such as the death of two of his children and his wife's discontentment, are nuisances, and he either ignores them or takes care of them quickly and distastefully, so that his life may continue on its uneventful course. Ivan Ilyich, it seems, has made a career out of moderation and unobtrusiveness. He marries Praskovya Fedorovna because it is considered by his friends "the right thing" to do; he doesn't like to win large sums of money at cards because it could arouse antipathy, which would disrupt the evening. And yet, by his very focus on making his life as placid as possible, he has lost track of what life really means. By suppressing his spontaneous impulses, he saps the vitality of his life. By avoiding unpleasantness, he makes its joys lackluster. A person cannot truly hate someone he has never loved, a person cannot experience ecstatic joy if he has never felt deep sorrow. Ivan Ilyich cannot understand his death because he never truly understood his life. And because he does not understand death, he resists it, increasing his agony still more. . . . —*Karen Lynn Estensen*

(continued)

e. e. Cummings: Rebel Poet

. . . Always searching for different approaches, Cummings also experimented with using words incorrectly. Adverbs could be adjectives, verbs could be nouns, and a pronoun could be a proper noun. His poem "anyone lived in a pretty how town" demonstrates his success in this area. This particular poem is quite a contrast to his visual poems in that it is certainly a poem to be read aloud, with its almost nursery-like rhymes and musical quality.

. . . The underlying theme of the poem is contained in a contradiction. The two lovers in the poem, "anyone" and "noone," are celebrating life and their love for each other. Their pronoun first names make them simultaneously individual and anonymous, hinting that anybody can attain the love and happiness they have. "anyone" is energetic and happy in his endeavours, regardless of failure or success: "he sang his didn't he danced his did." The two lovers are sincere, emotionally alive people and they wholeheartedly share their lives with each other. "noone's" love for "anyone" grows as she "laughed his joy she cried his grief." The other people in the town, the "women and men" and the "someones" and "anyones," do not live fully; rather, they go through the empty motions and thoughtless rituals. They are nameless people clumped together in their purposelessness. . . . —*Jennifer J. Renzel*

whole and realizing the contribution of the parts. But our comprehension moves into discussion as we ask: Now what is it all getting at? What are we to make of it? What does it all imply about love, death, war, religion, society, men, women, childhood, aging—about life? As we interpret, we reach for an understanding that satisfies our experience, that feels like it "fits the case." We try to get as close as possible to what we have read, felt, and thought.

We start to develop an interpretation, inevitably, during our first reading, just as we start interpreting what someone is telling us while we are listening. In both cases, we may well see afterwards that more was going on than we could have put into words right away. As we read or as we listen, we get *hunches*. Then we sort them out, seeing which ones seem to take us somewhere, which make more sense in the context of the whole. Having hunches, therefore, is a crucial part of understanding. What is more, our hunches bring an excitement along with them, a sense of possibilities. We start to expect something interesting waiting around the corner. Our own intelligence is aroused by a world of mind-ness that has drawn us into its realm.

While I will use the words more or less interchangeably, there is an advantage, I think, to talking about *commentary* rather than *interpretation*, although the latter is the more familiar word in the context of literary criticism. An "interpretation" is more likely to suggest an explanation which we wrest from a work; it may sound like the real point of it all, the result of decoding, or it may sound like an arbitrary offering: "just my interpretation." "Commentary" implies an exploratory and speculative process, supporting our experience of the work and bringing us back to it with satisfaction renewed. We explain a subject by talking around it.

We can understand the most basic problem about commentary or interpretation—the question of how meaning accrues and what it is like—by considering the relation between allegory and symbolism.

Allegory

Interpretation thinks about "the meaning" and says, "This is what I believe our fine author is getting at." Of course, we do have to interpret first of all what the words themselves mean, what the poem or story says is going on, what the characters are trying to tell one another: the *literal meaning* of what we read. Beyond that level, we pursue *thematic meanings*, or ideas the author is dealing with. Sometimes writers are quite explicit about their themes. This is most clearly true in the technique of **allegory,** where characters and places are labeled with the abstractions they "stand for." But even in good allegory, the more interesting meaning is tacit or suggested, as it is in most good works of any style.

A late medieval form of drama called the *morality play* is very obviously allegorical. The most famous example is the play called *Everyman*, in which the hero simply *is* "every man." After meeting up with a somber chap named Death, he seeks help desperately from characters named Kindred, Fellowship, and Goods.

EVERYMAN

O, to whom shall I make my moan
For to go with me in that heavy journey?
First *Fellowship* said he would with me gone°;   *go*
His words were very pleasant and gay,
But afterward he left me alone.
Then spake I to my kinsmen, all in despair,
And also they gave me words fair,
They lacked no fair speaking,
But all forsook me in the ending.
Then went I to my *Goods*, that I loved best,
In hope to have comfort, but there had I least;

> For my *Goods* sharply did me tell
> That he bringeth many into hell.
> Then of myself I was ashamed,
> And so I am worthy to be blamed;
> Thus may I well myself hate.
> Of whom shall I now counsel take?
> I think that I shall never speed
> Till that I go to my *Good Deed,*
> But alas, she is so weak
> That she can neither go nor speak;
> Yet will I venture on her now.—
> My Good Deeds, where be you?

> GOOD DEEDS
> Here I lie cold in the ground;
> Thy sins hath me sore bound,
> That I cannot stir.

Explicit allegory in this medieval manner occurs effectively in some later works such as Edmund Spenser's very long masterwork *The Faerie Queene.* Another example can be seen in a very short piece, also by an Elizabethan poet, a well-known love sonnet by Michael Drayton. In the second part of the poem, a lover insists with not very convincing pride that he is through with his lady, yet he cannot help but pathetically add his portrayal of love's own death-bed scene:

> Now at the last gasp of love's latest° breath,   *final*
> When, his pulse failing, Passion speechless lies,
> When Faith is kneeling by his bed of death,
> And Innocence is closing up his eyes,
> Now if thou wouldst, when all have given him over,
> From death to life thou mightst him yet recover.

Emily Dickinson's meaning is clear when she uses a similar allegoric method in the nineteenth century:

> Because I could not stop for Death—
> He kindly stopped for me—
> The Carriage held but just Ourselves—
> And Immortality.

In Nathaniel Hawthorne's short story "Young Goodman Brown," the Puritan title of address "Goodman"—the equivalent today would be "Mister"—helps to typify the hero as an upright member of his community. He goes forth into the wilderness one night to meet a man who is apparently the Devil and loses confidence in a lovely wife called Faith. Although much in the story is quite subtle, we should not miss the clearly sign-posted point that it is all about the experience of losing one's faith.

Allegory does not always deal with death and spiritual matters, but it does tell a story about figures and situations that clearly *are* what they mean. The allegorical story exemplifies aspects of life that are openly identified for us—but more importantly, it dramatizes the dynamic ways they relate to each other, which are likely to be more significant and more subtle, and it dramatizes similarly the ways we feel about the end of life, of love, or of faith—or any theme the allegory addresses.

Symbolism

Imagery is the presentation of anything coming to mind through the senses—something seen, heard, smelled, or felt bodily (including what are called "proprioceptive" images, sensations within one's body). Literary images are specific sights, sounds, and so forth as they are formed by words. A **symbol** is an image that tends to generalize itself, so that it evokes associations with typical qualities of life. Allegory is a form of symbolism operating through exact equivalences: The gentleman in Dickinson's carriage stands for *death*, Goodman Brown's wife for *faith*, Everyman for *every man*, and so forth.

Commonly we reserve the word "symbol," however, for an image that operates more through suggestions, associations, and qualities of feeling than through direct equivalences. These will be the more "mythic" symbols. Critics have produced very superficial interpretations of William Blake's "tyger" or Herman Melville's white whale Moby Dick by treating them allegorically as representations of divine power or of evil—or some other equally specific moral quality. These elusive beasts are too interesting in their own right, however, to be replaced by ideas. They are powerful *symbols*, we should say, rather than allegoric images: We explore them as we read, letting the work itself develop in our imagination its subtly changing, paradoxical perspectives.[3]

In contrast to allegory, symbols proper are to be imagined concretely, in the awe-inspiring confrontation with "tyger" and the obsessive pursuit of "whale." The meaning of the image lies in its specific qualities as we experience them, the tyger's "fearful symmetry" or the whale's unnatural whiteness,

---

3. Images with fixed equivalences are often called "signs." Critics influenced by the methods of structuralism and post-structuralism use the term regularly where I would speak in terms of "symbol." I prefer to reserve "sign" for arbitrary correspondences. A flag "stands for" a nation, but it probably does not express its nature the way that a love poem expresses the nature of love. The expression of love is intrinsic, in the poem. It is there in the very particular way that love is expressed by the poem's very particular words and rhythms.

for example. The author realizes these qualities (brings them to reality) and we realize them (appreciating their power). This kind of meaning is the symbol's capacity to be applied to various aspects of life, such as family relationships, ambitions, moral dilemmas, perplexities of alienation, and so forth. It is made clear to us through the relation to the image that the work itself establishes—Ahab's relation to the whale, Blake's speaker ("the bard of Experience") to his intense striped cat. In this way, symbolism lies not just in the beast but in the situation by which the beast becomes a human experience of "beast." This symbolic situation establishes a psychological or spiritual condition, a state of mind that typifies human life in some way. We can go even further to say that, reading, we ourselves enter a field of relationship: We take in the narrator Ishmael coming to know himself as he follows Ahab's obsessive pursuit of the whale. We experience something true in our own lives with Jim plus Huck plus Mississippi, man and horse and snowy woods.

Two short poems by Tennyson provide a helpful contrast between allegory and symbolism. In each case, I quote the first and last of four stanzas.

> Sunset and evening star,
> And one clear call for me!
> And may there be no moaning of the bar
> When I put out to sea,
>
> . . . .
>
> For though from out our bourne of Time and Place
> The flood may bear me far,
> I hope to see my Pilot face to face
> When I have crossed the bar.
>
> —*Alfred, Lord Tennyson*, "Crossing the Bar"

Sunset and evening star are the call of death, the end of life's day as one faces the endless expanse. Expanse of sky is matched by expanse of sea. The "moaning" of the wind upon the waters at the sandbar is subtly evocative, but it specifically indicates the barrier of emotion that holds us to life, whether a barrier of fear or of grief. The voyage over the waters will lead to God, "my Pilot," perhaps at the horizon, where sea meets sky. Parallels of image to idea are straightforward, and as readers we transpose the one to the other, making the poem basically allegorical. But see what happens in the poem that follows, in spite of its similarities to the first:

> Break, break, break,
> On thy cold gray stones, O sea!
> And I would that my tongue could utter
> The thoughts that arise in me.
>
> . . . .
>
> Break, break, break,
> At the foot of thy crags, O sea!

But the tender grace of a day that is dead
Will never come back to me.

—*Alfred, Lord Tennyson,* "Break, Break, Break"

The first poem expresses a brave determination not to grieve for oneself. This poem expresses grief for the death of another, "a vanished hand" and "a voice that is still" (from lines omitted here). The situation here calls for greater passion. Here the sea is being summoned to break upon the shore in order to convey the feeling powerfully. But is the sea death, is it the pain of grief, is it the sense of loss, is it rage or turmoil, is it the passage of time, is it nature, an indifferent universe? The answer is all of the above and none—for here we have an active symbol rather than allegory. The suggested "meanings" may be very different from one another, even contradictory. The symbol's full meaning lies in its own power to suggest such associations working in and out of each other and also working in and out of the state of mind, the personal drama. The speaker relates to the sea dramatically, involving himself in its power and involving his passion in *it*. He takes this overwhelming force into his anguish. Meanwhile, this personal drama stirs within us natural feelings about losing a beloved and recognizing the impact of death upon love—not vague feelings floating in our lives, but feelings conveyed precisely by precise language, imagery, and drama, which bring the symbol forth.

Looking within a work, we can make a handy distinction between intrinsic symbols like the whale or the tyger; focal symbols like Tennyson's breaking sea; and what we can call supportive symbols, which are especially common in modern literature. *Intrinsic symbols* are what the particular work is about; the work is inconceivable without the symbol, so we can say that, like *Moby Dick,* we have at hand an emphatically symbolic tale or poem. The *focal symbol* focuses upon the symbolic image to achieve a meaningful effect. Whereas Melville's story is about man plus whale, Tennyson's poem is about the speaker's grief, which is expressed through confrontation with the sea. He focuses his poem upon the sea in order to express the grief. *Supportive symbols* appear along the way, to suggest centrally meaningful qualities of a character's personality, of the place where the work is set, or of the central theme. Such a symbol may be the setting of the story, whether it is a forest, city, ocean, house, or room within a house. It may be an article of clothing, a picture on the wall, a piece of music, an animal that reappears, or even a typical gesture that a character makes. In Katherine Mansfield's story "Miss Brill," a timid English spinster living in Paris is surrounded with symbols that imply the feelings she cannot acknowledge, the identity she cannot claim for herself: the small room she lives in, the sensual fox fur-piece that she wears and treats as though it were alive, the coffin-like box in which she keeps the fur, a band concert in the park where she imagines herself an actress on the stage, and a slice of honey cake she fails to buy on the day she is humiliated and almost realizes it. One well-known thematic symbol is the strange sound in Anton Chekhov's play *The Cherry Orchard*—"as if out of the sky, like the sound of a harp string breaking, gradually and sadly dying away."[4] This is a unique sound with a unique quality; however, it is elusively also more than a sound. It seems to sum up all that is poignant in the play and, by extension, some fragility in all of us. If we chose, perhaps, we could say how the sound does this, but better to leave well enough alone and simply savor the image.

Sometimes a work is itself composed in a conspicuously "non-realistic" style that we can tell must be symbolic. The work is certainly meaningful, even though we cannot say how as easily as we might in allegory. We enter a world that seems dreamlike or hallucinatory. Our basic sense of fact is upset as we reorient our assumptions about how things happen, how people behave. The stories of Franz Kafka are all strong examples. A young man can wake up one morning transformed into a sizeable insect ("The Metamorphosis"); another can make a successful career from the fine art of not eating for a very long time ("The Hunger Artist"); the beleaguered mice folk may be spellbound by a vain and irritating singer in their midst ("Josephine"); detained at the gateway to the Law, a man can sit year after year until, as he is about to die, the doorkeeper tells him that this gate was only for him ("Before the Law"). We do not read such stories as curiosities about some strange cases: We sense their weirdness as all too familiar. Something irrational about us is being dramatized, and we connect with it subliminally.

Ultimately, all literary works are symbolic, for all represent life with a particular slant, which we interpret. All are versions of life that speak forth some dimension of our existence. And all are probably a little or a lot weird—disorienting, perhaps, or alarming, or surprisingly evocative of feelings that seep out of our unconscious minds. One man talking to a tyger, another talking to the sea. If you are tempted to read intelligently by seeing past such weirdness or explaining it away, don't! Cherish weirdness. There is the weirdness of sensationalism and perversion, of course; but this creative sort is oddly natural. It touches the innumerable ways that being human seems strange when we take a fresh look at ourselves: having bodies, having minds, having selves, having feelings, having very sticky relationships—and all that follows from these peculiar facts. A disorienting sense of the weird may be at the heart of literary meaning and the fascination that literature holds.

Several types of the specific symbol occur in literature: natural, conventional, psychic, creative, and iconic. As we'll see almost immediately, however, these types overlap.

---

4. From a translation by Robert W. Corrigan.

Natural symbols are entities and processes that occur in nature: flowers, deserts, starry skies, the sun and the moon, sunrise and sunset, rivers and oceans, and so forth. These have intrinsic values or qualities that our imagination responds to spontaneously. They are often cyclical, suggesting the natural cycles of our own lives or various stages in our cycles: springtime and winter, night and day.

Conventional symbols are images that have associations traditional within a culture. Sometimes natural symbols have become conventional, such as apples and serpents, roses and rosebuds. Some, like roses and rosebuds (as in Robert Herrick's "Gather ye rosebuds while ye may"), emphasizing the fragility of love and female beauty, belong to a poetic tradition that goes back to the ancients. Sometimes conventional symbols come from religion, such as apples and serpents again, crosses and spires, Christ-like heroes. Sometimes they come from mythology, such as hints about Oedipus's riddle or the master craftsman Daedalus. Sometimes they belong to folklore, such as horns of cuckoldry in Renaissance drama, lions as forest royalty (lions as hungry predators would simply be natural symbolism), and wily foxes.

Psychic symbols are images that psychologists have taught us to recognize as expressions of the unconscious, although they may be conventional or natural symbols in themselves. They may echo childhood memories, usually painful ones, associated perhaps with punishment or with conflict between one's parents. There are two well-known subtypes of the psychic symbol. *Erotic* (or *Freudian*) symbols suggest sexual parts of the body, like towers within bowers, or they may imply Oedipal tensions in family life. *Archetypal* symbols capture recurrent patterns found in myths and folktales. Common archetypal symbols are forests and oceans, suggesting the swarming unconscious itself; patterns of descent and ascent, which recall a mythical hero's journey to the underworld and hence rhythms of death and rebirth; demonic opponents; and perfect objects of desire, human and otherwise.

Creative symbols are images used symbolically in a particular work but sometimes recurrent within an author's writing. Creative symbolism may draw upon natural images and conventional or psychic associations but will do so with a new twist or a new range of ambiguities, as Melville does with his whale and Blake with his tyger. Or it may explore an image that is personally meaningful, perhaps from childhood, as D. H. Lawrence does in his poem "Piano." Or it may invoke an image that is not ordinarily thought of as poetic, like the poet Hart Crane's Brooklyn Bridge. It may refer us to another work of art, as W. H. Auden does in his poem "Musée des Beaux Arts," which is based on Pieter Breughel's painting "The Fall of Icarus." In all such cases, the work itself must teach us how to interpret the symbol, as associations and implications gather about it. This kind of symbolism has been a common feature of modern poetry.

Iconic symbols are powerful central images left to us by the great literary monuments. In fact, the greatness of such works involves their projection of this symbolism, a kind of after-image with a sense of given value, a defining quality that transcends the written text. To appreciate the *Iliad, Oedipus the King, The Divine Comedy, Hamlet, Moby Dick, Walden*— it is not enough to ask if they are good stories or beautiful poems or cogent theology. We retain, long after reading, the icon of Oedipus's ironic struggle to meet and to evade his identity as his father's killer and his mother's husband. Or of Dante's self-transforming quest through an elaborate vision of hell, purgatory, and heaven. A lyric poet like Walt Whitman can leave behind the iconic image of himself in his posture as poet: the author of *Leaves of Grass* as the American bard. Even people who have not read the "classics" inherit these icons as part of our cultural language. Each has cast its own spell, lingering among the culture's idioms.

Implications

Symbols of all these kinds are palpable to the imagination: We feel their meaning, which is emphatically qualitative. A better word than "meaning" when we deal with literary symbolism is, therefore, **significance.** When we talk about the significance of something, we talk about the *importance* that it has to us; we register its power and impact. At the same time, we explore its *implications,* just as we do for events in real life. Think of the range of implications that the Berlin Wall had, both the putting of it up and the tearing of it down; think of the implications of your going to college, the implications of an awkward remark you made to someone you are close to.

Interpreting through implications is most clearly appropriate when we ponder "creative symbols." It also fosters a creative attitude toward interpreting a literary work as a whole. Each novel, poem, or play can be seen most richly as a "symbolic form," having significance in much the way that a particular symbol does but with a good deal more complexity. (You might look ahead to the beginning of Chapter 4, where I go into this notion more fully.) Being verbal and mental, being shaped into form, literary works produce implications more actively than historical and personal events do. To a large degree, they control their implications. Their implications, that is, are more likely to be intended (but only *more likely,* not *bound to be*) and more limited in their range. They are more clearly *there* in the work, although they are suggested rather than dictated, and they can come to us in different guises—in shades and tones, in clusters of thoughts or in overriding realizations.

If we look back at our examples of allegory, we can see that, while on the one hand they assert specific meanings, they also achieve more subtle significance in the implications of those meanings. There is a first-level of allegorical images which we simply accept as starting points: Every Man, the Good Man, Death, Faith, Love. Then there are the processes by which we find these images interacting in a story to demonstrate typical patterns in life: the process of coming to terms with dying, the demise of a love affair, the loss of faith. But on a third level, we find the full significance of the imagery—the kind of meaning by which it has both its importance and its impact—in the story's specific features.

A commentary that realizes the significance of *Everyman* will respond to the poignance of the character's desperation, the all-too-familiar absurdity of his efforts to protect himself from death with worldly goods, and the modest dignity of his reconciliation with mortality—and a good deal more that makes this short play a work of sensitivity, charm, and power, that makes Everyman a character rather than an abstraction and his story a drama rather than a sermon. The apparently simple allegory is rich enough *symbolically* to evoke some subtly ambiguous qualities which we understand by implication (or by innuendo and nuance, as I put it in Chapter 3 under "Suggestion"). A comparison with Dickinson's carriage ride will show a similar situation: an encounter with Death that is made acceptable by a vision of timeless self-possession. The courteous gentleman caller interrupting someone's pleasantly busy life produces a comprehension of both death and life very different from that in *Everyman*. It is eerie and beautiful perhaps at the same time, a balance that your commentary may need to work out in order to fit your sense of the detailed whole.

What our commentary interprets, therefore, is the way in which the work itself interprets us. Expanding its images, portraying them sensitively, pointedly suggesting their implications from varying perspectives, the work is a concrete but many-dimensioned commentary on life. As critics, we conceptualize the concrete experience. The literary imagination grasps at forms of life that emphasize life's features. The *critical* imagination becomes conscious of what these features imply.

Implications of a work are of several sorts: let us say they move inwards, roundabout, and outwards.

Inward implications arise among the characters, situations, and events within the story. We say we read between the lines, because we have to understand so much more than we are told explicitly. What we are doing is working out the implications of what we do see and hear. We need to start out by taking in exactly what is in front of us (representing it to ourselves clearly). But we must also *appreciate* what we see, what is hinted at, what perhaps is only thought silently when characters try to conceal their feelings, what characters (including narrators) do not themselves even know they feel. We understand contrasts and parallels between characters that are simply shown to us. We infer characters' assumptions from their arguments, and we evaluate their attitudes toward life by watching what becomes of them. In order to understand what life is like for its inhabitants, we sense the *psychological environment* that a setting establishes. We notice symbolic objects, figures, or references that suggest connotations for the actions and the experience taking place.

Roundabout implications interpret the author's real world. They deal with the work's personal and social context. They may provide insight into the author's personality or character as an artist. We may take in implications about the social order of the day, the nature of religious assumptions, the relations between men and women or parents and children, or the dynamics of the political system—for good and ill. The author reflects assumptions of the day about what life is all about and how it is to be lived—often without realizing it because there is no reason to suspect alternatives. Or the author may be challenging assumptions normal at the time—or normal at any time.

Outward implications are what strike us as significant insights into life itself. Some works "imagine us" into their unique worlds and unusual characters more fully than other works do. As a rule, however, balanced against the literary work's own specificity is what I earlier called the symbol's tendency to generalize itself. We are compelled by the individuality of Hamlet or David Copperfield or Emily Dickinson's "voice," feeling we know them as persons, concerning ourselves in their plights, but we all—in our numerous and vastly different worlds—identify with them because each is also an Every-man or -woman demonstrating a basically human pattern of experience. All works, to pick up an earlier point, have an allegorical dimension. They reach out to us to tell *our* story. Almost always, the significant author is on our side.

Sense in Sensibility

The insights about life that a good work projects are not, of course, scattered at random. They gravitate about some central issue, tending into a kind of pattern, a more or less coherent set of attitudes, the sense of it all. We speak of a work's **theme** to focus upon a central issue like this (such as the plight of independent-minded wives in a conservative society, as portrayed in Kate Chopin's novel *The Awakening*) or the attitudinal pattern that emerges (Chopin's deep concern that creative women were stifled in her society or Chopin's condemnation of patriarchal marriage). Some textbooks speak of theme as a specific idea that the reader can extract. This approach gets dangerously close to a "message" or a "moral," and it also lets one speak too quickly from one's own point of view. In this vein, the theme of *The Awakening*, for example, might be that "one should not try to buck the system," or "patriarchal societies destroy women's lives," or "being too concerned for your own independence, you follow an illusion that can destroy both you and others." Or we might say that the theme of Robinson's poem "Richard Cory" shows that "we should not make assumptions about other people's lives" or that "the wealthy are often more unfortunate than the poor." These examples correctly show that a theme is not necessarily a definitive fact; one can come at the work's theme in different ways. Yet all these formulations are drastically oversimplified because they misrepresent the spirit, tone, or impact of these imaginative works. They court cliché.

The "theme" is more complex than what is usually called the work's *topic* or *subject:* the tyranny of patriarchal marriage, the gulf between social classes, or the misery of the rich. The theme deals with the way the work very specifically *treats* its subject, but it may need to be stated in a hesitant manner. Often it seems to me most accurate to say something like this: "The theme *concerns* the difficulty of life for a spirited woman in late 19th-century marriage"; or, with more breadth and strength, "the impossibility of self-fulfillment in society's terms." Of "Richard Cory's" theme, we might say it concerns the invisibility of inward suffering. The theme, then, picks up the work's essential viewpoint; however, it presents the problem through its implications. It avoids a simplistic statement that one might assert baldly. If you can reduce the theme to a statement, then the work itself seems unnecessary or is merely the means toward the end of "getting the idea across." The naive complaint that poets should "just say what they mean" is then justified indeed. A valid statement about the theme, on the other hand, immediately suggests implications that the reader might ponder, that the critic might write about.

If we look at a literary work itself symbolically, we can see the theme on four levels: for example, the specific fiction of *The Awakening,* the story of Edna Pontellier, extends itself to implications about its particular society, late 19th-century New Orleans; then to broader cultural relevance, traditional European-American family life; to applicability to a specific class of people, married women, or just women in the patriarchal society; to universal relevance, as the story tends to generalize itself (allegorically) about human nature, focusing on the inherent (and tragic) conflict between social order and the drive for self-realization. A diagram may be helpful:

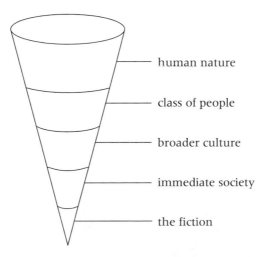

human nature

class of people

broader culture

immediate society

the fiction

Although one good reason for reading world literature widely is the marvellous range it provides for viewing life—through the cultural conditions of different epochs and the powerful temperaments of various writers—still there is a remarkable consistency to the themes we find. Realizing this can help if we think we should discover each time some arcane new ideas. We find, in fact, values that literature itself advances. In spite of exceptions and infinite variations, we can almost say there is a philosophy of literature. It sounds—and it *is*—quite different in Homer, in Dante, and in Hemingway, but it is also a re-viewing in each time and temperament of what are importantly humanistic values. Even explicitly religious works are about the *human experience* of being devout.

The themes of literature—their sense—explore and express the nature of human sensitivity, and that is the best reason of all, I believe, for studying literature deliberately and passionately. Nowadays, so many forces in our world work efficiently and successfully to desensitize us all, from the sterility of mass media to the facility of economic security. But throughout history, it seems, writers of all persuasions have expressed the human spirit's struggle to know and fulfill itself amid the varied obstacles it pleases life to grant us. They have shown how the nature of the spirit itself has made self-awareness difficult and dangerous, because of painful emotions, most likely, or the ways consciousness is naturally limited.

What I am calling *spirit* may be thought of as "spiritual" or "psychological," but what I mean is the full range of our feelings and awareness of ourselves *as selves*, our capacity for having experience, and our sense of ourselves *in the world*, reaching out and responding. The old word **sensibility** is still a good way of putting it. This includes our capacity for joy and love, for anger and bitterness, for grief and despair. It is one of the prime functions of literature to lead us through such feelings faithfully, imaginatively, and compassionately. Aside from feelings, sensibility includes consciousness itself—allowing us to focus upon the pain, the joy, the transforming power, and the responsibilities that follow from our awareness of ourselves and each other. Most helpfully, it means the qualities of our experience—the particular "textures" of our joys, fears, and sorrows. Significant literature keeps returning, then, to this one focus, in the nature and the value of sensibility. (This topic we will return to in Chapter 5.)

Attitudes

We can understand better how an author views a theme if we consider one aspect of literary imagination that may be so obvious we don't ordinarily think about it. The way we understand a work is controlled by attitudes that the author has built into it. In simplest terms, the author has decided who the hero is and who the villain. The decision may be unconscious, the author intending one effect and actually producing another, but if I feel that some fellow in a story is a rat, I assume he is detestable for the story, not just for me, even if you honestly feel that the story presents him as a misunderstood saint. In fact, the author is likely to conceive of a character *to be* a villain or a hero: the need for someone to perform the role probably comes first, depending upon the type of story being told. The attitude toward the character is an essential part of the characterization. However, it should not be confused with the *character's* attitude. If, reading well, we detest a character's opinions, that is very likely because we identify with the more enlightened viewpoint our author has built into the composition.

The attitudes towards characters, events, and places in literature become, of course, far more complex and subtle than that. They may be ambiguous mixtures of attraction and revulsion, admiration and disapproval. Attitudes may be compassionate, shocked, or amused, to different degrees—or even neutral. The important point is that our understanding depends upon the way we sense these attitudes, how we are led to feel toward the characters and so forth, how we relate consequently to the reality we are made to imagine. During the course of a work attitudes develop, going usually through various transformations, and our response flows along the current of these changes.

To a large degree, our interpretation of the text is precisely our interpretation of responses like these. The author induces in us feelings about the story being told, the scenes being observed, and our insights emerge as they are prompted by these feelings. We are given pictures of life, but they are pictures that highlight certain features and gloss over others. They draw us into sympathy with certain kinds of people while condemning others. Particular places are made to seem either desolate or delightful to help set a mood. The author will work out particular assumptions about ideas—perhaps philosophical or religious ones—by the weight that various personages carry. In other words, poems or stories always have viewpoints built into them, not just in characterization but in every feature of image, style, and theme.

Analysis

On the one hand, **analysis** puts us in the writer's workshop, looking over his or her shoulder to study the technology of the trade. Doing so gives us respect for real mastery (when it is there) and appreciation for fine workmanship. Analysis is how we account for the good (or bad) experience we have had. Recognizing our response, we ask what has produced it. Having absorbed ourselves into the literary world, we ask how its spell has captured us. Having been struck by its insights, we wonder what has evoked them.

But also, like commentary, analysis is simply a way of seeing clearly what is before us. As we look analytically at the product, we observe sensitively the ways in which parts make up the whole, we realize what effects truly consist of, we appreciate the fine beauties that the deft touch has produced. Even as we represent the literary experience vividly to ourselves and follow out its implications, we remember that literature is not life but art—not only because it is technical, but also because it is beautiful. We are not transferring our attention to mechanics for its own sake but to adroit sensitivities, lively craftsmanship, and elegant judgment. What we see in the work's artfulness is the capacity of articulate imagination to explore and recreate the manifold and intricate experiences of living—and to enjoy its own power to feel and know and make.

Some further aspects of analysis will come up in Chapter 6. Here, however, are a few general points that follow from our discussions of representation and commentary.

Style and Genre

One basic way to focus on the artfulness of art without making it sound too "crafty" is to appreciate some of the complications of **style.** In literature as in clothing, style is, of course, the manner in which the artist "fashions" the work. Most likely, that is a tendency to cut and stitch with a particular sense of what is beautiful, of what is appropriate for the occasion, and what is possible for the times. Style is a characteristic manner, a way of expressing oneself and adjusting to one's world. We think of literary style most commonly as a writer's characteristic use of language—particularly in sentence structure, rhythms, and diction—and here too it is importantly a way of responding to life. (You might look at the examples of language style in Chapter 3, pages 58–60.) More broadly speaking, style is a quality of the entire fictional world that one has created. A world carries, naturally, the manner of its creator.

What is the style characteristic of? Whose way of seeing is it? It is not enough to say it is the artist's. First, we should realize it belongs to the culture. We may be able to distinguish, most broadly, between Chinese, European, and native African styles. More specifically, we can see some typical traits that distinguish Elizabethan, English Romantic, and Victorian literary styles—as we would in the dress, in the politics, and most importantly, for our purposes, in the language of a period. A writer is always influenced by a fashionable style of the day, sometimes by several at a time, which express general assumptions, social conditions, values, and anxieties of the times. Such influence can also occur in reverse, when the artist changes the fashion of the day by opposing predecessors, as most good artists do at least to some degree.

Next, we can see that a work's style is also generic, determined to some degree by its **genre,** the *type* of literary work it is. (*Genre,* or *kind,* refers primarily to the major categories of literature: fiction, poetry, and drama—with their subgenres, such as the short story, the mystery novel, and the epic poem. The word is sometimes used more loosely to denote other kinds of classification.) A mystery novel, a love sonnet, an Elizabethan revenge play, a farce, a satiric epistle, a pastoral elegy each dictate certain stylistic features. These features will limit what a character can be, what feelings are likely to be aroused, how people speak, how action develops, and so forth—in short, what life *is* in the work and how life is seen through it. Such literary forms come to the writer with predetermined expectations, and the educated reader learns what to expect from them too.

Then, of course, we come to the style of the artist, but that is not such a simple matter either. It will express the artist's personality but also the artist's character *as an artist*. This is a matter of the position the writer takes in relation both to the going fashions of the day and to the traditions of the past. All writers belong to a literary community, sharing assumptions about how to imagine and how to speak, assumptions that influence what they do, what they refuse to do, and also what they quite literally could not conceive of doing yet. It is a community of contemporaries and also a community of past writers culminating in the present, so that what our author "means" is determined to some degree by the position he or she takes in a larger dialogue. The writer's style is, by and large, the individuation of a tradition. All this we understand well only by going on reading, expanding our repertoire, or by studying writers in relation to their time period and the sequence of literary history. Since we can't quite read everything, seeing how the process works in some instances gives us a sense of how it is probably working in others.

The writer's characteristic manner is also a matter of the range of experience one deals with, what one finds congenial or necessary to write about. And it is a matter of how the writer uses language as the medium out of which writings will be forged. Through these factors, each writer establishes an identity that we can recognize as Shakespearean or Miltonic, Dickensian or Dickinsonian. Each really creative writer, it has been said, teaches us anew how to read. While part of a cultural tradition, each writer reinvents literature. That, perhaps, is why generations must sometimes pass by before an author can be appreciated. It is behooving, therefore, that we keep our own assumptions open, letting our imagination teach us again and again how to respond, how to see life once more through the art of the work.

But a writer's style is likely to change in time, through maturity, response to outside influences, and continued experimentation. We see early, middle, and late stages in Shakespeare and in most other authors as well, if they lived long enough. In fact, we might say finally that each work develops its own style. The style of *Hamlet* is different from the style of *Othello* or *King Lear.* Although they are all major tragedies from Shakespeare's "middle period," the very quality of anguish is distinctive in each. In each, language is used somewhat differently to tell a different kind of tragic story about different kinds of people in different imaginary worlds. And each is a variation of Shakespeare's particular tragic vision.

In these different ways—culturally, generically, and personally—the artist recreates life in the particular way that style imagines things. The effect of style upon reality is **stylization.** Valid commentary and analysis both depend upon our

Stylization in the Visual Arts

Far left: Wood housepost figure. 43" high. Oceania. Polynesian. New Zealand. Nineteenth-twentieth century. The Metropolitan Museum of Art, The Michael C. Rockefeller Memorial Collection, Bequest of Nelson A. Rockefeller, 1979. *Center left:* An ivory handle (?) in the shape of a female figure. 13.3 cm high. Native American-Alaska. Nineteenth-twentieth century. The Metropolitan Museum of Art, The Michael C. Rockefeller Memorial Collection, Bequest of Nelson A. Rockefeller, 1979. *Center right:* Egyptian funerary model of a girl bearing basket of wine, meat, and ducks. Painted wood. Dynasty 11. The Metropolitan Museum of Art, Museum Excavations, 1919–1920, Rogers Fund, supplemented by contribution of Edward S. Harkness. *Far right:* St. James the Less. 1265–1280. Wood, polychromed and gilded. 77" high. German, Rhenish. The Metropolitan Museum of Art, Fletcher Fund, 1928.

perception of this factor. One of the most revealing kinds of analysis, therefore, shows how an author *stylizes* life into a work of art with its own atmosphere or flavor. In literature, this is done through a certain consistency in imagery, narrative, characterization, sentence style, sound patterns, symbolism, and on and on.

A clear and simple form of stylization everyone understands is caricature, as in cartoons that make fun of political figures so they will seem absurd. We can think of the process as *creative distortion,* transforming life's natural proportions. Always the method is to simplify and to emphasize, and the means to do so is an awareness of form. We focus upon some features of reality and ignore others, understanding the implications of the emphasis. The same principle operates in all visual art, as we can see in the conspicuously stylized sculptures shown on these pages. Playful, bizarre, devout, sensual, or stressful, we have here a reduction of features into design, but design with a capacity of expressiveness. Literature also communicates in this way, evoking complex responses through a consistency of style. We take in the author's characteristic manner with aesthetic pleasure and a gratifying sense that we are seeing the

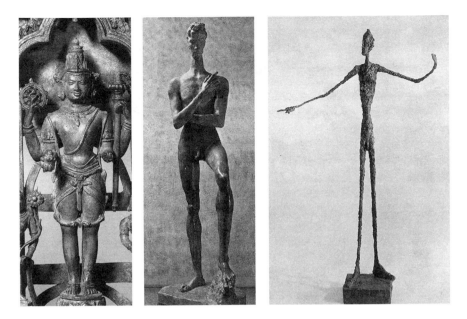

Left: Vishnu with consorts (detail). Bronze; Pala dynasty, tenth century. 17-1/4 inches high. Freer Gallery of Art. *Center:* Wilhelm Lehmbruck. *Standing Youth.* 1913. Cast stone, 7'8" × 33-1/2 × 26-3/4" including base. The Museum of Modern Art, New York. *Right:* Alberto Giacometti. *Man Pointing.* 1947. Bronze. 70-1/2 × 40-3/4 × 16-3/8", at base, 12 × 13-1/4". The Museum of Modern Art, New York.

world freshly. The bewildered blankness of Franz Kafka's characters, the curt restraint of Hemingway's, and the frenetic self-deception of Flannery O'Connor's all typify different mentalities that in turn characterize each author's way of experiencing life. And like everything else that the author gives us, this quality comes to us through a charactcristic kind of word-choice, syntax, sentence rhythm, and other features of language style.

Not only are all works stylized somewhat differently but some are more stylized than others. For literature as well as for visual art, we can think of a scale of stylization, with one end being photographic realism, an attempt to represent reality, and the other end being expressiveness in feeling and meaning. The energy of every work moves in both directions at once, but some go more emphatically in one way and some in the other. Towards the first end, we will find ourselves in a world that may look and sound like the world we see, hear, smell, and touch around us—or that we can well believe the world was like in a Victorian English village, a medieval castle. This tendency is *mimetic,* or imitative (*mimesis* is the Greek word for imitation). Towards the other end, the world seems much more clearly *mythic,* designed to be suggestive through its creative distortions. It is then likely to appear uniquely different from our reality while probing deeper forces within it. The style may, in fact, be symbolically potent simply because of how "apart" and how intense it is.

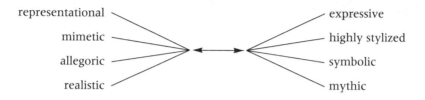

Individual works can fall anywhere on this scale and in any combination of positions at once. Particular literary modes and particular periods of cultural history favor different qualities and degrees of stylization. The kind of fiction known as *romance* (like Hawthorne's) is more stylized than the novel, Shakespeare's plays more than Arthur Miller's, farce more than domestic comedy. As readers we gauge the nature of the work's stylization while we read. This is one way in which we let the work teach us how to read it. We approach the work with a kind of diplomacy, a good will to adjust our expectations according to the assumptions and attitudes of the party we are negotiating with. We see how the opening of almost any work of fiction sets up the stylized world that the author will go on to build, especially in works that we're likely to regard as quirky or bizarre. Thus Charles Dickens introduces his amiable eccentric Mr. Pickwick with mock pomposity:

> The first ray of light which illumines the gloom, and converts into dazzling brilliancy that obscurity in which the earlier history of the public career of the immortal Pickwick would appear to be involved, is derived from the perusal of the following entry in the Transactions of the Pickwick Club, which the editor of these papers feels the highest pleasure in laying before his readers, as a proof of the careful attention, indefatigable assiduity, and nice discrimination, with which his search among the multifarious documents confided to him has been conducted.
>
> —*The Pickwick Papers*

We pick up the tone, seeing what game the author is playing with language and imagination, and we fall in with it. (For more examples, see pages 58–60.)

Obviously, the more readily we adapt to the mentalities of others, the more freely we negotiate among people. The wider the range of styles—and degrees of stylization—to which we can adjust our expectations, the better we can function as readers, the more literature we can experience and comprehend and enjoy, the more, in fact, we can ourselves *be.* Remember that deliberately realistic literature is rather modern and includes only a small proportion of the world's masterpieces. Until the 18th century, not many memorable writers—or their readers—would have seen any point in showing the world "as it is." The works of Homer, Dante, Shakespeare, and Milton achieve much of their power by being distinctly stylized in various specific ways, giving us something special that interprets life by intensifying its features. This is a point we easily miss if we see earlier authors as simply old-fashioned, not yet having learned how to write realistically.

Conventions

In highly stylized kinds of literature, we usually find specific **conventions** at work. We are all familiar with social conventions, like considerations of etiquette. We recognize conventions that we accept and conventions that we create for ourselves.

> [E]very love relationship is based on unwritten conventions rashly agreed upon by the lovers during the first weeks of their love. On the one hand, they are living a sort of dream; on the other, without realizing it, they are drawing up the fine print of their contracts like the most hard-nosed of lawyers. . . . In those first weeks it was decided between Karel and Marketa that Karel would be unfaithful and Marketa would submit, but that Marketa would have the privilege of being the better one in the couple and Karel would always feel guilty.
>
> —Milan Kundera, *The Book of Laughter and Forgetting*

By and large, conventions are systematic ways a culture expresses itself; however, they do not express only its social mores or its prejudices. Literary conventions are more or less fixed features of style that a writer works with, elements usually in an established literary manner. They may reflect assumptions out of which authors conceive their work, assumptions of what characters are, what story is, how one relates to one's readers, and so forth. There are three primary kinds: technical, cultural, and aesthetic.

Technical conventions are strictly matters of form. Sometimes they are dictated by circumstances in which works are written. Many features of Shakespeare's plays were determined by the physical nature of his theater—open-air, no curtain, little in the way of sets. His soliloquies were meant for actors who were able to see people in the audience and talk directly to them. Technical conventions include all sorts of fixed verse forms, like the blank verse and the sonnets that Shakespeare composed. Even the fact that a story has a beginning and an end is a convention, for episodes in our lives are not that discrete. So are facts that stories have central characters, not to mention heroes and villains; that novels have chapters and plays have acts; that characters generally know what they are feeling and can express themselves accurately, even when what they have to express is confusion or uncertainty.

Cultural conventions are attitudes, common at a time and place, that stylize how people think about feelings, manners, and values. In literature of the Middle Ages and the Renaissance, conventional conceptions of honor, love, and chastity play very conspicuous roles. Such conventions are sometimes called **sentiments,** meaning feelings that are regarded as values: for example, honor, sexual love, or empire as absolute goodness. They are forms of expression, but also modes of experience, ways in which people—as well as characters—have shaped their lives. Modern readers may find such old notions quaintly naive, but we might well wonder which conventions of our own day, invisible to us, future generations may find embarrassing. Knowing, then, the advantages of our own ways, we might ask what range of human feelings conventions of the past were able to express and explore, what sensitivities they embodied while leaving aside considerations that later generations pounced upon.

Aesthetic conventions are likely to reflect cultural conditions, but they have often produced what we can call stylistic systems, which unify the spirit of a work. An important example is **pastoralism,** a literary style popular in the Renaissance which portrays the simple lives of shepherds in the countryside with charm and grace. Derived from the Greeks and traceable down to modern times in various disguises (such as Garrison Keillor's radio tales from Lake Wobegone), it is a vision of ideal life imagined from the viewpoint of courtly or urban sophistication. Associated with pastoralism are some specific literary forms such as love lyrics, narrative tales, and *elegies* (formal laments for the dead, such as John Milton's *Lycidas* in the 17th century and Percy Shelley's *Adonais* in the 19th, both of which follow the pastoral tradition). In the 20th century, absurdist drama (by Samuel Beckett, Eugène Ionesco, Harold Pinter, and others) developed conventions of its own by inverting the technical conventions expected in drama—avoiding active plots, logically coherent dialogue, consistent characters, and so forth. (See "Unform" in Chapter 6.) The popular arts have always been rife with conventions, as in soap operas, situation comedies, horror movies, and comic strips (silently hostile pets, children with adult minds, unpronounceable bad words), and in popular literary forms such as the detective novel, spy stories, and science fiction.

Modern readers are commonly suspicious of conventions, assuming perhaps that they are substitutes for sincere feeling and original thought. But, like any other feature of style, literary conventions are in themselves neither good nor bad. They are forms for the imagination to play upon, means for exploring feelings and patterns of typical human experience. They can be dead and deadening; they can come alive with great charm and with subtly realized significance. Shakespeare and many other writers as well could take them seriously as vehicles for their art and make fun of them at the same time, as

Shakespeare does in *As You Like It*. What matters is whether a writer responds to them with a genuine quality of imagination, for creativity transforms conventions, adapting them continually to new needs. An appreciation for conventions reminds us of the artfulness of art. By enjoying such factors, the artist can express life rather than just copy it and we can relate ourselves to it imaginatively rather than just factually, to note what happens.

Evaluation

In your critical essays, by and large, you will express your **evaluation** of what you have read implicitly, by the way you talk about it. As you represent the experience with fine precision, as you pursue its implications into shattering insight, as you grasp its artistic achievement in exquisite detail, you will, one hopes, convey the fact that you are impressed. You will write with feeling for your text, grounding your enthusiasm (through representation) in a clearly thoughtful recognition of what is there.

Sometimes, however, you may be asked to—or may want to—write specifically about the literary quality of a work. In that case you need only recognize the fruits of your commentary and analysis to see what riches you have known. Occasionally, it's good for the soul to write a "hate" paper, venting your just rage (without sarcasm) at something awful. Hating the bad, of course, helps us love the good. But you will probably learn more and write better when you follow the trail that draws you onward, responding to a real interest with real curiosity.

Are there any rules to tell good literature from bad? One rule, at least: What *works* is good . . . but works toward what end? To express the tough sensitivity of the human spirit. What is *likely* to work? This book should make obvious what I think does: sensitive use of imagination, intelligent response to the capacities of language, an appreciation for the expressive conventions of art, sincere concern for the reality of human feelings, joy in the power of forging visions. Mastery of technique allows precise perception. Therefore, we stand in due respect before a true artist's mastery of craft in the seemingly natural flair with which grand gestures flourish, curlicues wind their way, or utterly simple truth bares its purity. We recognize the artist's vision as the symbolic epitome of an era or of some dimension of life difficult to name.

In order to be estimable, fortunately, a work need not be perfect. One excellent novel will be stronger in its intellectual power than in its craft. A story with clear weaknesses may be much more memorable for a single character than another that has no glaring faults but no brilliant features either. Still another will catch that moment of truth so sharply that we tolerate some silly dialogue in the foreground. A novel may be great in spite of a banal conclusion or a sickly streak of sentimentality. A writer's prejudices may not cancel out all the insight, even all the fineness of spirit, that may accompany them. A work's finest quality may lie in its synthesis of parts: a subtle view of city life may depend upon the perfect atmospheric prose. A work's virtues may well lie in camouflage: A story may strike us as simply funny at first and only later will we see the true depth of its feeling.

Hope is better than despair and joy is better than sorrow, but a hopeful and joyful work is not necessarily better than a despairing and painful one. If a happy ending were better than a sad one, all our great tragedies would be blunders. A book, of course, may be very important to you because of its ideas. It may even change your life, inspire you to greatness. It may even *be* a great book, but it is not great as a literary work for that reason. What matters most in literary terms is not just what it says or just how it says it, but *how* it says *what* it says. The point is not to be technically "literary," but to realize that a novel is itself a form of communication *as a novel*, a poem *as a poem*, and to see what it can do by being whatever it is.

A good writer impresses us with a sense of urgency about the affairs of life. Literature, of course, conveys values by which to live, but more importantly, we receive from the arts in general a sense of *value*: Life is valuable because sensibility is worth caring about; our feelings, intelligence, knowledge, and wisdom matter. The specific values that literature affirms are mostly concerned with authentic living, acknowledging the integrity of feelings and the fortitude of self-awareness. Such authenticity is portrayed through endless variations as the source of all real values because it is the basis of human value in itself.

The opposite of these values are the emotional fakeries of hoke and hype that flood the world around us, generated with more and more facility and dangerous expertise as the mass media become more and more proficient. At one extreme there is the **sentimentality** that strokes the mind with over-sweetened optimism and glibly idealized slogans. At the other, there is the **sensationalism** that intensifies feeling to the point of numbness, giving us excitement that has the sheer virtue of being exciting. Both, of course, diminish what we are.

When it comes to *evalu*ating literature, then, the most important thing is that we value excellence where we may discover it. That is simply to say that we value value; it matters that things matter. *Being* matters, and caring about it matters too. The value of the work, therefore, reflects directly upon our own value. When we appreciate a good mind, we are using our own good minds to do so. It takes sensitivity to know sensitivity. We appreciate then our own participation in the many worlds of art that are available to us. And if excellence matters, greatness matters even more. The richness of the great artist's vision, attainable because of the richness of art shaping it, is a tribute to our being. Our own tribute to genius, therefore, is fitting acknowledgment of what is for us ineluctably good.

A Final Word for the Chapter

Art, it is often said, is a way of knowing. Imagination tells us what fact and reason cannot grasp. Literature is interesting not just to read but to study because it *is* elusive, with a kind of meaningfulness that is more accurately suggested than stated. We are challenged to understand while we are teased by what we never quite pin down. Earlier, I suggested that *significance* is a more sensitive word to use about literature than *meaning*. In a somewhat different way, when we're talking about both life and literature, *meaningfulness* also can be more meaningful than *meaning*, for it emphasizes the importance our reading has to us. It matters that meaning matters. Such meaningfulness touches on the qualities of our own consciousness that we cannot put in words, that make us hold hands sometimes in silence, knowing something very strange about fear and desire, about our ability to feel both grief and utter happiness. Through the sensuality of images and rhythms, literature reaches our inner depths, and it is good to reflect that we know sensually what we are and that beauty is discovery as well as pleasure. Literature does not simply tell us what is true, it shows us what humanly meaningful truth *is*. It locates truth in the personal spirit caring about life, enjoying its own nature, and realizing its ability to see, know, and create, all at the same time, in the same process.

Chapter 2

Understanding *Understanding:* How Valid Is Interpretation?

Having and Knowing

The first chapter set forth the view that we understand literature by taking part in it. We know it by enjoying it, as we enjoy a meal—tasting, relishing, digesting, making it our own, part of ourselves in fact. Literature is a form of communication that comes in concrete images, as stories and characters, voices and accounts of places, as glimpses of life living. Because it is so concrete, we cannot translate it into abstract equivalences, for what literature communicates is not essentially conceptual. That is, we don't extract the message—a hidden meaning that has been craftily concealed. We take in a complex dramatic situation and think about its implications. We take in images and language movements that we experience both aesthetically and emotionally, sensing the ways the mind works, nudging us through life.

Reading (or sitting in the theater), we watch Romeo plummet into love with Juliet, forgetting his infatuation with Rosalind, while his friends and his family alike continue fuming about the Capulets—and we wonder about the beautiful power of young love and its vulnerability. We notice painfully the frustrating gulf that separates the social world of pride and rivalry from the private world of desire and delight. We feel deep sadness over the predilection of decent people for making life unlivable. And we dwell upon specific incidents, specific expressions of character, specific poetic images—such as the death of the lovers, Tybalt's energetic hostility, Mercutio's fantasy about Queen Mab—working out implications in their imaginative force and in their relation to other aspects of the play.

This is to say once more that we understand literature only as experience. We don't merely observe it from the outside, in the pages of a book; we reflect upon it as we enter into it. Reading imaginatively means seeing what is *there* in an imaginative work—seeing, smelling, hearing, feeling in the gut or on the sensitive skin. It also means experiencing *comprehension* of what we are taking in, as we perceive nuances and implications of the concrete world we are imagining. Such understanding may very well be subliminal. Criticism makes it explicit.

To some degree, we know a work of art in the way we know a dream. Although the form of a work of art is more determinate and consistent than that of a dream, our understanding is still based on the fact that the work lives in our minds, that we "have" it in the sense that we "have" a dream. As with dreams, we may actively seek to understand works of art, but we must also be passive, allowing ourselves to be acted upon. We respond, so to speak, to the stimuli in the images, which we receive according to our sensitivity to them. As we read well, we cultivate our sensitivities; and, obviously, as we open our minds to our fullest range of feelings and qualities of self-awareness, we are more alive to what we read, perceiving the images more sharply, feeling their emotional charge with more clarity, and noticing more of their implications. Our minds need to be highly tuned receiving instruments, though instruments alive with active energy.

Literature is unlike dreams, however, in two broad respects: It is communal (and comes from the community of the past as well as the present); and its construction is guided in part by the conscious mind, with its own willful intents. Literature also differs from dream in its involvement with ideas—issues philosophic, political, and so forth, that it may reflect or refute. Nevertheless, the communication it affects about these ideas is basically qualitative. Literature comes to us, that is, in the qualities of experience. Such qualities include what it feels like to think out ideas or to react to the conditions and quandaries that lead to such conclusions.

The view of literature as communication requires some further qualification. What the work itself communicates may not be what the author intended consciously. The writer may not, in fact, have consciously intended any communication at all to begin with. A poem, for example, may originate with a phrase, an image, even a rhythm that fascinates the poet, who then feels impelled to build a fantasy upon it. It would seem then that it is the image, phrase, or rhythm that is communicating, or working out its own implications. A reader, however, sees only the results and interprets according to the effects that they produce. Instead of asking *why* authors did things the way they did, therefore, it is often safer to ask *what effects they have achieved* by doing what they did. Many fine lyrics, furthermore, were written as songs, which ordinarily carry a communal voice: They are meant for everyone or anyone to sing. ("Lyric" comes from "lyre.") Rather than making a specific statement by the author, they communicate some variation or general sentiment, most likely about love.

One need not be in love, of course, to write love poetry, or even have a particular beloved in mind. Poems may also be written as imaginative excursions within a given convention rather than simply as self-expression— whether a sonnet in the Renaissance or a rock lyric today. The **carpe diem** theme was the kind of conceptual convention that spawned many a lyric, some of great depth and power, like Andrew Marvell's "To His Coy Mistress." Encouraging young lovers to "seize the day," the convention allowed Renaissance poets to explore an erotic theme and the imagery of nature. In following it out, however, they produced some beautiful celebrations of youthful energy as the basic spirit of life. Through skillful poetic craft, this sophisticated classical convention communicates an innocent delight in living.

Insight: The View from In

The kind of understanding we need in literature is *insight*. Insight is understanding that comes to us in the midst of experience. It's what we cannot get, ordinarily, from parents and teachers or older friends and siblings —as hard as they all try to give it to us. It is the wisdom we cannot have abstractly, in advance, even though we know the right words for it. It comes from being there, where life happens, from falling in love, from getting disappointing grades, from having a job for the first time, from losing a friend. Insight is experiential understanding.

We all value insightful people, and I suspect we all think ourselves especially conspicuous among them. The fact is, we *are* insightful. We all do see into the way emotions work, the ways people treat one another, the drives that lead us along our way. We need to sense what other people are feeling all the time to live with them or to do business with them, and it certainly helps to have some working knowledge of our own personal convolutions to get anywhere we want in life. Clearly, authors of literature need to be intuitive psychologists to convey and to explore the sense of life as it is lived. And good readers depend upon the same faculty as they imagine their way through the life of stories.

Can we learn, then, from experience we do not have? Although the cliché has it that we only learn from experience, we *can* have experience of an important kind vicariously. When friends tell us what they have been going through, we get a degree of insight into their situation as we imagine being them. We understand the past by imagining what it was like—we all hope that the human race can learn from history, even though history often seems to suggest otherwise. What I have been leading up to, of course, is that insight also comes from reading a good short story or poem. The writer of literature usually constructs the work as an imagined experience that deliberately induces insight in the reader. The capacity to suggest insight is built into the system. A character may achieve an insight that we too perceive as we imagine life through his or her experience: As our hero says, "Aha, I see the light at last . . . ," we are lit up as well. Or the insight may be implicit in the story, conveyed by the way it is being told to us. We are often led to see what some obtuse characters cannot take in or what dishonest ones obscure. In either case, it comes to us through our feelings as a realization about how things are. We have insights into specific characters and specific kinds of people and, speaking more generally, into how life works.

Such insight into literature depends on our observation of the real folk around us, but more importantly, on our own private awareness of ourselves. Good reading, that is, takes self-knowing as well as a good vocabulary. We bring to our reading our knowledge about living, something we are familiar with even if we cannot say we understand it. Conversely, what we see in a story reflects back upon our sense of what is true for us, of what we gather to be true for people as a rule. Hence, the story tends to generalize itself; the figures in the tale are symbolic to the extent that they stand in for us all, or for some aspects of us.

What we observe may be a matter of how emotions like love and hate are enmeshed with their opposites and how they change, how intimate relationships work (and do not work), how one's welfare affects one's values, how the changing body transforms one's outlook both in growth and in decline, how the need for self-fulfillment and the need for others frustrate each other, how weakness turns to violence and fear to power. These are age-old themes of literature because they are themes of life, dynamic principles by which we function. The insight may be simply a freshly rediscovered sense of basic feelings, such as loneliness or the fear of death. Some feature of life that always seemed obvious enough, like the pleasures of love, looks newly clear and vivid. Or the sympathies of imagination ease us into experiences painful to dwell on: humiliation, terror, death, and even torture. We are left feeling more open, receptive, and softened within our natural range of feelings.

The work gives us insight as we respond to the *vision* of life that it conveys. The work may either imply or state outright what the basis of its vision is; however, all the "ingredients" of the work, such as style and characterization, contribute to the vision, because they express attitudes toward what they show. This is how the literary world as a whole becomes symbolic, for it is shaped to reveal—through its medium—what we are to see in it. Literary vision is itself a "seeing" of life that illuminates life's nature. To say so is to use *vision* metaphorically, but we can follow the parallel further. The ordinary word means three things at once: a process of seeing, a view of what is seen, and a way of seeing. Being a process of seeing, literary vision is active and dramatic, something lively that we do. Being a view of what is seen, it is specific and interesting in itself. Being a way of seeing, it is a projection of the human mind (the author's writing and our reading), expressing the way the mind works as it sees, as it thinks and feels and grows. If we can interpret the work, that is because the work, as I've said before, interprets life. We interpret it by seeing just how it interprets us.

Responding, Reacting

If we want to avoid translating the imaginative work into abstractions, we can think, as I suggested in the first chapter, in terms of its *impact*. This is the effect the work has on us as we take in the experience we are led to imagine, the form in which it has been composed, and the kinds of meaning implied in its vision. The impact accumulates, word by image and image by word, until the form of the tale has evolved in the telling or the thrust of the lyric has fulfilled itself. Then we are left with an attitude about what we have seen and realized. We are sad, perhaps, even desolated, or outraged or shrewdly amused—but in the very precise mood that the (successful) piece has gradually evoked through its articulate presentation of imagined experience, delivered through a meticulously controlled tone. Our emotions blend with our sense of form and style, gratified by the execution of a skilled performance.

Receiving the impressions and insights of the literary experience is a matter of **response.** We allow ourselves to be acted upon, rather passively, accepting the communication. Response is also a creatively active process, however, if we think of ourselves as reaching out through imagination to recreate the experience for ourselves, so that it is vivid, fraught with specific pictures, emotions, and thoughts colored with our own interest.

Why, then, don't we all simply agree about everything we read? If we did, we wouldn't need criticism. Everybody would simply receive the communication and it would be the same for us all. There are obvious answers in our different backgrounds and personalities and the different ways we focus our attention at any time. But it is also helpful to distinguish between our *responses to* a work and our *reactions against* it. If response receives the communication, reaction, as I am using the word, blocks it. **Reaction** is our resistance to seeing what is there. It results from interference in the communication.

We react out of personal or cultural prejudice or because of irrelevant (or tangential) associations. We may misinterpret or dislike a work because our religious views set us against a character, because some peculiar woman reminds us of our mother, because of a similarity to a book we hated in fifth grade. We may feel dead set against the medieval world view because we cannot imagine why anybody would submit to a king when he or she could have been born in 20th-century America. Insisting on social realism to solve the world's problems, we dismiss myth and fantasy out of hand. And so on, in ways that may be conscious or unconscious, a matter of being simply modern, simply self-righteous, or simply oneself—in ways that our authors or their characters are not.

Primarily, therefore, response is active and reaction negative. However, we can *react positively,* in a sense, liking a story or poem for the wrong reasons—because it supports our prejudices or old limitations of taste. To love a sentimental love poem on a greeting card for its mushy clichés is—as literary judgment, at least—reaction. And we can *respond negatively,* in an appropriate manner, when we reject an insincere, clumsy, shallow, stupid, offensive, pretentious, and boring story by saying it is *bad.*

Of course, it is only human to have reactions. Perhaps life would be less interesting without them. But perhaps it is also a point of wisdom that we should try to be aware much of the time *when* we are having them. The distinction between response and reaction can help us see why there may be some implied experience or insight in a work that we are not getting—or why we are getting something that a critic or teacher is not. Our ability to interpret validly can be increased, therefore, to the extent that we recognize—and discount—reactions so that we can see what a true response might consist of. We may or may not be able to stop having reactions to what we read, but we can distinguish them from relevant interpretations. We read best by minimizing our reactions and maximizing our responses.

Knowing Dangerously

Implications can be extremely varied and even self-contradictory. A complex work will suggest more ways of seeing things than we are likely to recognize. Each of us will work out these insights at least a little differently.

Certainly, interpretation is something that each of us does as an individual. Tomorrow I might see implications from a different angle than I do today, and my sense of what is most important may shift from time to time. Yet all of us will want to argue that what we see is there, implied in the tale, in its wording, in its symbols, within the relationship of any of its parts.

Do we have any reason for faith in our own impressions? Can we assume that the meaning is in the work after all? If implications need to be read out of the text by each reader in his or her own way, isn't the idea of "meaning" just wishful thinking? Does literature *really* communicate? And then there is what often seems the most devastating question of all: Who's to say?

What better question to put an opponent on the defensive? The clever student challenges the dogmatic teacher, the generous-minded teacher challenges the formula-bound student, the quarreling friends invalidate one another, one rambunctious critic gleefully points a finger at another, the defender of liberty attacks the rigid authoritarian: "Who's to say?" Who's to say what it all means, what was in a dead author's mind? Who's to say that this book is better than that one, what we should learn in life, which character is right or has the better values? Who's to say what symbols mean, or poems that don't clearly state their message? Who's to say that I'm responding and you're reacting?

Through its vividly concrete imagery, characters, and situations, with all of its ambiguities and paradoxes, literature does communicate in a somewhat slippery way. In other areas of life, for that matter, communication is not nearly as straightforward as we might hope. We always interpret what we hear, relating it to what we know already. Yet, in spite of all our differences, we surely understand a good deal of what we say to each other or we would never talk. I would certainly not be writing this book if I didn't think I could convey to you my thoughts. And at the same time, I know you will probably receive some of what I say at least a little differently from what it means to me (although I must hope not too much!). It is not an all-or-nothing deal, as though you get it or you don't. Most of what we have to say to one another is not as specific as our bank statement or a final grade; most of the messages we exchange are not, therefore, posed simply in decipherable codes.

The important things we have to say are slippery because our experience of life is slippery. Our feelings and consciousness, our relationships and the events of our day are full of ambiguous and paradoxical features. Good talk and good literature both can be accurate and sensitive only because they can approach the elusiveness of life. Neither, however, is totally—or even predominantly—elusive. We do not need to defeat ourselves with unrealistic distinctions, no matter how logical they may seem.

Thinking about life always starts with seeing things from perspectives. That means "coming from" our own assumptions as we try to correct the assumptions of others. It also means starting with words that oversimplify things, then qualifying them, refining them, and balancing them out. It means speaking tentatively, subject to revision, knowing things by hunches, often sensing what "must be so" and elaborating our impressions alongside our memories. In other words, it means responding to what other folks have said in order to fill in what they have missed. It means taking the dreadful risk of discovering, alas, that we ourselves have been wrong, for wisdom comprehends its own fallibility.

Some people think that seeing from a perspective means not seeing truly, that any viewpoint is "merely subjective"—and therefore not meaningful. To be human is to have opinions, but even if we say our opinions are "*just* our opinions," we proceed on the assumption that they are valid opinions. We trust them in order to be ourselves, and so we must, even as we challenge and change them.

We can see our problem in more flexible terms than the either/or logic that tells us we can understand or else we cannot. Being more flexible in this way also means, I think, being more realistic. Honest understanding means understanding in the way that we live: personally, as persons, living in specific bodies with different backgrounds in life and individualized personalities, yet, in our own varied ways, having fundamental qualities in common simply because we are all human beings together. From individual perspectives, we all see with human eyes and respond with human awe, anger, or indifference. Individuality is at best, and fortunately so, a version of what we share.

We understand, then, by participating in the process of trying to know. We achieve "understandings," and these get us at the truth more or less successfully at different times. This doesn't mean our views are arbitrary, for they are ways of relating to the world we are in. We have all no doubt had the experience of coming to a clear realization of how wrong we were about something at an earlier stage of life, or yesterday for that matter. Surely such a process is more interesting and more humanly right than factual certainty would be. The possibilities of growth depend upon the probabilities of error. In the study of literature, this "uncertainty principle" gives to the work a capacity to communicate while letting us be humanly dumb, if we need to be. It also lets us come, as our selves, to the meaningful experience that is there for us to have—in the images, words, and voices—when we can best see and hear it. Rather than saying we cannot know truth at all, the uncertainty principle means literature is attuned to knowing life sensitively, accurately, and fairly, and we can participate, by insightful reading, in that knowing. And we can miss the point.

In other words, being human means having limited awareness, which is no big news. If for no other reason, it is true simply because focusing on one thing makes everything else peripheral. Our consciousness is always permeated with unconsciousness. Our thoughts and our feelings are always under the influence of others, of our culture, even the opponents we are determined to disagree with. We have a moral responsibility, I would say, to be as conscious as we can, aware especially of our prejudices and the needs of other people—the difference between our reactions and responses. Yet being responsibly human means grappling with our experience as best we can, considering all the difficulties that the human mind creates for itself. When our opinions are generously open-minded and open-hearted, we can see often enough that they are authentically human judgments that deserve our allegiance because of their humanity. Most literature fosters precisely such an attitude.

If this idea of knowing is clear enough now, we need to see the two important differences between life and literature which complicate things for us even more. The ambiguity—or slipperiness—of life is not exactly the ambiguity of literature. Because literature is composed of specific words, we should expect it to be more definite and definable than life. On the other hand, because there is no truly living reality in the book, as there is in my house and in yours, we should expect it to be less so. Both of these factors, however, reflect the fact that the symbolic forms of literature are shaped by their authors to convey something about their subjects. They emanate from life, and they are made to be different from it, so they can *mean*. It is all the more clearly true, therefore, that our determinations of meaning can have an appreciable validity.

Have we answered then that burning question: Who's to say? Surely, ONE is to say. It is one's own need and one's own right to say what seems to be true and to argue that it *is* true. Of course, as in all things, it helps if one's opinion is cultivated with knowledge: knowledge of literature, knowledge of life, and knowledge about how the two come together. Understanding literature, as we have seen, involves some knowledge about—or some feel for—all these important factors: cultural context, the nature of language, artistic conventions, and the qualities of sensibility. Our goal is to cultivate (in a phrase of Northrop Frye's) "the educated imagination."[1] It doesn't follow that if we study literary history deeply, our opinions will necessarily be valid, but if one does know about the author's cultural context and concept of style, *one* has a better chance of knowing what one is talking about—at least if one doesn't let one's intuition get overwhelmed and one's human sympathies washed out. It is that delightfully simple, and that complex. One exercises one's judgment. This method is hardly infallible, but neither is it necessarily arbitrary. It is both the way we cope and the way we understand. What is

---

1. It is the title of a book (Bloomington: Indiana University Press, 1964). I am using the phrase a little differently than Frye. He is talking about the imagination as itself a means of knowing that should be vital to our education.

more, this is one of the factors that make life—and literature—particularly interesting, more interesting, we must think, than if our minds were either computers or divine oracles, and more interesting than if we were truly all isolated side-by-side in separate universes. One does the best one can—and may achieve some very nice, even remarkable, things.

PART TWO
Imaginative Reality

Chapter 3

How Language Becomes Literature

Living Language

People often have difficulty doing literary criticism well, I believe, because of certain misleading assumptions built into our educational philosophy. These assumptions, which I refer to in the Introduction as a subject-object split, just don't work for us when we study literature. They make us say things that we don't mean. They make us write (and teach) criticism that has nothing to do with what really moves us when we read, what makes us want to read more and to study literature seriously. I think that this factor often makes it unnecessarily difficult for people to develop their writing skills in general as well as their faculty for thinking about what other people have written.

We can see a source of this problem in our assumptions about language, the material that literature is, of course, made of. What is true of language will have to be true of literature. Objectively, we may think of words as tools that we take off a shelf, use according to the manufacturer's instructions, and put back until we need them again. This makes us regard words in some limiting ways:

- As things existing in themselves, as foreign objects we observe and handle (and translate into meaning) . . . whereas they exist in our minds and are thoroughly involved in our sense of reality;

- As individually meaningful units of sense, with fixed equivalents . . . whereas they come into their full meaning as they are used together in the web of language that is continually reweaving itself, in phrases, sentences, and the movement of discourse;

- As stable devices that will perform their expected offices, constant in their nature . . . whereas they change through time as we do and as human history does, emerging, transforming, and receding—containing, moreover, as we do, their lively past always vital in their present;

- As neutral and impartial witnesses of our meanings . . . whereas they come to us with their own energies, demanding respect.

- As only serious objects to work with . . . whereas they are very good to play with as well;

- As substitutes for our thoughts . . . whereas they are, working together, carriers of consciousness, running in and out of our changing states of mind, engaging us together in all sorts of social actions, reaching out among us to affect one another's lives.

Or, subjectively, we may think of words as symptoms of our feelings, like sighs and groans, that utter our state of mind and create mirrors in which only we can see ourselves . . . whereas they are coin of the realm, liable to counterfeiting, adaptable for new forms of exchange, but always available on the public market.

Essential in what all this must mean to us is that we know language (and therefore literature) experientially. Meaning carries *meaningfulness* along with it, and that is a quality we can only know by experience. We understand language by our participation in it, and we can participate in it only because it comes to us from beyond, from the minds of others, who have been sharing language through the centuries as they have found out and promulgated multifarious kinds of meaning.

To be sure, a simply objective or simply subjective view of matters is a lot easier to understand and apply. But the writing that makes literature doesn't operate on such assumptions. When we read with deep understanding and write with real satisfaction, I think, it is on the basis of my "whereases." For language is integral to our sense of ourselves in life. We are born without it and occasionally people have survived without it. For practical purposes, however, we live *in it*, both communally and solitarily, mumbling, arguing, planning, watching television, buying and selling, loving, and writing English papers. We don't just think with language; we think to a considerable degree *languagely*—in ways that language makes possible. We swim in language as in a sea and can float buoyantly in it. But that too suggests that we are inside it; actually, it permeates our minds like the water in our bodies. And it is outside us, in the minds of others, in the cultural tradition, in the voices on radio and television, and in a great deal of printed matter.

The fact of literature—the capacity of language to extend our intimate nature throughout time—depends absolutely on all the reasons *whereas* language is as close to us as it is and as subtle. Thus, to read and to write more meaningfully, what we most need is not more information or simpler rules but a clearer relationship to language and the things made artfully out of it. For that, it helps to realize how much language is already part of our selves, how sensitive we already are to its ways and its means and also how sensitive it is to convey our nature.

Word Painting

Just as we appreciate the brushstrokes, textures, tones, and proportions of the painted apple or sunflower, we appreciate the textures of wordstuff wrought and crafted by the literary artist. If we look at a head sculpted in clay or cast in bronze, the medium, we know, modifies our experience of this earthy or this metallic person. So too, the literary reality lives in its language, exploded out of words but limited and controlled by them too.

The various features of language make up the literary reality in such a way that it will be precisely vivid and uniquely intricate—features of language such as its mélange of sound effects; its projection of things, thoughts, places, and persons; its capacity for many types of meaning, gross and subtle, suggested and affirmed. We may think back easily on a Hamlet, Scrooge, or Prufrock drifting disembodied in our fond memories, but properly, of course, their home is in their words: what they say, what they hear, what is said about them, and all the language that makes up the fabric of their universe. Literature (literally, *letter-doing*, or simply *letter-ing*) invites us to marvel at the peculiar and wonderful capacities of words, these blobs and droplets of sound that conjure so much so richly in our minds.

Because we use words casually and continually, even in our dreams and our mumbling to ourselves, we are used to looking right through them to what they mean. The closer writing is to practical, informative use, the more naturally we read transparently to see what's on the other side, as though we were looking through clear glass. The more "poetic" writing is, on the other hand, the more it stops our vision, like stained glass, so that we are struck by the light-transfigured colors that form the patterned picture-shapes. As a result, meaning in literature is not something we find by looking through the words to ideas beyond them, or by uncovering hidden secrets or cracking coded messages. Rather, meaning comes to us in our direct experience of language as we participate in the speeches, descriptions, narrations, and rhapsodies that make up the literary text. Reading the words imaginatively, we experience them as though they cast forth our own thoughts and yelped our own feelings. Reading a little more consciously, we notice the state of mind we are in as we think and utter them. Words are vehicles of consciousness itself.

In literature, words "see" for us, but what words see is not what eyes see. Literature sees creatively, as art, interpretively and with elegance or style. Language may have to see one item at a time, in a sequential accounting— the eyes, then the nose, then the mouth—while eyesight knows them all at once, integrally: the single complex thing called a face,[1] but though words cannot see all that eyes can, they focus fine and complex discriminations. The way language describes is itself a commentary on what we are to see. It can be penetrating, suggestive, and precise in a way that develops *authorial* vision. Language can see in time and transformation. It can put us inside other minds (or give us the illusion of doing so) and it can explore minds interacting. It can give us a special clarity and concentration of consciousness and fold levels of awareness upon one another. Besides expressing and describing, it can analyze, socialize, and negotiate.

The language of literature can be studiously banal, delicately coarse, voluptuous, precise and pure, stately, tumultuously chaotic, or playfully coy— or follow in style and tone almost any human mood and temperament or combination thereof. Think how you would characterize these passages of modern prose (all of which are opening passages except for the one by Morrison):

> In this refulgent summer, it has been a luxury to draw the breath of life. The grass grows, the buds burst, the meadow is spotted with fire and gold in the tint of flowers. The air is full of birds, and sweet with the breath of the pine, the balm-of-Gilead, and the new hay. Night brings no gloom to the heart with its welcome shade. Through the transparent darkness the stars pour their almost spiritual rays. Man under them seems a young child, and his huge globe a toy. The cool night bathes the world as with a river, and prepares his eyes again for the crimson dawn. The mystery of nature was never displayed more happily.
>
> —Ralph Waldo Emerson, "The Divinity School Address"

> The store in which the Justice of the Peace's court was sitting smelled of cheese. The boy, crouched on his nail keg at the back of the crowded room, knew he smelled cheese, and more: from where he sat he could see the ranked shelves close-packed with the solid, squat, dynamic shapes of tin cans whose labels his stomach read, not from the

---

1. As a visual art, of course, painting can do some of what language cannot, while language can do some of what painting cannot. Drama and film get advantages of both but are limited to the interpretation of performance.

lettering which meant nothing to his mind but from the scarlet devils and the silver curve of fish—this, the cheese which he knew he smelled and the hermetic meat which his intestines believed he smelled coming in intermittent gusts momentary and brief between the other constant one, the smell and sense just a little of fear because mostly of despair and grief, the old fierce pull of blood. He could not see the table where the Justice sat and before which his father and his father's enemy (*our enemy* he thought in that despair; *ourn! mine and hisn both! He's my father!*) stood, but he could hear them, the two of them that is, because his father had said no word yet. . . .

—William Faulkner, "Barn Burning"

Boys are playing basketball around a telephone pole with a backboard bolted to it. Legs, shouts. The scrape and snap of Keds on loose alley pebbles seems to catapult their voices high into the moist March air blue above the wires. Rabbit Angstrom, coming up the alley in a business suit, stops and watches, though he's twenty-six and six three. . . .

The ball, rocketing off the crotch of the rim, leaps over the heads of the six and lands at the feet of the one. He catches it on the short bounce with a quickness that startles them. As they stare hushed he sights squinting through blue clouds of weed smoke, a suddenly dark silhouette like a smokestack against the afternoon spring sky, setting his feet with care, wiggling the ball with nervousness in front of his chest, one widespread white hand on top of the ball and the other underneath, jiggling it patiently to get some adjustment in air itself. The cuticle moons on his fingernails are big. Then the ball seems to ride up the right lapel of his coat and comes off the shoulder as his knees dip down, and it appears the ball will miss because though he shot from an angle the ball is not going toward the backboard. It was not aimed there. It drops into the circle of the rim, whipping the net with a ladylike whisper. "Hey!" he shouts in pride.

"Luck," one of the kids says.

—John Updike, *Rabbit, Run*

The day is coming when great nations will find their numbers dwindling from census to census; when the six roomed villa will rise in price above the family mansion; when the viciously reckless poor and the stupidly pious rich will delay the extinction of the race only by degrading it; whilst the boldly prudent, the thriftily selfish and ambitious, the imaginative and poetic, the lovers of money and solid comfort, the worshippers of success, of art, and of love, will all oppose to the Force of Life the device of sterility.

—George Bernard Shaw, *Man and Superman*

What was taken by outsiders to be slackness, slovenliness or even generosity was in fact a full recognition of the legitimacy of forces other than good ones. They did not believe doctors could heal—for them, none ever had done so. They did not believe death was accidental—life might be but death was deliberate. They did not believe Nature was ever askew—only inconvenient. Plague and drought were as "natural" as springtime. If milk could curdle, God knows robins could fall. The purpose of evil was to survive it and they determined (without ever knowing they had made up their minds to do it) to survive floods, white people, tuberculosis, famine and ignorance. They knew anger well but not despair, and they didn't stone sinners for the same reason they didn't commit suicide—it was beneath them.

—Toni Morrison, *Sula*

In the remote border town of Q., which when seen from the air resembles nothing so much as an ill-proportioned dumbbell, there once lived three lovely, and loving, sisters. Their names . . . but their real names were never used, like the best household china, which was locked away after the night of their joint tragedy in a cupboard whose location was eventually forgotten, so that the great thousand-piece service from the Gardner potteries in Tsarist Russia became a family myth in whose factuality they almost ceased to believe . . . the three sisters, I should state without further delay, bore the family name of Shakil, and were universally known (in descending order of age) as Chhunni, Munnee and Bunny.

And one day their father died.

—Salman Rushdie, *Shame*

How does Emerson's language capture both joy and awe? What makes Shaw's character sound both intellectual and passionate? How does Faulkner capture the young boy's turmoil and make it sound like the mystery of life? What in Updike's language sustains his restless tension? What makes Morrison compassionate and painfully reflective? What makes Rushdie both whimsical and sardonic? What makes them all in their own ways so intense? It is not just what they are saying but how they are saying it. It is a matter of the style through which each temperament finds its own response to thought and experience. We notice the sort of words used and the ways they are brought together, the directness or convolution of sentence structure, the play of thoughts modifying other thoughts, the rhythms of phrasing that echo the human voice exploring the human mind, the building up of parts into a whole, the effort to bring word structures closer and closer to emotion or perception.

As we make such discriminations, responding to such a range of articulate possibilities, we appreciate more and more the writer's palette, the good writer's virtuosity, and that extraordinary phenomenon *life-in-words*. We realize that language is something that happens within us *dramatically*. Language takes on a life of its own, also dramatically, as it struggles to know and to feel with clarity, embodies states of mind, works out conflicts of fear and desire, comes up against its own consciousness of itself, and greatly enjoys its power to see, its power to sing. "Hello" *means* a particular phase in the experience of meeting up with someone; as I say it, it enacts my recognition of your existence. "I hate you" *becomes* the specific blend of revulsion, anger, perhaps fear and humiliation, that the occasion requires. In literature this dramatic factor is especially telling. Taken as a whole or taken phrase-by-phrase, the poem means the experience of thinking those words and of being in the specific state of mind that thinking them establishes. These are all resources of language exploited by the author's style.

The Language of Literature

To comprehend anything, of course, we need to know what kind of a thing it is. We ask different questions of a real apple and a painted one, the apple of Eden and the apple in a supermarket ad. What it *is*, in each case, is a question of what it is for, what it is made of, and how we imagine it to exist. The short story is imaginary, but it is *there*. What kind of reality does it derive from the factors that make it up and put it there? Literature, certainly, is made out of language—but what kind of language is it made of?

The good news is that it's the same kind of language we've been using all our lives: those bits of sound all strung together, which allow us—incredibly— to talk, listen, read and write, talk with ourselves (even in dreams), become engrossed in conversations dumb, funny, frustrating, stimulating, depressing—helping us through all our days together. Earlier modern English, as in Shakespeare and the King James Bible, will seem strange if we're not used to it. Some modern authors like Gerard Manley Hopkins or James Joyce write in especially tricky ways. Some authors use dialect, like Robert Burns's Scottish English or Langston Hughes's African-American English. In the 18th century, some poets favored a class of words called *poetic diction*—"How doth the finny pilgrim through liquid depths propel?"—instead of How do fish swim? Still, the power of any effective literary style arises altogether from its base in the language of ordinary speech and thought. If we don't always recognize every word or expression, we are easily familiar with most, especially those basic words like helping verbs, pronouns, and prepositions on which sentence structure is based. We see how words are built into phrases and phrases into clauses and sentences. We recognize emphasis, exclamation, questioning, and other forms and shapes that expression of mind takes on.

If that's the good news, the even better news is that the language of literature is the same stuff made still more interesting—interesting not because it is
old, quaint, or tricky, but because it is well-crafted and sharply realized. Literary
language becomes particularly interesting in several ways. They are all involved
in one another, but we can see a separate emphasis in each.

Precision

The apt phrase, the right word, the compact expression. Getting a subtle
feeling or elusive thought just right. Thinking and observing accurately
through language. Taking advantage of the resources of language, which are
literally infinite: the vast vocabulary available, the turns of expression, the
subtleties of connotation, the associations that expressions have with particular experiences, the capacity of language to reshape and renew itself. Precision depends, of course, on a sensitivity to diction, but it depends as well on
all the means by which a writer "gets it just right."

A good writer is alert to the full range of implications that a word may
have, in order to draw on them for specific purposes. Often poets take advantage of a word's etymology or its literal meaning when we have become used
to its extended sense. In "Ode to the West Wind," Shelley refers to the "steep
sky's commotion," making us notice that *commotion* is a kind of *motion*, a mix-
ing together of things. A few lines later, he calls storm clouds borne by the
wind "angels of rain and lightning." It adds something to the verse if we know
that *angel* comes from a word for *messenger*—although we wouldn't want to
lose the more obvious image in this striking metaphor. In the same poem,
Shelley describes autumn leaves driven by the powerful wind as:

> Yellow, and black, and pale, and hectic red,
> Pestilence-stricken multitudes . . .

Confused by *hectic* here, a modern reader might have to learn that it has
here an older meaning, "feverish"—although, as is very often the case, the
following term *pestilence-stricken* provides a good clue. Towards the end of the
poem, Shelley calls upon the wind to merge with his spirit: "Be thou me,
impetuous one!" *Impetuous* comes from *impetus* and originally meant "moving
very forcefully." Thus many words in very common use have been extended
metaphorically from old literal meanings, often weakening their sense. Consider: *redemption* ("buying back"), *occasional* ("for a specific purpose"), *terrific*
("inspiring terror"), *phenomenal* ("about experienced events"), *fantastic* ("of
fantasy"), *plastic* ("shaping, creative"), *secretary* ("keeper of secrets"), *eccentric*
("off center"), *synthetic* ("bringing parts together"). We can all easily guess the
literal meanings of such common words as *business, foundation, understanding,
realize, elementary*—but rarely stop to think about them.

It may be difficult for a reader today to grasp, without some help, the nice precision of Shelley's word choices, although each of his words has a dramatic feeling that in itself is stirring to the imagination. Even if we don't know the origin of *hectic* or *impetuous*, the familiar sense of the word gains from unfamiliar use an intriguingly mysterious aura.

Often a poet's precise language grasps an elusive thought, like Wallace Stevens's "Death is the mother of beauty" from "Sunday Morning." Or a comic one. In *Don Juan*, Byron writes

Man, being reasonable, must get drunk . . .

but then he tricks us by interpreting the line with the more serious one that follows:

The best of Life is but intoxication . . .

—"intoxication" suggesting in this broader context something more than alcohol can give us. Precise language can be utterly clear and simple, however. At an intensely dramatic moment of complex passion, an author may hit the right note with a simple deft touch, as when King Lear, about to die in agonizing grief, interrupts his lament for Cordelia with: "Pray you, undo this button: thank you, Sir." What could be more precise than Hamlet's "To be or not to be" or "The readiness is all"?

A poem's precision may be merely descriptive. In this little piece, William Carlos Williams presents a very simple action through conspicuously natural words placed in careful stanzas with very short lines, unrhymed and unpunctuated. His style emphasizes the deliberate precision with which the deed is acknowledged.

THIS IS JUST TO SAY

I have eaten
the plums
that were in
the icebox

and which
you were probably
saving
for breakfast

Forgive me
they were delicious
so sweet
and so cold

Sometimes a writer's precision consists of getting exactly the wrong word—in the mouth, that is, of the right character. *Malapropism* is an error someone makes in ignorance, usually trying to sound impressive, relishing a word without quite understanding it. It is named for Mrs. Malaprop (after the French *mal apropos*) in Richard Brinsley Sheridan's 18th-century comedy *The Rivals*. She laments "how few gentlemen now-a-days know how to value the ineffectual qualities in a woman"; the gentleman who flatters her is "the very pineapple of politeness"; her niece—the romantic heroine—is "as headstrong as an allegory on the banks of the Nile." In *A Midsummer Night's Dream*, Bottom the Weaver, a superstar among bumpkins, looks forward to rehearsing with his fellow-actors "most obscenely" in private (he may have meant "most seemly," but God knows), crystallizing his proud and joyful dumbness. He promises to "aggravate his voice," instead of moderate ("attenuate?") it.

Suggestion

We all know that language can "say" more than it says—partly through figures of speech, partly through connotations and associations, partly through restraint, clearly holding back our thoughts, or by allowing pictures and memories to play upon the mind. We express ourselves in hints and implications—sometimes grunts or sighs—to help us speak. Intonation is often more "telling" than the words themselves. We let body language talk for us, in a raised eyebrow or a wave of the hand, sometimes more than we know. In all of these ways, we probably feel we want to say something we can't get into words. By the suggestiveness that is part of language in itself, the good writer elicits a subliminal or unconscious quality of awareness that may seem more real or profound than the talking about it—glimpsing such "mysteries" as love and death and a sense of the sacred, which sometimes seem betrayed by mere descriptions.

There is the kind of suggestiveness in which a poet dramatizes what he is talking about by the way he says it: "Tomorrow, and tomorrow, and tomorrow. . . ." Meaning may depend more upon doing than saying. Good reading requires, therefore, an alertness to innuendoes and nuances of expression, which speak with the subtlety of what is *almost* said. **Innuendo** is the hint that one does intend silent meaning. A little imagination goes a long way when we read that "the congressman employed many attractive secretaries who didn't stay on the job long." Sexual innuendo need not be snickering, however. When in an earlier story a woman said something like "You don't respect me anymore," we understood well enough what we didn't need to see in sweaty detail.

And, although it does seem particularly helpful when dealing with "unmentionable" subjects, innuendo need not always be sexual. When an unhappy character stares into space, for example, and announces a long journey, we know this person may not be long for the world. For an example of innuendo subtly at work in modern fiction, see Grace Paley's story "Debts" in Appendix 1 at the end of the book.

Nuance is, first of all, tone or shading of meaning, the kind of precision with which subtle distinctions are perceived, the curves of words. We often color our self-expression with the nonverbal nuances of our gestures. A good writer conveys nuances of meaning in specific words or combinations of words, even in the silence with which one character listens to another. Nuance can be the telling quality in any form of expression. A well-chosen metaphor conveys a specific nuance of meaning. There are nuances of innuendoes and innuendoes of nuances. And the precise word in the seemingly necessary place comes across with the exactly right nuance. The aging lawyer who narrates Herman Melville's "Bartleby the Scrivener" describes his astonishingly reticent employee as "pallidly neat, pitiably respectable, incurably forlorn." Each combination of adverb and adjective is delicately adjusted, and the three terms play off against each other into an effective sequence, conveying a precise impression. "There was something about Bartleby," the lawyer writes, "that not only strangely disarmed me, but in a wonderful manner, touched and disconcerted me." He wants to define very precisely the effect that this strange man has upon him as he responds to those same few words that Bartleby utters every single time he is asked to do anything: "I would prefer not to." To his coworkers this repetition is merely unheard-of obstinacy, but to the lawyer (and through him the reader) it accumulates, in its human context and in its very minimal form, a weirdly familiar note of desperate resistance to the human condition.

Aside from a precise phrase, a nuance can be a subtle feeling or thought delicately conveyed by a whole poem, a passage of description, or an argument. The nuance is an insight conveyed with a very light touch. It may accumulate gradually. Such subtlety can be seen in the simplest of poems, such as the following poem by a Japanese child. Perhaps it is what makes them effective *as* simple poems, giving us an electrical twinge when we can hardly tell why.

MY MOTHER'S BREAST

I love to take a bath with Mommy.
I hold her breast in my mouth for fun.
It's very soft.
Soft as a rubber mattress?
Soft as a rubber ball.
When I put my cheek against it
I remember when I was a baby.
Mommy is smiling.
I feel shy and let go of her breast.
Her breast is such a good thing.

—*Okito Junko, age 7*[2]

---

2. From *There Are Two Lives: Poems by Children of Japan,* edited by Richard Lewis, translated by Haruna Kimura (N.Y.: Simon and Schuster, 1970).

Why is the rubber mattress a question and the rubber ball an answer? No answer. But what does the change let us experience in the child's mind? What is the movement in time back to infancy, then back again to ripe old childhood? The memory, the mother's smiling, the big child's shyness, the letting go? Facts simply stated, or a natural and touching emotional progression? What, finally, is the nuance of the final line, so simply and delicately put, that a stronger statement would butcher? What can "such a good thing" convey only because of all that comes before it, all that would be lost without the rest of the poem as context?

We may see something similar in William Carlos Williams's bare poem about the stolen plums (page 63). How would one feel leaving such a message on a refrigerator? ("Forgive me . . .") A bit guilty, a bit embarrassed? About having taken the plums or about having enjoyed them? Is the "probably" perhaps a touch hopeful? Does the careful hesitancy of the poem's style suggest a conflict of feelings like this: I shouldn't have done this to you, but I'm glad I did? Does the poem's utter simplicity understate what is tactfully left unsaid? We may disagree about what a poem suggests, but suggestions, notice, can be as precise as statements—even when we record them most accurately as questions or suspicions or ambiguous possibilities. The responsive reader can pick up such nuances or innuendoes, sensing (sometimes just suspecting) they are there because they are part of our natural expressiveness, part of the way language works.

Elegance

If the mathematician can speak of an elegant proof and the physicist of an elegant hypothesis, surely the critic can remind us of elegance that characterizes language when it is delicately pruned and trimmed, or when it is seized upon with inspiration. Language composed well has *grace,* which is part of its effectiveness and therefore part of its meaning.

> Lay your sleeping head, my love,
> Human on my faithless arm;
> Time and fevers burn away
> Individual beauty from
> Thoughtful children, and the grave
> Proves the child ephemeral:
> But in my arms till break of day
> Let the living creature lie
> Mortal, guilty, but to me
> The entirely beautiful.
>
> —*W. H. Auden,* "Lullaby"

This is, in a way, a poem *about* grace of a very personal kind. Even ugly thoughts can be expressed with grace, however. In Shakespeare's *Troilus and Cressida,* the wretched Thersites is eloquently disgusting in his curses: "I would thou didst itch from head to foot; and [*if*] I had the scratching of thee, I would make thee the loathsomest scab in Greece."

Certain modern writers deliberately avoid sounding beautiful, to convey the idea that beauty is artificial and makes grim truth sound too good. But when their work is appreciable, it too has its own sort of elegance, for elegance, or grace, is a sense of mastery in which style grasps experience with rightness and with an impression of utter competence. Grace, in this sense, is not decoration or beautification but sensitivity to feeling and fluency of perception. It is also a kind of sociability, a willingness to work with the reader, drawing us into a world we are glad to enter—just as social grace makes possible a sense of community, even between two people.

Point

Good language has something to say. Even nonsense poetry expresses something important, the very meaningful joy in play. If it is good nonsense, like Lewis Carroll's "Jabberwocky," it conveys that spirit with the elegance and precision which makes true play joyful (as in the play of sports or of musical performance). More commonly, literary language grasps at subtle insights that matter to us. Sometimes, these insights are stated directly by the author or by a character who seems to be speaking for the author, as in W. B. Yeats's

> . . . nothing can be sole or whole
> That has not been rent.°   *torn*
>
> — "Crazy Jane Talks with the Bishop"

Sometimes, they are conveyed as a poem's speaker or a story's character comes into a state of realization. These lines are also from Yeats:

> When such as I cast out remorse
> So great a sweetness flows into the breast
> We must laugh and we must sing,
> We are blest by everything,
> Everything we look upon is blest.
>
> —"A Dialogue of Self and Soul"

Or an insight may come through a question, as when Yeats concludes "Among School Children" by asking "How can we know the dancer from the dance?"—a question that says more without an answer than an answer would say in response to it.

Throughout such work, language probes the further corners of life, evolving intricate visions of experience. Of course, characters and stories and imagery do all this in a more obvious way. They exist for us, however, only insofar as language can bring them forth, making them expressive and penetrating.

Richness

I have left this topic for last simply because it needs more detailed discussion than the others. Later sections of this book (in Chapter 6) will explore the sensual richness of language in qualities of sound and structure. What I have in mind here is language's capacity—sometimes its need—to enrich expression by speaking imaginatively. Language often conveys experience through metaphors and other **figures of speech,** ways in which language reaches meaning more firmly by going roundabout. Whenever writing means something without making sense literally, we are in the presence of figures. They are as much functions of literary language as individual words and direct descriptions. It is perhaps easier to demonstrate figures of speech in poetry; however, they are important features of literary prose as well (although, when they occur conspicuously in prose, we sometimes say the author is being "poetic"). In the following sections, I will distinguish figures (primarily) of perception from figures (primarily) of logic—although we should perhaps call this second type "figures of *il*logic."

Figures of Perception

Figures of perception are imaginative ways of seeing, hearing, smelling, and so forth. Here, images appeal to the senses in ways that extend ordinary perceiving.

Metaphors

In **metaphor** two kinds of reality blend to form a new reality that exists only for the moment, in the imagination, creating a fresh perception which appears as a sudden insight. The English critic I. A. Richards called the two sides of the metaphor its "vehicle" and its "tenor." These terms help to clarify not only the distinction between the two but also their relationship. The *vehicle* is the image the poet brings forth to *carry along* the subject. *Tenor,* in this sense of the word, means the *theme* or *point* being communicated. If this term is difficult to keep clear, we can create a proper metaphor by calling it the "passenger," which the vehicle carries.[3] If I say, for example, "Her hat is a chocolate layer cake," it is more than likely that I am talking about the hat: It is my subject, my "tenor" or "passenger" taking a ride. The cake is the "vehicle" with which I convey my impression of it, driving it down the street of your imagination.

---

3. Or, to try again, the "burden," a word that has both the physical meaning of what is carried and the abstract sense of a theme or subject.

In his "Intimations of Immortality" ode, William Wordsworth writes

Our birth is but a sleep and a forgetting:
The Soul that rises with us, our life's Star,
   Hath had elsewhere its setting,
   And cometh from afar:
   Not in entire forgetfulness,
   And not in utter nakedness,
But trailing clouds of glory do we come
   From God, who is our home:
Heaven lies about us in our infancy!
Shades of the prison-house begin to close
   Upon the growing Boy,
But he beholds the light, and whence it flows,
   He sees it in his joy . . .

Birth is a form of sleep, in which our immortality is forgotten. The soul is a star.[4] Immortal glory is a cloud. The cloud is a cloak, which trails behind us. (Here we have a metaphor for a metaphor—the cloak for the cloud for the soul—as well as what is known as an *implied metaphor* because the cloak is not actually mentioned.) Our loss of immortality is a kind of nakedness. God is a home. Mortal life is a dark prison. (We go straight from home to jail.) A child still sees the light of heaven, although the darkness soon closes about him.

For a poet such as Wordsworth, metaphor, it is often said, is a kind of thinking. But it is a kind of thought that undermines "realistic" distinctions between things in order to get at a *creative* truth. Souls and stars are radically different kinds of things. To interpret the metaphor, we translate the vehicle into its tenor: "star" into "soul" and so forth. As we *imagine* the metaphor, however, we merge the two sides into a soul-star unity. Rather than being merely a way to say something else, therefore, the metaphor takes us to a new level of experience established by the combination itself: in this case, a fully spiritual experience of soul-starness. The poem is about knowing that special reality, with its own nuance and its own pleasure. Similarly, when Shakespeare chooses these metaphors to characterize love, he means what his metaphors say *as metaphors:*

> . . . it is an ever-fixèd mark°   *sea mark*
> That looks on tempests and is never shaken;
> It is the star to every wand'ring bark,°   *ship*
> Whose worth's unknown, although his height be taken.°   *measured*

---

4. The star is usually said to be the sun, its previous setting in an earlier life.

He is not simply composing a description or making comparisons. He does indeed mean that love is "an ever-fixèd mark / That looks on tempests" and so forth—and it really is.

Similes

My point about the special reality of metaphors might become clearer if we contrast them with **similes.** In a simile the distinction between the vehicle and the tenor is explicitly preserved, as in Robert Burns's "My love is like a red, red rose." Not *is,* only *like*—or *as,* or *as though:* "She tripped downstairs like an avalanche." "He sings as a piccolo chirps." "He glared at me as though he were a locomotive fast approaching." Edwin Arlington Robinson's old Mr. Flood, sitting meditatively on the hill above his town, sets down his jug of whiskey "as a mother sets her sleeping child / Down tenderly, fearing it may awake."

> And only when assured that on firm earth
> It stood, as the uncertain lives of men
> Assuredly did not, he paced away

and delivered a fond oration to himself ("Mr. Flood's Party"). William Blake tells us of the child born into a world of grief "like a fiend hid in a cloud" ("Infant Sorrow"). Richard Eberhart describes the reality of life that we must all someday face as "the truth wailing there like a red babe" ("If I could only live at the pitch that is near madness"). In Part One of *Henry IV,* Falstaff and Prince Hal have a good time getting Falstaff's mood just right:

FALSTAFF:	. . . I am as melancholy as a gib-°cat or	*neutered*
	a lugged° bear.	*captive*
PRINCE:	Or an old lion, or a lover's lute.	
FALSTAFF:	Yea, or the drone of a Lincolnshire bagpipe.	
PRINCE:	What sayest thou to a hare, or the melancholy	
	of Moor Ditch°?	*an open sewer*
FALSTAFF:	Thou hast the most unsavory similes, and art indeed the most	
	comparative, rascalliest, sweet young prince. . . .	

In *Othello* Iago poisons his commander's susceptible mind with similes, picturing Othello's wife's supposed intercourse with the lieutenant Cassio:

> It is impossible you should see this,
> Were they as prime° as goats, as hot as monkeys,   *aroused*
> As salt° as wolves in pride°, and fools as gross   *lustful; in heat*
> As ignorance made drunk.

He forces Othello to imagine what he cannot see so he will believe what he imagines. (We know it has never occurred and should be unthinkable.)

An *epic simile* (to be found in epic poems, naturally) paints its image loftily on a large scale. John Milton watches from afar as Satan flies toward the Gates of Hell:

> As when far off at sea a fleet descried
> Hangs in the clouds, by equinoctial winds
> Close sailing from Bengala, or the isles
> Of Ternate and Tidore, whence merchants bring
> Their spicy drugs; they on the trading flood
> Through the wide Ethiopian to the Cape
> Ply stemming nightly toward the Pole: so seemed
> Far off the flying fiend.
>
> *—Paradise Lost,* Book II

In this example, the scale of detail supports the scale of the subject. The point of the place names is that they are exotic and far from English readers. Bengala is Bengal in India, Ternate and Tidore are islands now in Indonesia, the Ethiopian is the Indian Ocean. Thus the distant perspective frames the diabolic journey with a tremendous sense of space.

Metaphor and simile, we can see, are different states of mind. In metaphor we enter an imaginative world where two disparate things become one. In simile we think with our conscious intelligence about a particular similarity, remaining aware that the similarity is a limited one; the effect may even depend as much on the difference, as in Mr. Flood's jug and the sleeping babe. A simile is an explicit comparison; a metaphor is a two-fold identity.

Some teachers and critics regard the symbol as a figure of speech, like metaphor and simile.[5] I have chosen to treat it earlier in the book (see Chap-

---

5. Formally, it is easy to tell metaphor from simile. However, if we accept the idea that they are different states of consciousness, this rhetorical distinction may yield to a more important one. Some similes are as tightly unified as most metaphors, and some metaphors are as intellectually self-aware as most similes. In "Dover Beach," Matthew Arnold compares the world to "a land of dreams" and says "we are here as on a darkling plain": Both figures have the form of similes but the imaginative quality of metaphors. In "She Dwelt among Untrodden Ways," Wordsworth describes a girl now dead first through a metaphor ("A violet . . .") then through a simile ("Fair as a star . . ."):

> A violet by a mossy stone
>   Half hidden from the eye!
> Fair as a star, when only one
>   Is shining in the sky.

She *is* a violet; she is *like* a star. Isn't the metaphor here as slack as the simile, a clearly rational comparison? Like the Arnold, my earlier examples from Blake and Eberhart are also unusually "taut." Blake would probably insist that the child *does* become a fiend hid in a cloud. This point, about the qualitative reversibility of some metaphors and similes, I have from the philosopher Philip Wheelwright's chapter "Metaphoric Tension" in his book *The Burning Fountain* (Bloomington: Indiana University Press, 1968).

ter 1). The basic point, at any rate, is that while metaphor says love is a rose and simile says love is like a rose, symbol simply gives us the rose in such a way that it is highly charged with the implications and associations it develops within its imaginative context.

> O Rose thou art sick.
> The invisible worm
> That flies in the night,
> In the howling storm:
>
> Has found out thy bed
> Of crimson joy:
> And his dark secret love
> Does thy life destroy.
>
>   —*Blake,* "The Sick Rose"

Two further points about metaphor and simile. First, we have in our language many instances of what are called *dead metaphors*. There is nothing wrong with them: they are simply expressions that no longer call up imaginative experience: "This puts things in a new light." "Go to the head of the class." "Now we get to the heart of the matter." The poet does not "get credit" for dead metaphors, so they do not get explicated as figures. Second, what appears to be a simile may be a factual comparison: An apple *is* like a pear in certain respects, a man like a woman, many adults like children. Coleridge's Ancient Mariner and his crew-mates greet the albatross "As if it had been a Christian soul": simply the way they did it.

Conceits

Two variations on the simile, sometimes hard to tell apart, are the conceit and the analogy, both also being explicit comparisons. A **conceit** (related to *concept* and *conceive*) is always explained as an extended simile. Many features of the comparison are brought out, the poet dwelling lovingly on the relationship. The Metaphysical poets of the early 17th century, particularly John Donne, are notable for their development of this figure. The most famous example is in Donne's "A Valediction: Forbidding Mourning," which concludes with a sixteen-line comparison between the movement of a pair of compasses and the poet's experience of journeying away from his wife (circling around without separation and coming back in the end). Here is a modern example in a one-sentence sonnet by Robert Frost, "The Silken Tent":

> She is as in a field a silken tent
> At midday when a sunny summer breeze
> Has dried the dew and all its ropes relent,

So that in guys it gently sways at ease,
And its supporting central cedar pole,
That is its pinnacle to heavenward
And signifies the sureness of the soul,
Seems to owe naught to any single cord,
But strictly held by none, is loosely bound
By countless silken ties of love and thought
To everything on earth the compass round,
And only by one's going slightly taut
In the capriciousness of summer air
Is of the slightest bondage made aware.

Donne's comparison is strictly rational. Frost's is less so, almost subliminal in fact. The lady is like a silken tent (not for your usual camping trip!), under very specific conditions at that: at midday, in summer, with a breeze that has "dried the dew," causing the guy lines to slacken ("relent" has this literal meaning, however, it also carries a personal feeling). The central tentpole, which is raised toward heaven, "signifies the sureness of [her] soul." The surrounding cords are "loosely bound / By . . . ties of love and thought" and suggest her bond to others. The contrast between *slack* and *taut* parallels her movement between self-containment and connection to the world outside.[6]

Analogies

An **analogy** shows the way in which one process or situation is like another. It is more clearly a form of reasoning, with one similarity leading usually to another. Byron composes a beautifully phrased simile when he writes

She walks in Beauty, like the night
Of cloudless climes and starry skies . . .

—"She Walks in Beauty"

In this next passage, he draws an analogy that is equally fine:

. . . the sword outwears its sheath,
And the soul wears out the breast,
And the heart must pause to breathe,
And love itself have rest.

—"So We'll Go No More A-roving"

---

6. This is a good poem, incidentally, on which to practice following the structure of a complex sentence in verse, an essential ability for good explication. How does the predicate of each clause relate to its subject?

Matthew Arnold's "Dover Beach" is based on a double analogy: "Our" watching the sea from Dover is like Sophocles' perception of life's tragic nature as he looks out on *his* country's sea, the Aegean; and both these bodies of water are like the "Sea of Faith," which Arnold saw receding in his own day. His poem simply juxtaposes these three thoughts without explaining the connections.

Synecdoche and Metonymy

Two cousins of metaphor, the pair synecdoche (sin-NECK-duck-key) and metonymy (met-AH-numb-me), are less appreciated, although they are common enough in everyday use. They are sometimes indistinguishable and some people don't bother trying to tell them apart. However, a useful distinction can be made in principle and in many examples. **Synecdoche** lets part of something stand in for the whole: "He fell for the first pretty face he saw." He may have, actually, but a little more than her face was probably involved. "Some of the best minds in America are assembled here today." They were probably bright enough to bring their bodies along with them. "I'd like a word with you." Some words can be very effective by themselves, but it sounds like some exchange is expected. Less commonly, the whole stands for the part: "England beat France in the soccer match." We may hope that only the teams played.

In **metonymy** a subject is represented by a specific object readily associated with it: "The pen is mightier than the sword." "The crown of England is rapidly losing its glitter." "The White House is finally negotiating with Capitol Hill." "She is the brains in the family." (Notice the difference between this and the "best minds" example in the previous paragraph.) Several good examples of metonymy can be found in "The Collar," by the 17th-century clergyman-poet George Herbert. The title of the poem refers to the clerical collar and therefore stands for Herbert's position in the Church. (A collar is also a restraint. And the word has also been seen as a pun on both "choler," meaning anger, and "caller": At the end of the poem the voice of God summons gently after the poet has vented resentment at the restraint his calling calls for.) Within the poem, Herbert writes:

> Sure there was wine
> Before my sighs did dry it; there was corn
> Before my tears did drown it.
> Is the year only lost to me?
> Have I no bays to crown it,
> No flowers, no garlands gay?

The wine and the corn (the second meaning "wheat" in British usage) stand for food and drink and the pleasures offered by both. The sighs and tears represent all the poet's grief and frustration. "Bays" is a conventional image referring to a poet's laurel crown, so it stands for his life as a poet. The "garlands gay" should bring to mind the good times of country living in ages gone.

Personification

Personification can be seen as a kind of implied metaphor. It describes something that is not human as if it were human (not, however, as if it were another animal—when Carl Sandberg's fog "comes on little cat feet," it is simply metaphorical). If the poet speaks of a storm as raging in a tantrum or of a gentle breeze tiptoeing beneath the trees, we are reading about natural phenomena in terms literally appropriate only for *persons.* In *The Rape of the Lock,* Alexander Pope describes the river Thames as surveying "with Pride . . . his rising Tow'rs." Robert Browning says "the sun looked over the mountain's rim" ("Parting at Morning"). Personifications (like metaphors) are often embedded in the language as common expressions which are not, therefore, part of the poet's figurative technique: "Winter is approaching; the end of the year will soon arrive." When Gwendolyn Brooks begins a poem "Abortions will not let you forget" ("The Mother"), she is on the borderline, it seems to me, between explicit personification and familiar idiom. She is taking advantage of both and of the difference (or the tension) between them: Something common and familiar is also dreadful and dramatic.

Synesthesia and Transferred Epithet

Our survey of figures of perception concludes with synesthesia and the transferred epithet. **Synesthesia** blends different senses, such as seeing and hearing, into a single image: a deafening red, a violet whisper in the cool light of morning, a pastel sonata of fur, the acrid stench of his music. (This is fun!) Robert Hayden remembers that

> On Sundays too my father got up early
> and put his clothes on in the blueblack cold . . .
>
> —"Those Winter Sundays"

Later in the poem, Hayden describes "the cold [air] splintering, breaking."

In a **transferred epithet,** an adjective ("epithet") that should logically describe a person is transferred to a noun in the person's context. It is usually a human feeling that is made to describe the time, place, or situation. I speak of "my young days," when, of course, I mean the days when I was young. Similarly, one speaks of a "sad result" and a "desperate maneuver." I might say, "He made a greedy fortune"; "She walks an anxious path." Revolted by his mother's marriage to his uncle, Hamlet refers to the "incestuous sheets" of their bed, but upset though he may be, he knows the sheets are not at fault. In *Paradise Lost,* Satan summons the other fallen angels where they "Lie thus astonished on th' oblivious pool." It is his colleagues, of course, who are oblivious because astonished (literally, "thunderstruck"), although the pool is probably not too conscious either. Here the artificiality of expression fits in with Milton's elevated tone of epic dignity.

Note that between metaphor and any of these other figures, there are gray (or perhaps, more interestingly, mauve) areas. The critic often makes distinctions that the poet doesn't need to bother about.

Figures of Logic

What I have called figures of perception can be seen as ways of thinking, but as my term suggests, the figures of logic are played specifically against logical expectations. They are apostrophe, irony, paradox, pun, understatement, and overstatement (or hyperbole). I could argue that simile and analogy should go here too, but I won't.

Apostrophe

You know what **apostrophe** means in punctuation ('); in poetics it means addressing something that can't hear you, usually because it is not human—or, if human, then not on the scene or not alive. The effect is typically a formal one, but it can be playful as well. Macbeth's "Out, out, brief candle" is one good example of very serious use of apostrophe. Sir Philip Sidney, on the other hand, begins a love sonnet by talking whimsically to the moon: "With how sad steps, O moon, thou climb'st the sky." (The "O"—not "oh"—is a traditional way of addressing something, although it can also let the poet hold forth in a lofty tone.) Apostrophe is illogical because it makes no sense to talk to something or even to someone who can't hear you, yet it expresses the speaker's state of mind with dramatic force. Note that when John Donne writes, "Go, and catch a falling star," he is not apostrophizing but addressing the reader. When Robert Herrick begins "Corinna's Going a Maying" with "Get up, get up for shame," he is talking to a fictional character that we imagine being there to hear him.

Irony

The other main figures of logic are familiar from everyday use: verbal irony, paradox, overstatement, and understatement. They all belong to the general "illogic" of **irony,** which turns ordinary logic upside down. Irony says *more* by not meaning what it says. It suggests an alternative way of seeing things that seems closer to the truth. A kind of tension is established between two perspectives, conveying their sharp difference by implication, a tension that holds the writer's real meaning. Irony is, therefore, not just intellectual, for the gap is effective dramatically, making the meaning happen in what can be a startling reversal. It can even express the pain of resistance to the way things are, like Hamlet's account of how happy he is:

> O God, your only jig-maker! What should a man do but be merry? For look you how cheerfully my mother looks, and my father died within's two hours.

Alexander Pope's schoolmaster boasts:

> We ply the Memory, we load the brain,
> Bind rebel Wit, and double chain on chain,
> Confine the thought, to exercise the breath;
> And keep them [youth] in the pale of Words till death,
> Whate'er the talents, or howe'er designed,
> We hang one jingling padlock on the mind.
>
> —*The Dunciad*, Book IV

Sarcasm is a very weak form of irony, saying more about the speaker than the subject, expressing, as it does, the speaker's nasty feeling: "You think you're really something, don'tcha!" Good irony is likely to be much more subtle, sly, and adroit. The tone is shrewd and often caustic, bringing us to a subtle perception. The literary ironist speaks in a tone of intellectual detachment, a sophisticated capacity to see through others, with a justified sense of superiority. Irony can express, therefore, a strong sense of character, a voice that is knowing and penetrating but also committed to its values in a confident manner. In works of satire, the satirist, one may say, is the hero, whose intelligence we are pleased to share, as we take shelter ourselves from insidious innuendoes.

VERBAL IRONY In its most obvious form, irony appears as *verbal irony*. It is a pretended logic, in which the speaker means to fool the unwary but invite us clever folk into the game. The writer plays with the way he says things, so we need to be alert to the logic of thoughts and phrasing. Shakespeare's fools (what we usually call "jesters") make their living at this. When, in *As You Like It*, the young ladies are invited to enjoy a wrestling match, the fool Touchstone comments with mock admiration

> Thus men may grow wiser every day. It is the first time that ever I heard breaking of ribs was sport for ladies.

Sometimes a character's remarks are unconsciously ironic, as we can tell from the context. When Polonius in *Hamlet* advises his son, "To thine own self be true," we don't dismiss the sentiment but we do consider who is talking and how his words are betrayed by his behavior. In a medieval crucifixion play, the soldiers crucifying Christ swear by Christ while they are concentrating conscientiously on their labor. Seduction poems, a sophisticated pastime in the 17th century, were commonly ironic. Through a kind of pretended naiveté, the eager lover offers various logical reasons why the young beauty should assent to his ardors. The following argument is based on the belief at the time that the sex act mixed together the partners' blood.

> Mark but this flea, and mark in this
> How little that which thou deny'st me is;
> It sucked me first, and now sucks thee,
> And in this flea our two bloods mingled be;
> Thou knowst this cannot be said
> A sin, nor shame, nor loss of maidenhead . . .
>
> —*John Donne*, "The Flea"

In Andrew Marvell's "To His Coy Mistress," however, the argument outweighs the seduction, dramatizing a powerful reflection on mortality.

Here is the celebrated opening of Jane Austen's *Pride and Prejudice:*

> It is a truth universally acknowledged, that a single man in possession of a good fortune must be in want of a wife.

It is a "truth" that is really acknowledged "universally" only by parents (rather well off themselves) with marriageable daughters they would like to dispose of. The narrator pretends to share the sentiment, as though it were indeed a self-evident law of life, but it is a self-conscious pretense. Stylistically, the sentence starts off in the language of philosophy but follows through with a distinctly unphilosophical proclamation. The ironic effect is a kind of droll anticlimax. After this, through the rest of the brief first chapter, we move to verbal irony in dialogue. Mr. Bennett, father to five such young ladies, pretends not to understand his wife's frenetic curiosity about the young gentleman in question:

> ". . . A single man of large fortune; four or five thousand [pounds] a year. What a fine thing for our girls!"
> "How so? How can it affect them?"
> "My dear Mr. Bennett," replied his wife, "how can you be so tiresome! You must know that I am thinking of his marrying one of them."
> "Is that his design in settling here?"

"Design! Nonsense, how can you talk so! But it is very likely that he *may* fall in love with one of them, and therefore you must visit him as soon as he comes."

Mr. Bennett cannot criticize his wife directly, since she will not get the point, so he amuses himself (and us), comforting himself for having to put up with her. Although he fully intends to visit his new neighbor the next morning, he cannot resist exasperating his wife into further absurdity. This is irony in action.

Mr. Bennett is functioning in the role that the Greeks called the *eiron,* a figure who pretends modesty in order to express a natural superiority. Making little of himself, the *eiron* acts *ironically* as he exposes or deceives or ridicules or simply provides a contrast for a character called the *alazon,* who is usually a pretentious fool glorying in exaggerated virtues. Typically, the *eiron* is a trickster, merrily drawing his victim into a well-deserved disaster. Mrs. Bennett is a mild case of the *alazon.* Her husband plays upon her motherly self-importance and her illusion of social refinement; however, she is too much the flibbertigibbet to be a full-blown example. Thus, she is spared disaster and is immune to exposure. Better examples of the alazon are Molière's "saintly" Tartuffe (before his true nature as a con artist is revealed) and Shakespeare's Malvolio, in *Twelfth Night.* The sanctimoniousness of the one and the pomposity of the other are clearly puffed up to be deflated. We watch, with pleasant malice, as they get closer and closer to the banana peel. Polonius is *alazon* to Hamlet's *eiron,* meeting disaster enough in death. Prince Hal serves as *eiron* to Falstaff's *alazon,* but part of Falstaff's special genius lies in his ability to be both at once, as he plays the role of *being Falstaff* for the self-satisfaction of others.

STYLISTIC IRONY The opening sentence of *Pride and Prejudice* is a brief example of what we can call *stylistic irony.* Here, an author deliberately adopts a style or a tone that is sharply opposed to his or her true viewpoint. Feelings are held back, to be suggested by innuendo. Jonathan Swift's "A Modest Proposal" is a complete work in this mode. We are given an earnest argument that Ireland's poverty should be remedied by raising and selling Irish children as food. Behind the ironic earnestness and the "modesty" of the tone, we should be hearing Swift's outrage at England's failure to treat the Irish humanely. In a metaphoric sense, the children of Ireland already are being slaughtered and devoured by their wealthy English landlords.

One much-loved form of stylistic irony is **parody.** In the best-known kind, a famous writer's style is ridiculed by mock imitation. When almost everyone knew the beginning of Carl Sandburg's brief poem "Fog" ("The fog comes / on little cat feet), the verse-humorist Odgen Nash gave us "The frog comes / on little flat feet." In the following excerpt, William Faulkner parodies himself, pretending to be a ghost-writer, Ernest V. Trueblood, who is "really" responsible for Faulkner's own notoriously convoluted style (see the real thing on pages 58–59). The two are discussing what Trueblood will write for Faulkner the next day, when they hear that the boys have set fire to the pasture. Faulkner springs up

> . . . referring to his own son, Malcolm, and to his brother's son, James, and to the cook's son, Rover or Grover. Grover his name is, though both Malcolm and James (they and Grover are of an age and have, indeed, grown up not only contemporaneously but almost inextricably) have insisted upon calling him Rover since they could speak, so that now all the household, including the child's own mother and naturally the child itself, call him Rover too, with the exception of myself, whose practice and belief it has never been to call any creature, man, woman, child or beast, out of its rightful name. . . .

to quote just the first half of the sentence.[7] Parody can be playful, then, as well as critical. Sometimes it can be very serious. Donald Justice's "Counting the Mad" imitates a familiar nursery rhyme with poignant force, reducing our respect for the original not a whit.

> This one was put in a jacket,
> This one was sent home,
> This one was given bread and meat
> But would eat none,
> And this one cried No No No No
> All day long.

Here is a purely stylistic parody in which George Bernard Shaw skewers a cherished institution:

> Marriage is the only legal contract which abrogates as between the parties all the laws that safeguard the particular relation to which it refers.
>
> —"The Revolutionist's Handbook," *Man and Superman*

Imitating the dense style of a legal contract, Shaw conveys the paradoxical trap of marriage with serious wit.

DRAMATIC IRONY In a broad sense, most stories are ironic. At the end, plots reverse expectations the author has created in the beginning, or they upset our assumptions about how things are supposed to work in this world. The

---

7. The whole piece (and, of course, many more in this genre) can be read in *Parodies: An Anthology from Chaucer to Beerbohm—and After,* edited by Dwight Macdonald (N.Y.: Random House, 1960).

love between Romeo and Juliet *should* reconcile their families and allow everybody to live happily ever after. It reconciles them, all right, but only in the deaths of the lovers. In the narrative line of Edward Arlington Robinson's poem "Richard Cory," the wealthy, gracious, and much admired gentleman in town should be eminently pleased with life, but he kills himself. Irony doesn't have to be a let-down, however. In Emily Dickinson's poem about the gentleman called Death, we are made to see what should be appalling as, strangely, rather agreeable.

In *dramatic irony* the author lets us know what a character or narrator cannot see coming, putting us on a superior level as we watch someone about to fall into the thorns while expecting a rosy future. We can see how dumb the character is or just how unduly optimistic. An important variation of dramatic irony occurs pointedly in *Oedipus the King*. This more specific technique is known as Sophoclean irony in honor of that play's author, Sophocles. Early in the play, Oedipus proclaims a kingly curse upon the foul being who has polluted Thebes and brought down a plague upon the city. The rest of the play shows Oedipus getting a clearer and clearer picture that he himself is the nasty one. Ironically, the judge is the criminal, the detective has "done it." Sophoclean irony is more than a nuance of language, therefore: It suggests through events something absurdly dreadful at the heart of life. It is common in the Greek myths. Consider the predicament of Cassandra, princess of the doomed city of Troy. To win her love, Apollo gave her the gift of prophecy. When she refused to yield to his advances, however, he ordained that no one would ever believe her. She who knows what is coming is mocked and punished for saying so.

And if there is tragic irony, there is comic irony as well, in at least two forms: the excesses of a villain or a pretentious fool bringing about his or her own humiliation; and suffering reversed into joy, as in Christian belief the Crucifixion leading to the Resurrection.

Variations on Irony

If we regard puns and paradoxes as forms of irony, we can see that in **paradox** contradictory aspects of reality are collapsed into one concept, whereas in puns, distinctly different kinds of truth are broken out of individual words.

PARADOX Wordsworth's "The Child is father of the Man" is a paradoxical metaphor. In a line of Lord Byron's quoted earlier, paradox plays upon the nature of logic itself: "Man, being reasonable, must get drunk." It is only rational to need an escape from reason. William Blake sees a painful paradox in the self-congratulation of charitable souls: They get more out of being noble towards the poor than they would by relieving poverty through social reform.

Pity would be no more
If we did not make somebody Poor;
And Mercy no more could be
If all were as happy as we.

        —"The Human Abstract"

In the very different paradoxes of Byron and Blake, the tension lies between a socially "normal" attitude and an insight that finds that attitude hypocritical. In Byron's the revelation is a merry one; in Blake's it is painful to consider. Byron's line says that strict logic is not good sense: It must allow for self-gratification. The irony in Wordsworth's line reflects the inadequacy of ordinary reason and ordinary social relations to grasp an almost mystical intuition: the knowledge we are born with that gets lost as our minds mature.

The most compact form of paradox is *oxymoron*, which occurs in two words, usually a noun described by an adjective meaningfully at odds with it: "She is horribly beautiful." "His entrance was a dramatic anticlimax." "Our leaders are honestly corrupt." A happy critic? Oxymoron has a pithy punch.

PUNS In a tribute to his "beloved, the Author Mr. William Shakespeare," Ben Jonson **puns** affectionately on the master's name when he speaks of his plays "shaking" a stage and of his verses as shaking "a Lance, / As [though they were] brandish't at the eyes of Ignorance." Puns are common in Shakespeare's plays. The very first line that we hear from Lord Hamlet is, in fact, a double pun: "A little more than kin and less than kind." He is referring to his usurping uncle's stagey show of kindness toward him as being (a) unbefitting a relative, (b) unnatural, and (c) ungracious—all three meanings being implied in Elizabethan understanding of "kind." For Hamlet, the pun expresses an unbearable conflict among the different views of his situation that he must struggle with. Neo-classical critics were later to deplore Shakespeare's puns (called "quibbles" then), but they are often not just a trivial playing around with words (like some of my titles). In Sonnet 65, Shakespeare asks about physical beauty, "Shall Time's best jewel from Time's chest lie hid?" Time's "chest" is both the jewel box and the coffin. Could it also be the chest that contains one's heart? In either case, the pun combines in one thought the richness of beauty and its mortality. The effect is both poignant and horrifying (an effect sometimes called "the Metaphysical shudder," after the so-called Metaphysical poets like Donne and Marvell, who favored it.)

OVERSTATEMENT In *overstatement* (or **hyperbole**), the language says more than it means literally. We can see that our casual use of words like "incredible" and "devastating" is (fortunately) overstatement if we think about what they really say (which we don't). When a Renaissance poet compares his mistress' eyes to the sun, he is clearly overstating his case to express how far beyond reasonable understanding is both her beauty and his adoration.

Shakespeare plays upon this *trope* (or traditional figure) when he declares his own "mistress' eyes are nothing like the sun" (Sonnet 130). His "Dark Lady," as she is known, has her problems, but she is a human being. Alexander Pope describes a fashionable young lady according to the same trope:

> Bright as the Sun, her Eyes the Gazers strike,
> And, like the Sun, they shine on all alike.

> —*The Rape of the Lock*

However, Pope is teasing in a different way. By his day the idea is a stale one, but when in the second line he suggests that her attentions are as indiscriminate as the sun's, he gives it a new twist. In fact, he is being doubly ironical. (No surprise: Pope is the master of irony among English writers.) The overstatement is turned upside down, implying the pretty young Belinda's vanity and empty-headedness. The tone of reverent praise is a sly dig.

Actually, this entire long poem, *The Rape of the Lock,* belongs to an inherently ironic genre called the **mock epic,** or *mock heroic poem.* Throughout, Pope adopts, in pretense, the lofty tone, the nobly heroic actions, and the mythological framework of ancient epics like the *Iliad* and the *Aeneid:* His purpose is to overplay the self-importance of this elegant society, to expose its shallowness (not, however, to mock the epic form). The central action takes place upon the battlefield of a card game, when a dastardly young man "rapes" a lock of Belinda's precious hair. All delightfully overstated. Another typically Popean form of irony occurs when her trivial pursuits are listed, in a deadpan style, along with truly serious matters. She is watched over by (totally ineffectual) airy spirits, whose job it is to forestall disaster:

> Whether the Nymph shall break Diana's law,
> Or some frail China Jar receive a Flaw;
> Or stain her Honor or her new Brocade;
> Forget her Pray'rs, or miss a Masquerade;
> Or lose her heart, or Necklace, at a Ball;
> Or whether Heav'n has doomed that Shock must fall.

(The "nymph" here is Belinda herself, regarded mythologically. The goddess Diana upholds chastity. Shock is Belinda's lapdog. The literal meaning of *rape,* "carrying off," is often taken for granted in classical literature. The exaggerated importance Belinda places upon her gown, the masqued ball, or her necklace is a form of hyperbole. Seen from the other direction, however, Pope himself *understates* her pretensions, ironically deflating them. The main point is her inability to distinguish what truly matters. This kind of deliberate inappropriateness with which words are set together is called *zeugma.*)

UNDERSTATEMENT **Understatement** is most commonly a turn of phrase, often cautiously dry in tone. In *As You Like It,* the fool Touchstone misses court life when he is living in the forest: "When I was at home I was in a better place." His simple word understates how much better it really was. Understatement can also be gently pathetic, as in Old English poetry, where it lends a kind of austere dignity to a life of hardship, a life in which gratification does not come easy. In *Beowulf,* the monster Grendel attacks King Hrothgar's mead hall, devouring sleeping thanes: "Thereafter it was easy to find the man who sought rest for himself elsewhere, farther away." Hrothgar is praised as "a king blameless in all things until age took from him the joys of his strength—old age that has often harmed many."[8] In this way, minimizing a situation actually heightens its pathos. When Isaac is expecting to be sacrificed by his father Abraham in one of the mysteries (or Biblical plays) written later in the Middle Ages, the boy says of God:

> He might a° sent me a better destiny   *might have*
> If it had a be° his pleasure.   *had been*
>
> —The Brome *Sacrifice of Isaac*

This is understatement very close to *euphemism,* an expression evading unpleasant associations. However, we sense that Isaac really means what he says as he says it. A less equivocal example of ironic euphemism occurs in Shakespeare's *The Winter's Tale* when the merry thief Autolycus pretends innocence, characterizing himself as "a snatcher up of unconsidered trifles." The tone of understatement is not necessarily dry, however. In his poem addressed (in apostrophe) "To an Athlete Dying Young," A. E. Housman calls the dead youth "Townsman of a stiller town." The effect is appropriately subdued.

Two illustrations that I used before can be seen now as fuller versions of understatement: William Carlos Williams's plum poem and Swift's "A Modest Proposal." Both speak less than they mean. Williams's tone is factual in an obviously simple manner, but he cautiously withholds delicate feelings, that tinge of delicious regret that we can feel without hearing it spoken. By its very modesty, "A Modest Proposal" goes very dramatically in the opposite direction from the powerful outrage it intends. A common form of understatement occurs in metaphors that deliberately downplay their subject. On the other hand, "A Modest Proposal" can also be seen as hyperbole, for its tasteful cannibalism provides a metaphor for civilized laws that exploit the poor. The rich English landlords are not *quite* eating the Irish babies . . . but almost.

In the image from Housman's "To an Athlete" quoted above, death is an extremely quiet sort of village. Frequently in poetry one comes upon an expression calling death a form of sleep, another understated metaphor, as Ham-

---

8. Translation by E. Talbot Donaldson.

let realizes when he thinks closely about "that sleep of death." Also from Housman is this complete poem, the first line of which doubles as the title:

> With rue my heart is laden
> For golden friends I had,
> For many a rose-lipt maiden,
> And many a lightfoot lad.
>
> By brooks too broad for leaping
> The lightfoot boys are laid;
> The rose-lipt girls are sleeping
> In fields where roses fade.

Perhaps the "lightfoot boys" and the "rose-lipt girls" understate the whole life span of these old friends in a way that stresses the pathos of their passing first into age and then into extinction. The carefully restrained word "rue," which means both "regret" and "pity," is verbal understatement for clearly deeper feelings. (Wordsworth, you may recall, reverses the idea completely when, in his "Intimations of Immortality" ode, he calls *birth* a sleep.) John Crowe Ransom gives us a fresh modern variation on the understatement of death as sleep when he describes a dead child's pose in the coffin as a "brown study"—which means a deeply thoughtful mood:

> There was such speed in her little body,
> And such lightness in her footfall,
> It is no wonder her brown study
> Astonishes us all.
>
> —"Bells for John Whiteside's Daughter"

"Tactfully," like the guest he is before another family's grief, the poet restrains his show of feeling to let it sound truly sincere.

A twist on understatement is *litotes* (lie-TOE-tees), a kind of double negative canceling the opposite of the real meaning: "She cast me a not unfriendly glance." Literally, "not unfriendly" just means "friendly," but we should catch the innuendo of something rather more sly. The irony is a little sharper than in ordinary understatement. The technique is not uncommon in Old English. When Beowulf sets sail for a meeting with the monster Grendel, "very little," we are told, "did wise men blame him for that adventure." They praised him very much indeed. After the meeting, visitors come to gape at the dead creature's footprints: "Nor did his going from life seem sad to any of the men who saw the tracks of the one without glory." The men are tickled to see them—to coin an understatement.

The uses of understatement quoted here should make clear the real power of subtlety. As in all figures of speech (well used), the poet is indirect not just to be obscure or to sound super-refined but to express more realistically the nature of feelings, which simply *are* sensitive in the privacy of our own being. And for this we must be grateful. Emily Dickinson defends the indirect method of telling it "slant" as a more basic need. In things that matter, it is the only way of being really truthful.

> Tell all the truth but tell it slant—
> Success in Circuit lies
> Too bright for our infirm Delight
> The truth's superb surprise
> As Lightning to the Children eased
> With explanation kind
> The Truth must dazzle gradually
> Or every man be blind—

Summing Up

By using figurative language, the skillful author captures what cannot get into factual language: moods, tones, subliminal perceptions, and the all-important sensation of having one's own experience. Thus, through figures, words can conjure what they cannot say. Even a cliché can be more accurate than a literal statement. If I say, "I could eat a cow" or "You are as lovely as a sunset," the absurdity of the cow and my aesthetic self-consciousness about the sunset show the intensity of my passion: They dramatize what feels dramatic. Also, they express the way I feel about my passion: the silliness of my "desperate" hunger, the sweetness of my grand amour.

Tying the right tag around the neck of an expression should help us to notice that it *is* a figure of speech and to appreciate the fact that figures do come in varieties. If you want to see how a poem is working, however, this should be only the first step. It is more important to explain the logic of the figure: exactly what it is that the two parts of a metaphor or simile have in common, why an irony is ironical, a paradox paradoxical, hyperbole hyperbolic. This kind of analysis is one of the main features of explication. More important yet is describing and accounting for the effect that the figure has. What does the poet achieve by using this figure? What exactly does it convey in our experience of the piece? And, in fact, what does the poet get out of using this particular kind of figure? What does a given synecdoche express by being synecdochic, an understatement by being understated? Byron's simile (from "She Walks in Beauty") allows the lady to remain herself, in her own beauty, while evoking the atmosphere of a cloudless, starry night sky to suggest particular qualities of that beauty: delicate, calm, clear, mysterious, and more than we can put in a few adjectives. Macbeth's apostrophe to life, "Out, out, brief candle . . ." expresses *as apostrophe* the desperation with which he is confronting his mortality. As implied metaphor—candle for life—it expresses pathetically the insubstantiality and vulnerability of life together with the warmth and light of its possibilities, which seem slight indeed under the circumstances. The combined effect should leave us moved and perhaps also appalled by Macbeth's combination of disgust, disillusion, and despair.

The most important reason of all for studying figures closely, however, is a broader one and does not end with the instances in themselves *or* their names. Seeing how all these possibilities play in imagination makes one far more aware of the general richness of language that a writer can draw upon for precision, for intensity of awareness, and for the sundry forms of beauty.

Chapter 4

How Literature Expresses Our Reality by Making Its Own

Symbolic Reality

Out of one world the author forms another. They are not completely separate worlds, although there are essential differences in the kind of reality that each has. How we understand this special world-in-art depends upon its relation to our own; however, we need to see how it is both like and unlike our own. In fact, we need to see how it is real in one sense and unreal in another. This relationship gets clearer if we think of the literary work in terms of symbolism.

In the first chapter, we thought about symbols; now we are talking about a broader concept. Specific symbols are important elements in literary works: crosses, albatrosses, flowery bowers, and phallic towers. In a fundamental sense, however, all of literature—and even all of culture—is symbolism. A culture consists of various symbolic languages and the various works formulated (or "stated") in those languages. English, French, Tagalog, and Hindi are obvious kinds of language, but it is useful to consider algebra, history, chemistry, music, and poetry as symbolic languages as well—all the systems we have, in fact, to represent our experience in the world and share with one another our comprehension. In these various languages, we create **symbolic forms,** individual works such as equations, scientific hypotheses, symphonies, and poems.[1]

The kind of reality we wish to identify in a literary work is first of all, therefore, a *symbolic reality.* The world we enter when we read is a symbolic world. It is a world made not of actual time and space but, in Langer's word (coined before the advent of computer technology), of *virtual* time and space.[2] Characters are virtual people living in virtual houses. They are real "as it were." While objective truth is valid or invalid, symbolic truth *tends to be true.* Your portrait is not real in the same sense that you are real, but it is, nonetheless, a real portrait. And by looking like you, it tends to be you, conveying a real sense of you. But it should have its own interest for you as well, as a portrait. Its value depends on the way it strikes you with its own reality while reflecting yours. Is it interesting *as a picture?* To say that literature has a symbolic reality is to say that it is both real and unreal at the same time, both typical and unique. We get familiarity and we get fantasy. Literature, on one hand, reflects us and reflects upon us; on the other, it invites a special kind of joy in the imagination.

The virtual time, space, and people of literature are not merely replicas, therefore. They serve a need that the real thing cannot possibly fulfill. There is a lot that characters cannot do, like talk to us in any words other than the ones their dialogue is made of, like die accidentally before their authors need them to, like have any past life other than what the author cares to give them. However, we can be more sure than we can of ourselves that they live in a meaningful universe—even if that meaning should say that life itself is meaningless. Their meaning has to do, of course, with their relationship to us. In its own world, the symbol carries some essence of ours. As interested as we may be in their own odd stories and in their own quirks and squabbles, we find they capture something of our nature. In Chapter 1, I defined *symbol* as an image that tends to generalize itself. Now we can say that every story has a tendency to generalize itself, suggesting typical predicaments of human experience. Every character is something of an *everyperson,* projecting some recurring facet of our selves.

---

1. These ideas are based loosely on the views of Susanne K. Langer and Ernst Cassirer. For Langer, see *Philosophy in a New Key: A Study in the Symbolism of Reason, Rite, and Art* (Cambridge, Mass.: Harvard, 1942); for Cassirer, *An Essay on Man: An Introduction to a Philosophy of Human Culture* (New Haven: Yale, 1944). Cassirer speaks of the systems themselves as "symbolic forms." Langer would object strenuously to my calling them (metaphorically) "languages."

2. This term is used in Langer's books *Feeling and Form* (New York: Scribner's, 1953) and *Problems of Art* (New York: Scribner's, 1957).

Consider one of the most imaginative of works. Shakespeare's *A Midsummer Night's Dream* is a very real play about very real—though not, we may want to say, realistic—characters. We have a mythical duke (Theseus) who sounds smugly middle-aged. We have a quartet of willful adolescents who are purest poetry. We have the local weaver who is gorgeously dumb and winds up with a donkey head on his shoulders. And we have a crew of fairies who can fly through the air. They serve a fairy king and queen who squabble like any married couple, although *their* squabble turns the weather dreary. We relate to these creatures in at least four ways at once—humanly, aesthetically, imaginatively, and meaningfully:

- They all speak and behave with vivid personality;
- They charm us with their creator's virtuosity;
- They impress us with their own existence, as a species unto themselves;
- They reflect the delightful absurdity of our own existence and its evanescence.

They are *of* us and they are *about* us, they are themselves and they are art.[3]

The two worlds—the one we live in and the virtual world of the work—are held together by the process of symbolic projection, which draws out the one from the other. The imagination projects, and projection (literally) casts something forth. The work is known only in relation to minds imagining it—both ours and the author's, for symbols are fraught with feeling and consciousness. The work finally becomes an artful thing, however, through the resources of language, becoming very much itself. Thus the personal world of the artist and the social world round about are projected into the special world of the literary work, which has its own ecology in the imagination. A novel carries the author's society and creative personality along into its own world. It also carries over the feelings of living that constitute the human spirit. A love poem is a loving poem; Lear's tragedy (I hope to show) is also our own. Meaning has everything to do with this relationship—and this difference. The world of art is a stylized world, a world of interpretive transformation (remember the discussion of stylization in Chapter 1), but there is some consistency in transformation, just as we remain ourselves through all the transformations of our lives.

Thus symbolic meaning is both interpretive and creative. The symbol (or symbolic form) does not *have* meaning; it *makes* meaning. It "symbolifies" rather than symbolizes; meaning is a process rather than a statement. Unlike

---

3. I am returning, with some difference, to a theme in Chapter 1, discussed under "Sense in Sensibility."

a symbol, a sign, like the flag, refers simply to something outside itself; it stands for something, and we understand it by translation. The symbol, on the other hand, is complex: it has a lot to do for itself. (It is common nowadays, in my view, for critics to oversimplify symbols by treating them as signs or codes.) To express the intricate realities that we are, a symbol must have an intricate reality of its own, and it must interest us in what that is. To express the processes of our lives, it must enact its drama for us.

Because symbols are real and unreal, creative and reflective, the idea of symbolic form suggests an integral approach to the study of literature. In the symbolic form of literature, the author, the reader, and society interpenetrate; aesthetics, stylistics, psychology, social structure, and intellectual history all come together. The work expresses its author, its society, and its cultural traditions. Critics who take a strictly psychological, sociological, or historical approach to interpretation often treat characters as though they were people and the imaginative world as though it were the kind of time and space all around us. (For some explanation of contemporary critical approaches, see Appendix 1 at the end of the book.) If you acknowledge the broader picture, however, you can emphasize any feature of the symbolic reality, according to your bent, without losing a sense of proportion or a sense of aesthetic values. Art is about life, but if we take art *as* life, we lose a lot of beauty, a lot of meaning, and the good faith of communication.[4]

A World View

Pictures, sounds, sometimes smells, and bodily sensations. Sunsets and flowers, of course, eyebrows and golden hair, but also mob scenes and guns, sandwiches, bald heads, sneezes, scissors, and sewers. The taste of a pastry, sexual stirrings. Literary language projects images, and a scattering of images can suggest the essential nature of people, places, and moods. Images can also establish the mind as it perceives details, deciding what *is* the essential nature of things. Literary language continually constructs a work by focusing, arranging, and exploring images, providing matter for all the imaginative senses,

---

4. The relevance of deconstruction theory is more complicated. In order to express direct experience, symbols need to be partially different from it. Expressing our minds, they convey our unconsciousness as well as our consciousness. As Thomas Carlyle said (thinking in metaphysical terms), symbols reveal and conceal. Deconstruction focuses on the concealment (of what it prefers to call "signs") and depreciates the revelation. Symbolic theory can accommodate what I think is valid in deconstruction, therefore, without getting trapped in what many see as its negativism. For more on this argument, see my book *Between Blake and Nietzsche*.

whether such images are part of the literal scene where the action is taking place or they are metaphors or symbols—the moon of lovers or of loneliness or the moon of a cool night sky. Through vivid images, we are struck, perhaps, that things and conditions really are what they are, even boredom, emptiness, and ugliness.

Characters are images of a sort, especially a character in a particular episode, alone or with others, posed and moving through a process of action— thus Romeo below Juliet's balcony or Hamlet leaping into Ophelia's grave. The tense court setting that opens the second scene of *Hamlet* or a battle scene or a storm at sea may also be thought of as a complex image composed of many things to see and hear and feel. The imagery adds up to a world whole and unique that is more than the sum of its parts: a Victorian London as seen by Charles Dickens with his own quirky eye for what is delightfully or dreadfully grotesque, a medieval Denmark made from scraps of Elizabethan England, a totalitarian America of the next century, and so forth. All are imaginary projections out of what is known, what is conjectured, and what is made up fresh in the free-floating theater of the mind. Through evocative imagery, the author's language "worldifies," let us say, conjuring an environment that may seem as much alive as the characters in it.

We are tourists in such worlds, with a fixed itinerary—but with some differences. We are shown all that there is; we are asked to truly *see* what we are looking at. We compare what we see with what we know of our home planet and with what we have seen elsewhere. It is a world to enjoy, and it is also a world to interpret. What are the laws here? The laws of time and space as well as the laws of politics, certainly the laws of psychology. We are talking not only about a Victorian England or an Elizabethan—the *author's* environment—but the stylized fictional world of a Scrooge or a Hamlet. What holds things together imaginatively? How do characters, those humanoid ideas, behave toward each other? Most importantly, what does it feel like to be alive here, to experience oneself within this whole image of society, living its customs and thinking its characteristic thoughts as we "know" our way into its specific realm of experience?

The Cultural Context

A literary world is drawn to a large degree out of forms and images from the author's culture, including the culture's political, religious, and social institutions. As a result, we can *sort of* live in Homer's time or Shakespeare's, comparing the lifestyle of the day with our own. We have the vicarious experience of being kings and queens, saints and murderers, and also of living amid the kind of poverty or warfare or political oppression that most of us have escaped by the luck of birth—without having to take any of the consequences. Reading works from a different culture helps to put us there, but not just (to improve what I said before) as tourists looking; rather, we have the privilege of being within people's minds in a world that opens up aspects of life different from those we are used to, aspects fostered not only by different traditions but also by different attitudes toward tradition.

We do not just come to see how people live elsewhere, therefore; rather, we comprehend what it is *like* for them to be living their lives, with a direct realization regarding why they live as they do. If we let our imagination go where the author leads us, we understand how naturally the lives of others have taken different shape from ours—while at the same time, we sense how like us they are under it all, how we might have lived in such a different manner and been just as rightly human, and how, under all the differences, things haven't changed all that much anyway. Aside from the experience we have via whole worlds of characters, furthermore, we get to know life through the particularly acute minds of authors who bring us perspectives on being human that we are not used to, perspectives that let us see things with unusual penetration and feel the heightened energy of our own intelligence.

The past of our own culture is also to some degree another culture. There too we are inner tourists, or travelers in a time machine that can put us in the heads of people, and there too we have the privilege of living with a difference. In "Young Goodman Brown" and many of Hawthorne's other works, like *The Scarlet Letter,* we make a psychological visit to American origins in Puritan New England. Hawthorne imagines what this world was like and also what it must have been like to live in it. However, his interest is not primarily in a realistic portrayal. His old Massachusetts is a world in the imagination, conceived and shaped to *interpret* the Puritans and their influence on later American culture.

Visiting the past in this way, we are likely to discover that it has both advantages and disadvantages as a way of life, that each period makes possible certain aspects of human expression (or self-realization) at the expense of others. The cultural unity of earlier times, for example, provided the stability and the sensitivity of a generally shared faith, which modern life has sacrificed. Modern culture, however, is based upon a more or less open-ended view of life's possibilities that most of us would not care to sacrifice for the unity that we've lost. It is perhaps a trade-off.

In an important sense, the past is always with us, deny it as we may. Visiting, you seem to remember having been there before. You don't quite fit in but feel compelled to poke around, watching for an important realization about who you are. If you read early literature with an open mind, you may recall that familiar sense of strangeness we experience in dreams, when feelings and viewpoints of which we are not ordinarily conscious seem restored to us. People who love older literature often feel they are rediscovering lost parts of themselves, important capacities to think, feel, and see the world that complement and broaden modern culture's ways of being conscious.

The study of past literature clarifies the nature of literature itself, as well as the nature of life. By reading writers of one or two generations together, we better understand the communal nature of literature: seeing how writers respond (with variations) to the challenges and pressures of their times, how they draw upon the authors before them, how they debate with one another the possibilities of imagination. We understand the assumptions writers share in a "school of thought" or tradition, the way they respond to ideas that are in the air; nor is this only a matter of intellectual information for us, for we can sense the urgency of intellectual discovery and debate, the impact of ideas upon people's lives. The nature of literature reflects, therefore, our own communal nature—our interactive relation to the world around us and the world behind our backs.

By studying together a selection of the writers within a cultural movement—Romantics, say, or Neoclassicists—we learn something essential about what a culture is. By studying epochs in sequence, we appreciate the dimension of time, which is equally important to cultural identity. In a culture, as in each of us personally, the past adds up, pretty much, to the present. To understand what we are, we must know what we have been, for the past is always in us—the good and the bad of it, what we have held onto and what we think we have lost. The past serves therefore as *analysis* of the present, to a very large degree, showing us what its elements are and how they have come together.

Because each stage of life—for a culture as for a person—is a response to the stage before, change is probably more a matter of transformation than invention. Assumptions of one age become explicit in the next. Major realizations turn into obvious sidelights. Last year's undercurrents become this year's obsessions—and vice versa. A theological doctrine, like the Puritan conviction of innate sin, becomes for a later New Englander named Nathaniel Hawthorne a fascination with the psychology of guilt. Even revolutionary ideas are based upon the old ideas that they turn inside out. If you say, "Yes, but on the other hand . . . ," what the "other hand" is all about still depends upon the "yes." To understand the *angst* of existentialism, for instance, it helps to understand the survival of Victorian optimism into the 20th century and the growing unease of the Victorian world as well (as in Matthew Arnold's "Dover Beach"). To understand the humanistic vitality and the tragic sense of the Renaissance, it helps to understand both the spiritual vitality of the Middle Ages and that period's strain of popular humanism (as in Chaucer). Each age needs to be known for its particular kinds of vitality, as well as for the tensions that will be played out differently in the future.

Part of the fascination of literary study, therefore, is seeing how works evolve under the spell of previous works, which, of course, have been themselves spawned by previous ones, and so forth. One certainly can study literature just because one likes to read good books. However, seeing books in their creative context opens up their greater power to stimulate and move us. We are all the more deeply impressed then by the symbolic energies of language and the acuteness of the mind.

Having a sense of cultural context, needless to say, also makes individual works much clearer. There is no reason to believe you should always be able to interpret a poem in an anthology, without any context, immediately. Part of the language in which any work is composed is the language of literary conventions and traditional styles and the language of a society's social institutions. The latter include political, religious, and economic ways of organizing life, which convey the values and assumptions of the times. To read well, you need to have some awareness of such "languages" just as you need to understand the words and syntax of the literal language, the English or French or whatever, that you are reading.

A World unto Itself

The spirit of every play, story, novel, or poem arises through its *psychological atmosphere*. The author starts us out with a very conscious selection of suggestive details. Often a symbolic image or a line of dialogue establishes the work's sense of reality, explicitly summing up all that we expect to be reminded of. The atmosphere may emphasize feelings sensual, hopeful, genial, repelled, bewildered, complacent, furtive, angry, morose, and whatever else occurs to you—in a way that is likely to be also foreboding and tantalizing. These become qualities in the work's very specific world, but they also carry over into its essential view of life. As the work establishes its own world, it brings us into its ambience. It selects, intensifies, and fantasizes about elements in the world at large, dramatizing their relations *in a tone, with an attitude,* leaving us to face the world in a focused state of mind. The atmosphere moves between the personal and the social, between the human presence and its environment. Most likely, the sense of place serves the sense of self. The atmosphere focuses the character's or the author's experience of being human.

This is the case even in autobiographical fiction like Thomas Wolfe's story "The Lost Boy," which begins, as many stories do, with a symbolically charged setting described in a symbolically emotive style:

> Light came and went and came again, the booming strokes of three o'clock beat out across the town in thronging bronze from the courthouse bell, light winds of April blew the fountain out in rainbow sheets, until the plume returned and pulsed, as Grover turned into the square.

He was a child, dark-eyed and grave, birthmarked upon his neck—a berry of warm brown—and with a gentle face, too quiet and too listening for his years. . . .[5] He turned and passed along the north side of the Square and in that moment saw the union of Forever and of Now.

Light came and went and came again, the great plume of the fountain pulsed and winds of April sheeted it across the Square in a rainbow gossamer of spray. The fire department horses drummed on the floors with wooden stomp, most casually, and with dry whiskings of their clean, coarse tails. The street cars ground into the Square from every portion of the compass and halted briefly like wound toys in their familiar quarter-hourly formula. A dray, hauled by a boneyard nag, rattled across the cobbles on the other side before his father's shop. The courthouse bell boomed out its solemn warning of immediate three, and everything was just the same as it had always been.

The story is about the child, but it is also about the teller of the tale, his brother, who is searching to place the child in his own life. And it is about light and time and space, memory, the gulf between a familiar environment and the world beyond, sounds that drifted into silence many years before, a community, a child's father. Grover died not long after the episode that is begun here, so the story is about death, childhood, and aging. And it is about love within a family. All of these themes are there in the images surveyed and in the feeling with which they are evoked. Whatever will happen to the boy and to his brother later in the story will grow out of the seeds planted here, in the boy's imagined knowledge of himself within a vividly specific but universal world.

Often an author simply reflects the world round about quite naturally because that is the material at hand, the given environment, with all its limitations and prejudices, simply there along with its power and glory, on the assumption, perhaps, that that's the way life is, a mixed blessing (or in Christian terms, a fallen state). At other times, the society's ills—its power, in fact, to corrupt life—will be the deliberate subject in a spirit of social protest or of satire. William Blake and Charles Dickens both created fictional or mythic worlds that epitomized the gruesome impact of the Industrial Revolution on English society.

Blake's "London" grasps his world's social forces so concisely that the energy packed within its imagery seems about to explode.

I wander thro' each charter'd street,
Near where the charter'd Thames does flow,

---

5. The passage I've omitted describes the boy's well-worn clothing.

And mark in every face I meet
Marks of weakness, marks of woe.

In every cry of every Man,
In every Infant's cry of fear,
In every voice, in every ban,
The mind-forg'd manacles I hear.

How the Chimney-sweeper's cry
Every black'ning Church appalls;
And the hapless Soldier's sigh
Runs in blood down Palace walls.

But most thro' midnight streets I hear
How the youthful Harlot's curse
Blasts the new born Infant's tear,
And blights with plagues the Marriage hearse.

In a dreadful vision, Blake dramatizes the impact of contemporary social institutions upon people's lives: the law of the land, or "charter," seems an oppressive burden upon the great river itself (the Thames) as well as on the crowded residents of the city, the church of the day ignores its responsibility for helpless poverty, the royal palace protects its prerogatives with the blood of impoverished soldiers, marriage (with little possibility then of divorce) fosters prostitution with its accompanying despair and disease.

Although this poem is understood well only with some knowledge of social history, its ultimate power lies in its symbolic capacity to dramatize in the images of his own society this continually recurring factor (which Blake called the state of "Experience"): the human talent to distort and even pervert life with the help of depersonalizing institutions and through the kind of self-protection that gives us power over others. This vision of life Blake captures by the "woldifying" (or mythmaking) quality of the poem itself, although it is set in a specific city at a particular time in history. He selects images that crystallize each of the social ills around him, looking past any signs of comfort and pleasure that another observer might dwell upon. He not only condenses his images but compacts them into inescapable relationships: the chimney-sweeper's cry (calling out his trade in the streets but also weeping in his misery) appalls the church (casting a "pall" over it but also making it appalling), blackening it with the guilt shed by the children's filthy sweepings. Each crystallized picture comes so fast upon the next that they all seem to merge into a single image. The insistent parallelism ("In every cry . . .") intensifies this effect. The result of all these features of the poem—the selectivity of images, the crystallization and condensation of detail, and the reiteration of style—is a very tight little world of imagination, unique and concrete, unmistakable for the world of any other poem or for what anyone else would have projected as a vision of London at that time. The poem's tone of pained outrage consolidates the emotional temper of this world. This visionary "London" is clearly and dramatically a grim and pathetic place. It is also an intensely human place, both in the cruel indifference it portrays and the empathy with which that is perceived.

Long Live Dead Authors (and Live Ones, Too)!

A literary world is shadowed by the presence of its author. Reading good books, obviously, we are reading good authors, and we are likely to be interested in these remarkable people themselves. There is undoubtedly some fascination (and perhaps a sense of romance) in learning about great authors' lives and personalities, even when we have more questions about them than facts—whether we are wondering about Marlowe's sexual preference, Shelley's treatment of the women in his life, Emily Dickinson's seclusion, Hemingway's machismo, the premature deaths of so many poets, or even the question of whether Homer actually existed. Interesting writers tend to be interesting people (except, I suppose, for the possibly nonexistent Homer). We may expect that it is the qualities of genius they expressed in their works that will remain what is most interesting about them, but we needn't ignore them as people in order to concentrate on their art.

There is, to be sure, an element of gossip in such topics, and it is certainly no substitute for studying what the people wrote. We need to be careful about what we think such biographical information explains, and we should be aware of our inclination to construct a clearer picture than our knowledge warrants. Authors' personal lives and their works often do illuminate each other, but we need to be careful not to oversimplify parallels between the two: Symbolic truth and historical fact work very differently (and what is "fact" in anybody's personality is a ticklish question).

An author's life may tell us about a story's source, but it won't tell us about its meaning. That thousands of readers have identified with it proves as much. For this kind of shared understanding, we go back to the symbolic reality the author formed out of his or her personal struggle. The particular environment that Thomas Wolfe remembers from his childhood becomes for the rest of us the sense of place itself, of time itself, of mysterious loss that bewilders us all as we look back. We may get some insight into the obsessive paranoia of Franz Kafka's stories by learning how keenly he felt humiliated by his father even as an adult[6]—but it is only a "genetic" explanation. Drawing

---

6. See the "Letter to His Father" he wrote—but never delivered—when he was thirty-six.

on his heightened sensitivity, Kafka delineated a strangely familiar kind of paranoia that seems all too normal in life, in modern life especially, and has helped give the "Kafkaesque" style its puzzling magnetism.

Nevertheless, to read literature is clearly to involve oneself in the aura of authors. We feel the power in their skills and in their vision. The author cuts a figure as craftsman, as sage, *and* simply as a person who has the power to impress his or her sense of being upon us. And this sense of being is always unique, as any strong person's is, with a quality as identifiable as a particular style and as deep as the works' particular range of feelings. In the artist, we see the personal strength that goes along with a passion for art, a passion that most folks refuse to take seriously at all. The successful author seems often a kind of hero in himself or herself, standing forth with a risky commitment to something that may be as revealing as it is creative. When we read, we share the author's reality, even in the case of someone we might not like in person. If, as in some earlier times, all literature were anonymous, we who love our books would feel a good deal poorer, I think. We wish we could know about Homer: Our interest in the authors is part of our response to literature as a human phenomenon.

Life and Art

Our look at literary reality leads naturally to a point that may be obvious enough on the surface but that is also an elusive paradox. What is most extraordinary about literature, and most intriguing to try to understand, is the fact that it is both life and art. At the same time that a literary world is made entirely of language and entirely of imagery, it is made up also entirely of the human spirit and human experience. On the one hand, it elicits an aesthetic response to articulate forms, crafted in a specific medium with beauty and precision; on the other, it engages us in our most intimate personal concerns, our most pressing social problems, and the timeless anxieties of our species.

Literature's capacity to have theme, to have application to our lives—or, simply put, to *say something*—depends upon the presence in the work of the forms that life takes: kingdoms, families, and friendships; occupations, travels, and wars; disappointments, accidents, illnesses, realizations, survivals, and on and on. And interpretation requires sensitivity to the medium, an alertness to the way it operates, its inner logic and the subtle stimuli of its intricate forms. It also requires some real experience in living—and recognition of the experience we have had. Literature, as we have seen, is made out of the human mind thinking thoughts and imagining images. It requires appreciation of the forces of passion but also respect for the value of illuminating thought. It requires, in fact, some wisdom, just as it delivers some.

Critics who treat literature as though it *were* life sacrifice, I think, not only the aesthetic pleasure of interpreting literature as art but also a peculiar kind of knowledge that literature attains in its own right. As specific acts of imagination, a good story or poem can give us not simply abstract generalizations about life's problems but a sense of life as it matters, which is life *as it is lived*, with presence, in process, suggesting multitudinous subtle nuances and angles of awareness.

Thus we do not go to literature only to learn about life. We go to it for literary experience—for the pleasures of language-art and for a kind of knowledge that is native to the imagination. The central questions of criticism should be then: How do art and life relate to each other in individual stories, novels, poems, and plays? How does language-stuff get to be so potent and so "telling" in the shaping hands of the skilled author? What qualities of the creative mind permit this to happen? How does the art evoke and interpret the life? How does the life of one's own mind draw from the particular features of art a way of seeing into its own nature?

There are no direct answers to such questions, of course. But whatever answers there are depend, I believe, on the way that, in the symbolic reality of literature, form takes on a sense of self and self takes on form. However it may be that this happens, we witness and we share in the strange meeting of life and the stuff of the artistic medium, through which both are transformed. In this process, a mutual inspiration takes place. Form is inspired—in the literal sense of having life breathed into it—and life is inspired—in the common, extended sense, as the substance of experience is reaffirmed. With such an emphasis, it may be possible for literary criticism to attain once more a sense of wonder and to recognize thereby that wonder is a natural faculty of the imagination, coming alive in the love of reading. The following pair of chapters will explore this relationship between literary form and the sense of a living self, looking at many of the features of literature in its light.

PART THREE
Self and Form

Chapter 5

Being Self-ish: How Literature Depends upon Consciousness

Reading Consciousness

The last chapter emphasized differences between the literary world and immediate reality. At least as important is the relationship *between* them, for we are talking about a similarity-in-difference—a transformation that alters things significantly (both *importantly* and *meaningfully*) rather than giving us something wholly new. Of course, as we saw, awareness of our social and cultural world carries over meaningfully into the work, and the author's personality does as well. The most important factor in the relationship between life and art, however, is carryover of the sense of self: the intrinsic subjectivity of human life, which is arguably the source of all meaning and values.

A symbolic (or *symbolistic*) approach to the reality of literature starts with the premise that every work exists in a process of projection. Just as the beam of light from a movie projector is continuous with the image on the screen, so the mental activity of projecting symbolic forms is continuous with the story or poem projected. This mental activity arises out of the integral personality (of reader as well as author), where intelligence is at one with emotions, perceptions, and awareness. The symbolic world of culture is inseparable, therefore, from being human—while at the same time it takes on its own kind of reality. It is like the dreamworld, which we enter while also it remains oneself.

A more common word for what I mean by "projection" is imagination. The images of literature all exist only in the mind *imagining;* they are made up *of* imagination. Projection is literally a "casting forth" from the mind, and the images that are imagined stay rooted in the mind imagining them; they are of its nature, mind-born and mind-fleshed. Two more ways of saying this are that literature (and any other symbolic language) exists *in our response to it* and *as experience.* When we take in the literary world, we are taking in our own experience of it, for the literary work exists only to recreate itself in our minds, through the images we *imagine,* through feelings, sensations, and ideas that come to us detail by detail as we read. It needs us to feel and to realize in order for it to mean.

As I am using the word now, *experience* is very close to words I've empha-sized before, *sensibility* and *subjectivity.* Another related term, with a different shade of meaning, is *consciousness.* Consciousness emphasizes our awareness of what we are experiencing and our capacity to comprehend it. It is con-sciousness that gives one the sense of being a person, and it is our attention. It is most significantly, therefore, consciousness that is the intelligent life in literature. We care about the work when we find such life in it. This is the full sense of presence, of somebody there, of some self *being.* When we read a poem, we recreate the speaker's voice; when we read a story, the narrator's. In either case, through our own silent voice reading, we imagine a life con-scious of living. We are conscious of the various characters' consciousness, conscious in fact *through* each character's consciousness. Also, at least as im-portantly, we participate in the *story's* consciousness of the characters within it—which interprets them for us, leading the way to meaning. There is an outer personality enveloping inner personalities.

As we are conscious of the story's consciousness, we are experiencing our own. We are aware of our own lives living, with the particular slant that the work has developed. Thus the story generalizes (or tends to allegorize) its implications: What feels true in the story *and* feels true in me would tend to be true of people as a rule. We may be reading about people whose circum-stances in life are extremely different from our own—the suffering in a Soviet or a Nazi prison camp, for example, or the pleasant society of Renaissance courtiers. Nevertheless, if the work works for us, it will be because we can imagine this pain or this pleasure *humanly.* We may comprehend a good deal about basic human capacities for abomination on the one hand and for fulfill-ment on the other. That these two words don't say very much shows how much we need the works themselves, in all their intricate specificity, to say it for us with the sense of solid presence that carries meaning and conviction.

Consciousness also implies its underside, *unconsciousness.* Within a work of fiction, an author commonly creates characters whose unconsciousness we need to grasp consciously. We need to see, in other words, what they don't see. In older works, according to earlier modes of character stylization, *self-ignorance* is generally a more accurate term. However, not just the characters but the work itself may have its unconscious side. Every vision has its limitations or blindspots. Every style and every epoch—including, we may be very sure, our own excellent times and the styles that we favor—breed their peculiar forms of self-deception. Very simply, through its symbolic resources, the mind needs to focus, so a great deal is bound to be out of focus or out of range. This can be dangerous, or it can be merely a natural limitation that makes creative living possible. An author may be interesting, therefore, for what he or she fails to see—although, if we are suitably humbled by recollecting our own fallibility, it befits us to keep such awareness in proportion to the positive side: what the vision does see, what an author's accomplishment does achieve.

Being Self-ish

To be conscious is to be a self. In art, as in life, the height of experience comes in our ability to have some essential consciousness of another person's experience, to perceive another as a self. Great portraits, like those on page 106, are not necessarily pretty faces, they are not only elegant designs, and they are not always good likenesses. As a rule, they are, however, expressions of the subject's inner being. They capture with exquisite sensitivity the particular pathos or pleasure of a personality as it is known to the person. As we gaze into the eyes before us on a museum wall, we feel that someone is really there amid the conglomeration of mere brush strokes, and over a gulf of centuries perhaps, we are moved that we can know a long-gone stranger so intimately.

So it is with the more interesting characters of literature. Much of the beauty of what we read lies in the capacity of language, like paint, to capture *being* or *inwardness*. Although characters are not real people, they can be formed subtly by the author to give us this impression. We enjoy the lovers enjoying one another's company and imagine their anxieties, failures, and pleasures. We hear their voices and sense what it is like to speak their thoughts, just as actors do when they are performing in a play. The voice of narration enveloping the story or poem becomes our comprehending voice as we read in mimicry.

In many works, the **hero** is not a particularly admirable person, but still is (and should be defined as) the center of consciousness through whom we experience the others. In our own reality, we are surrounded by a swarming cast of characters whose being in themselves we cannot continually think about. They are *our* others, *our* minor characters. Similarly, there are some forms of literature, like melodrama and satire, in which most or all characters

Presence in the Visual Arts

Top left: Portrait of a bearded man. Egyptian. Second-century Roman period. Encaustic on wood. 39.4 ×
19.3 cm. The Metropolitan Museum of Art, Rogers Fund, 1909. *Top right:* Head of a girl (broken from a
marble relief). Roman period (Augustan). First century B.C.—First century A.D. The Metropolitan
Museum of Art, Rogers Fund, 1918. *Bottom left:* Johannes Vermeer. *Portrait of a Young Woman.* Oil on
canvas. 17-1/2 × 15-3/4 in. The Metropolitan Museum of Art, Gift of Mr. and Mrs. Charles Wrightsman,
in memory of Theodore Rosseau, Jr., 1979. *Bottom right:* Attributed to Peter Paul Rubens. Detail from
Four Studies of a Negro's Head. 1617–1620. Oil on Wood. 10 × 25-1/2 inches. Collection of the J. Paul
Getty Museum, Malibu, California.

are conveniently portrayed as *other* people. This distinction is a matter of stylization, and admittedly one that may be relative in literature as in life. In a story about a woman, the man may very well be portrayed as her "other," and vice versa. It may be imaginatively appropriate for us to enjoy the suffering of a villain and the absurdity of a jackass, without having to worry (as we might want to do in real life) what life is like for them. We can enjoy the excitement of an adventure story because we don't have to realize all the hardship and pain the characters would be going through if they were people. Sometimes we get great characters, like Shakespeare's Malvolio in *Twelfth Night* or Cervantes' Don Quixote, whom we can laugh at and sympathize with at the same time, or like Shylock, in *The Merchant of Venice*, whom we can be horrified by and also feel for, simultaneously or alternately. Comic villains like Malvolio and Shylock are sometimes said to function as *scapegoats* upon whom the comic spirit can release its exuberance without our having to take them too seriously as people (although Shakespeare is not content to leave these particular fellows completely to such indifference).

This function of the imagination can be distressingly racist, sexist, or supernationalist, at least when it affects the way we live, but within the fictional "world," it may be more like the "catism" in the cartoons, when the pussycat gets smashed by the mouse or the doggie by the cat. The stylization through which we imagine such scapegoats allows us different standards of judgment than we would apply to other people in real life. It can keep them safely within the realm of imaginative projection (or fantasy). We judge partly by the quality of malice with which such villains are portrayed but also by the stylization through which they are imagined. (Remember too that the story itself may be criticizing the character without saying so explicitly. A novel about a sexist may very well not be a sexist novel.)

In great works, there are always minor characters whose problems simply cannot get much attention within the economy of a story, where we have to see what happens as it affects the hero. Shakespeare allows Hamlet first to kill Polonius and then Rosencrantz and Guildenstern without giving any of them much concern; they are made to seem ridiculous enough or slight enough so that their deaths should not matter to us too much. We might care if they were *people*, but as characters they are stylized simply as others to the selfhood of Hamlet, in which we are fully engrossed. It is like hurting people in our daydreams. That this is an artistic choice is clear if we compare *Hamlet* with Tom Stoppard's *Rosencrantz and Guildenstern Are Dead*, a brilliant modern job of turning *Hamlet* inside out. Here R. and G. are in the foreground, so we experience them as selves, while they try to figure out what that Danish prince, mumbling weirdly in the background, is up to. Shakespeare allows us into King Claudius's experience when he is attempting to pray, but most of the time he has externalized him as villain-scapegoat. In *Macbeth*, it has been said, Shakespeare sets us fully and sympathetically into the selfhood of a character who is in something like Claudius's position, letting us know how dreadful life can be for the poor tyrant.

Making Selves

When we want to pay close attention to the portrayal of characters (as in a formal character study), we consider several factors: how the characters are seen—by the narrator and by other characters; how the characters see them- selves; how they behave, what their behavior expresses, and what it conceals; and, our present interest, how they experience themselves, what it is like for them to be who they are. Sometimes analysis evaluates the character's *round- ness* or *flatness,* in terms introduced by the novelist E. M. Forster.[1] It is useful to combine this distinction with another common one, between *dynamic* and *static* characters. Flat characters have a single basic characteristic, and they are not capable of change. Round characters, contrariwise, are more like real people, with multiple interests, conflicts, feeling patterns, imaginable histo- ries, and ways of relating to others. According to the distinction I made in the last section, they have more clearly a sense of self, while we are content to experience the flat as "others." Forster emphasizes that round characters are capable of surprising us. He also points out that the distinction is not an abso- lute one. Some basically flat characters tend toward roundness. (They are, we may say, more-or-less oval.) And he makes the further important point that flatness is not bad. There are many marvellous flat characters, especially in comedy, like Forster's ideal example, Charles Dickens's Micawber. (This dis- tinction, of course, applies only to characters, not people. To call a *character* flat is a very different proposition from calling a *person* boring or limited. We can have a round characterization of a dreadful bore.)

Discussions of characterization commonly focus on **motivation,** often explained in terms of the conflicts with others or the social pressures to which the character is responding. To my mind, the projection of consciousness is a far more interesting and telling aspect of characterization. It gives "motiva- tion" far more depth, for one thing, since it shows people driven by factors inherent in human nature rather than acting simply in response to events, circumstances, other people, or isolated impulses. Also it is more profoundly suggestive of a work's meaning, and it more fully engages our imaginative interest.

A focus on consciousness also makes more interesting the feature of nar- ration known technically as **point of view,** the relationship between the teller, the telling, and the told. We distinguish *first-person narration,* in which

---

1. In *Aspects of the Novel* (New York: Harcourt, 1927), pp. 103–118.

the teller is speaking as the "I" who knows all about it because he or she was there, and *third-person narration*, in which the narrator simply *is* a narrator, reporting events that have occurred on their own. A first-person narrator may be the main character, someone else participating in the action, or someone who saw it all and reports it as the experience of seeing it. Third-person narration is said to be *omniscient* when the teller, like God, knows everything that everybody does, says, or thinks. It is said to be *limited* when it is, well, limited.

No matter which point of view a story uses, the narrative strategy establishes a field of consciousness among teller, telling, and told, with tensions that are particular to each case. It is one more opportunity for the author to evoke a world and bring us into it at the same time. The opening sentence of Toni Cade Bambara's story "The Lesson" already shows us how this can work in the first person:

> Back in the days when everyone was old and stupid or young and foolish and me and Sugar were the only ones just right, this lady moved on our block with nappy hair and proper speech and no makeup.

The first-person narrator is often reminiscing like this. As a result, the impact of time comes into play, in this case as the older self's awareness of her younger self, the mature woman knowing herself through her awareness of who she was and how she then experienced herself to be. We get the young girl's sense of who she is in relation both to her peers and to "this lady"—her competitiveness, her restless and aggressive energy, her sharpness of perception, her youthful smugness, her self-protective judgement, and basic to all of that, her keen self-awareness. And, simultaneously, we get the mature woman's attitude toward the brash girl she once was, implying how far she has come, with what wisdom she can look back—nostalgic, tolerant, amused, a little embarrassed maybe, and glad for the change. The irony of her style conveys the narrator's distance from what she sees but her closeness to it as well. The girl felt these feelings, but it takes the woman to put them neatly in these wry terms.

The projection of consciousness can be at least as subtle when a character's mind is out there in the third person, as it is received through someone else's awareness. Look at how Hawthorne introduces his Goodman Brown, whom we have thought about several times already:

> Young Goodman Brown came forth at sunset, into the street of Salem village; but put his head back, after crossing the threshold, to exchange a parting kiss with his young wife. And Faith, as the wife was aptly named, thrust her own pretty head into the street, letting the wind play with the pink ribbons of her cap while she called to Goodman Brown.
>
> "Dearest Heart," whispered she, softly and rather sadly, when her lips were close to his ear, "prithee put off your journey until sunrise and sleep in your own bed to-night. A lone woman is troubled with such

dreams and such thoughts that she's afeard of herself sometimes. Pray, tarry with me this night, dear husband, of all nights in the year."

"My love and my Faith," replied young Goodman Brown, "of all nights in the year, this one night must I tarry away from thee. My journey, as thou callest it, forth and back again, must needs be done 'twixt now and sunrise. What, my sweet, pretty wife, dost thou doubt me already, and we but three months married?"

Without yet knowing what is special about this one night of the year, we readily sense the young wife's anxiety, the husband's determination, and the combination of both into a worrisome feeling of urgency. The intimacy between them makes them both seem like admirable young folk, but it is also a temptation that would restrain him, against which he is pulling away. His insistence on the rhetorical question at the end of the third paragraph evokes foreboding for the reader, but it also betrays, perhaps, some uncertainty in himself. (We may often think as we read that certain feelings *seem* or *tend to* be there, so that a weaselly "perhaps" may actually make our reading more accurate.)

The final paragraph of the story portrays a much transformed young man, for in the forest he beheld the decent folk of his town, including finally Faith herself, in the Devil's midnight communion:

> Had Goodman Brown fallen asleep in the forest and only dreamed a wild dream of a witch-meeting?
>
> Be it so, if you will; but, alas! it was a dream of evil omen for young Goodman Brown. A stern, a sad, a darkly meditative, a distrustful, if not a desperate man did he become, from the night of that fearful dream. On the Sabbath day, when the congregation were singing a holy psalm, he could not listen because an anthem of sin rushed loudly upon his ear and drowned all the blessed strain. When the minister spoke from the pulpit with power and fervid eloquence, and with his hand on the open Bible, of the sacred truths of our religion, and of saintlike lives and triumphant deaths, and of future bliss or misery unutterable, then did Goodman Brown turn pale, dreading lest the roof should thunder down upon the gray blasphemer and his hearers. Often, awaking suddenly at midnight, he shrank from the bosom of Faith; and at morning or eventide, when the family knelt down at prayer, he scowled and muttered to himself, and gazed sternly at his wife, and turned away. And when he had lived long, and was borne to his grave a hoary corpse, followed by Faith, an aged woman, and children and grand-children, a goodly procession, besides neighbors not a few, they carved no hopeful verse upon his tombstone, for his dying hour was gloom.

Adjectives describe Brown's state—*stern, sad, darkly meditative, distrustful, desperate*—but they also help to evoke that state through their insistent iteration. As he listens to the minister, unable to forget what he has seen and heard in the forest, recoiling from the night's lesson—"Evil is the nature of mankind. Evil must be your only happiness"—his pain and horror are palpable. Finally, we should appreciate the burden under which he has carried on to the end, with his children, grandchildren, and aging Faith about him. The gloom of his dying hour does not comes to us as a fact noted or observed: It culminates the inner desolation towards which the whole story has moved.

Such a view of the story can be reached only if we follow out the attitude toward the character that the story has developed subjectively. The best way to block such a response is to try to be objective and give advice: He should lighten up, he should trust his wife, he should not believe the vision. Oedipus should have asked more questions, Hamlet should have asked fewer. Neither one should have gone around killing people. Everyone should learn to compromise.

It is well worth noting how often an author maintains a sympathetic neutrality when we are tempted to moralize. Sometimes a story or a play clearly evaluates the actions of characters, but they are usually contributory characters or obvious subjects of satire. As a rule, you can take it as a rule: Never, but never give advice to characters. For one thing, they can't hear you. For another, it's too late. For still another, you probably don't like people giving *you* advice. (Advice, after all, is for *other* people.) Furthermore, if the characters had done otherwise, *we wouldn't have the story:* The story comes out the way it does because of what it expresses *this* way. Ultimately, advice is irrelevant to literary knowledge of experience. Central characters in particular follow out their inner necessity, giving the story meaning through the development of their consciousness. Advice is about people's *behavior,* what they *do*—unless, of course, you have the audacity to tell people what they should feel. Meaning in literature comes more often from the inevitable unfolding of what the characters do feel. Their actions are the living out of their states of mind. Goodman Brown's development of despair demonstrates what despair, the loss of faith, *is.* Like most deep states of being or passions that literature represents, such as love and hate, this despair is confronted in absolute terms in order that it *can* be known. The story conveys, through the character, a consciousness of its utter reality; it is given to us as a fact of human experience that we need to know if we are to comprehend our nature.

Hearing Voices

Because the projection of consciousness is the life blood of literature, the most important aspect of literary language is its capacity to convey **voice.** In voice we directly experience the presence of consciousness, the somebody at home, the life that it's all about. We know this well enough in ourselves and in anyone we listen to. How one says what one means comes through quite spontaneously in the structuring of phrases, the choice of evocative words, and the interjection of qualifying expressions as we reach for emphasis, balance our terms to hit the right fit for the occasion, try to say enough without saying too much, and express our reactions to what we're hearing. Subliminally, at least, we adjust our part in conversation to the tone we are hearing come at us. A great deal we understand from what is *not* spoken as we pick up on someone's effort to suppress some feelings just beneath the surface. When we overhear a conversation, we can often tell what each party *must* be feeling while the other is holding forth. When someone is speaking to us with feeling, much we may be expected to get, whether we want it or not, by innuendo.

In actual speech we understand **tone** to a large degree by the pitch and stress of utterance. By the tone of voice, we can tell whether someone is joking or serious. Emotional burdens of all kinds can be placed upon a sentence that looks innocent enough, such as "Pass the salt." But when we are reading (and as writers ourselves), we need to recognize that tone can be built into wording and phrasing; the ability to maneuver tone is one of the most important skills a writer can draw upon. " 'Please pass the salt,' she said shyly as, uneasily, she faced his steady gaze." If you read "Will you please pass that damn salt already!" you just might detect a note of impatient irritability. What do you hear in this: "I wonder whether you would be so kind as to let me have a bit of your salt"? Nearly unbelievable timidity? Sickening humility? Or sarcasm, conveying by innuendo more of that impatient irritability? Taking the sentence by itself, we can't say for sure, but it is certainly not neutral, like "Pass the salt." It has a definable range of possibilities. It is seriously servile or ironically nasty. Presumably, the immediate context would lead up to just the right expression we need when we come to this profound line.

In the dialogue of fiction or plays, in the speaking presence of poetry, we can hear a mind thinking the words and finding the fit phrases. It is not that we read *between* the lines: we need only to read sensitively *in* them. Ernest Hemingway wrote powerful short stories told largely in curt dialogue with revealing silence weighing heavily around it. In "Hills Like White Elephants," a young couple travelling in Spain are discussing the need for an abortion (although the story never mentions the word):

> "It's really an awfully simple operation, Jig," the man said. "It's not really an operation at all."
>
> The girl looked at the ground the table legs rested on.
>
> "I know you wouldn't mind it, Jig. It's really not anything. It's just to let the air in."
>
> The girl did not say anything.
>
> "I'll go with you and I'll stay with you all the time. They just let the air in and then it's all perfectly natural."
>
> "Then what will we do afterward?"
>
> "We'll be fine afterward. Just like we were before."

"What makes you think so?"

"That's the only thing that bothers us. It's the only thing that's made us unhappy."

The girl looked at the bead curtain, put her hand out and took hold of two of the strings of beads.

"And you think then we'll be all right and be happy."

"I know we will. You don't have to be afraid. I've known lots of people who have done it."

"So have I," said the girl. "And afterward they were all so happy."

As the narrator, in perfectly neutral terms, describes Jig listening, we begin to imagine the feelings and the understanding building up together in her mind. As the dialogue continues, we experience what each character is going through, hearing as well as speaking. In the young man's repeated oversimplification of the process, we hear his fear of the reality—both the reality of the operation and the reality of what is happening between them—and we hear the urgency with which he's trying to wipe out both. In her terse responses, we feel how much she cannot say to him, because presumably he will not hear it. Her last statement quoted here would certainly sound positive enough out of context, but as we come to it, we feel as we read it a touch of very sad sarcasm, as she realizes, in spite of his reiterated protests (or because of his obtuseness), that their relationship is as dead as the symbolic "hills like white elephants" they have been looking at across the valley.

Self in Play and Poem

In dramatic dialogue we have nothing but a pattern of voices impacting upon one another. Without narration, we are directly involved in the perspective of everyone: As a whole, drama is about the things people do to each other and to themselves as they follow the drives of their own being. Through competing voices, tensions grow. Through voices in harmony, tensions resolve themselves. Through uncertainties, frustration builds up until it bursts. Consider how Shakespeare opens *King Lear,* coming in suddenly, as he likes to do, in the middle of a conversation.

KENT: I thought the King had more affected [liked] the Duke of Albany than Cornwall.

GLOUCESTER: It did always seem so to us; but now, in the division of the kingdom, it appears not which of the dukes he values most, for qualities are so weighed that curiosity in neither can make choice of either's moiety.

The final clause in Gloucester's speech means that neither man, thinking carefully about it, has reason to prefer the other one's share. Although you probably needed someone to explain this to you, it should be interesting to see how much you may have picked up without understanding all the words. The best way to begin understanding what's going on in Shakespeare is, very simply, to *listen to the voices*. What states of mind are people conveying through the way they are talking to each other? In this very brief passage, we pick up a nervous energy sparked by bewilderment and surprise about important events occurring in the kingdom. Immediately, we are involved in the mounting excitement of people eager to see what's going on here. ("Division" is a key word in the passage, with more possible meanings than one; we will wait to see how they develop.) Kent's opening is a simple but somewhat perplexed statement as I hear it. Gloucester's rather convoluted response is more clearly troubled. Strangely, the fact that the king is treating the two dukes equally, which might ordinarily seem fair play, is seen as frustrating and ominous. Whom the king "affects"—and how he decides whom—is going to be a matter with very heavy consequence in this play, so we are already focusing upon a central thematic issue, although we may realize this only in hindsight. Through this brief exchange, then, Shakespeare establishes a "psychological atmosphere" for his main plot. As soon as he has done this, he goes on to do something similar for the subplot, which directly involves Gloucester himself.

In a poem we may have a fictitious voice speaking as a distinct character, a **persona** (literally meaning "mask" and giving us "person" and "personality"), such as the Duke in Robert Browning's dramatic monologue "My Last Duchess." Disgusted by his wife's good-hearted modesty, the Duke of Ferrara in Renaissance Italy "gave commands" and now she is somehow dead.

> She had
> A heart—how shall I say?—too soon made glad,
> Too easily impressed; she liked whate'er
> She looked on, and her looks went everywhere.

A persona provides a perspective that we need to evaluate as we would do for any fictional character. How sane is that Duke of Ferrara? How fairly did he judge his wife? This particular "voice" is a classic example of an *unreliable narrator*, a kind of character encountered more commonly in short stories. (The term itself has the distinctive virtue of defining itself.) We need not always regard a poem's speaker as a persona, however. Often we hear the poet's own voice modified as a poetic presence. We can call this the voice of *authorial authority*, with which a writer commands (and needs to justify) our interest: This is my poem and I have a right to be heard, because I have interesting things to say. And besides, I got here first.

Lyric poems are concise nuggets of experience—literary experience, of course, presenting a poet's (or a fictitious character's) feelings, insights, or memories in heightened language. Because they often are so condensed, generating a complex of implications, lyric poems can be, as we all know, difficult. It is all the more important, therefore, to appreciate the realization of voice that brings them to life. Through the styles of all ages, even when the thoughts are conventional and the words now obscure, we should be able to enter the mental world of a lyric by taking up its voice. Consider the rhymed delicacy of Chaucer in medieval England:

> Madame, ye ben of al beaute shryne
> As fer as cercled is the mapemounde,°   *world map*
> For as the cristall glorious ye shyne,
> And lyke ruby ben your chekës rounde.
> Therwith ye ben so mery and so jocounde
> That at a revell whan that I se you daunce,
> It is an oynement unto my wounde,
> Though ye to me ne do no daliaunce.
>
> —"To Rosemounde"

Or the American boldness of Walt Whitman's free verse:

> Beat! beat! drums!—blow! bugles! blow!
> Make no parley—stop for no expostulation,
> Mind not the timid—mind not the weeper or prayer,
> Mind not the old man beseeching the young man,
> Let not the child's voice be heard, nor the mother's entreaties,
> Make even the trestles to shake the dead where they lie awaiting the
>   hearses.
> So strong you thump O terrible drums—so loud you bugles blow.
>
> —"Beat! Beat! Drums!"

Or the relative plainness of William Wordsworth, sober in ecstasy:

> I wandered lonely as a cloud
> That floats on high o'er vales and hills,
> When all at once I saw a crowd,
> A host, of golden daffodils,
> Beside the lake, beneath the trees,
> Fluttering and dancing in the breeze.
>
> —"I Wandered Lonely As a Cloud"

Or the passionate ingenuity of Gerard Manley Hopkins:

> How to kéep—is there ány any, is there none such, nowhcre known some,
>   bow or brooch or braid or brace, láce, latch or catch or keep to keep
> Back beauty, keep it, beauty, beauty, beauty, . . . from vanishing away?
>
> —"The Leaden Echo and the Golden Echo"

Or the many voices of ethnic American dialect, as in this passage of counterpoint from Langston Hughes:

> When I was a chile we used to play,
> "One—two—buckle my shoe!"
> and things like that. But now, Lord,
> listen at them little varmits!
> ·
>
> > *What don't bug*
> > *them white kids*
> > *sure bugs me:*
> > *We knows everybody*
> > *ain't free!*
> >
> > —"Children's Rhymes"

Actually, to convey a range by such examples is futile. We would go on a long time to be accurate, for every poet's voice is different from every other's, and the voice is often different in poems by the same poet. In the excerpt from Hughes, for example, two voices speak, both presumably fictional.

I am myself partial to a style that runs from Sir Thomas Wyatt in the 16th century to many of the major poets of the early 17th, a style of dramatic presence in vigorous voices:

> It was no dream: I lay broad waking.
> But all is turnèd through my gentleness
> Into a strange fashion of forsaking . . .
> —*Sir Thomas Wyatt*, "They Flee from Me"

> For Godsake hold your tongue and let me love,
>   Or chide my palsy or my gout,
> My five gray hairs or ruin'd fortune flout,
> With wealth your state, your mind with Arts improve,
>   Take you a course, get you a place,°   *a position in the royal court*
>   Observe His Honour, or His Grace,
> Or the King's real, or his stampèd face°   *as on a coin*
>   Contemplate; what you will, approve,
>   So you will let me love.
>
> > —*John Donne*, "The Canonization"[2]

---

2. This stanza demonstrates something that one needs to be able to do particularly when reading older verse: to recognize and follow out the structure of an English sentence in spite of the fact that it has been rearranged. Natural word order has been in some positions inverted here to adapt the sentence to a stanza form. A lesser poet may use the technique awkwardly, but here it has an elegance that does not detract from the poem's strong energy. In such a case, simply identifying the subject of a clause and its main verb, when you are confused, can make things instantly clear.

I struck the board° and cried, "No more;   *table*
   I will abroad!
 What? Shall I ever sigh and pine?
My lines and life are free, free as the road,
   Loose as the wind, as large as store.
 Shall I be still in suit°?   *in service*

       —*George Herbert,* "The Collar"

We can see this style working beautifully in the first part of a famous sonnet by Michael Drayton, a contemporary of Shakespeare's. I quoted the rest in Chapter 1 when I was talking about allegory.

Since there's no help, come let us kiss and part;
Nay, I have done, you get no more of me,
And I am glad, yea, glad with all my heart
That thus so cleanly I myself can free;
Shake hands forever, cancel all our vows,
And when we meet at any time again,
Be it not seen in either of our brows
That we one jot of former love retain.

An affair is over. The lover is leaving his lady for the last time, insisting it doesn't bother him a bit: He will have no trouble letting her go. But our man seems to be working pretty hard to say he doesn't care. We can feel him hoping that she'll say she's sorry first. "Since there's no help" suggests, of course, that he'd like some. In his repetitions he seems to be talking himself into a strong, manly pose, but meanwhile, his mind goes tenderly over the scene he can't let go of: "Shake hands forever, cancel all our vows." In the strong stress on "either" and on both syllables of "one jot" he reaches with difficulty to imagine the indifference that is still beyond him.

Here and in all the passages I've just quoted, the poet achieves the vigor of his drama by taking advantage of natural phrasing in English. We still recognize immediately the ways that the speaking mind works as it sorts out thoughts and feelings and reaches for understanding by another mind. We hear insistent exclamations, phrases building upon phrases, the sentences striving for emphasis, and, through all this, the tension between feelings working themselves out in a voice that is surprised perhaps by its own self-realizations.

Getting to Be Mortal

Although feelings are various and personalities complex, the patterns of literary experience come down to a basic view of the human situation. Over and over again, we find the same kinds of feeling driving characters, crossing them up, and getting between them. Through infinite variations, we have love stories, we have tragedies of self-induced ruin, we have competitions for power, we have struggles for self-fulfillment. This regularity of experience occurs in literature, apparently, because it also appears in life. In our own lives, the patterns may be less clearly defined, for our lives are more hesitant and confused and vague, while the lives of characters project our tendencies into perceptible shapes. Where we hesitate and compromise, characters go all the way, living out what is potential within us, showing us meaning that lurks in our uncertainties. We do something similar in our fantasy life, letting our feelings go in order to see where they want to lead us. And at the same time, our fantasies measure the frustrated desire and anxiety out of which we project them. Our dreams of glory, that is, are as extreme as our sense of help-lessness, and they let us know just what that hurtful feeling is all about.

In simple terms, the stories of literature seem to remind us, we live be-tween desire and fear, between vulnerability and resistance—within a field of consciousness that can be represented something like this:

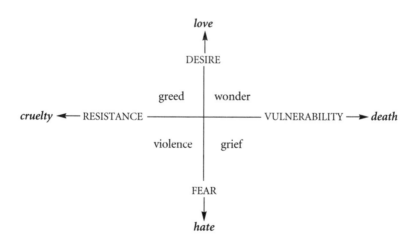

In all aspects of life, we are impelled by desire—for love, of course, but for the gratification of all sorts of appetites, for power, for recognition and self-respect, for comfort and the amelioration of pain, perhaps for mere survival; and we are daunted by fear that our desires will lead us nowhere—fear of failure, of shame, of self-doubt, of loss, of death, of aloneness, of lovelessness. That we feel fear in the midst of desire makes us keenly vulnerable, physically or emotionally or both. Our physical vulnerability exposes us to pain and death; our emotional vulnerability exposes us to such awkward feelings as guilt, loneliness, and humiliation. But personal fulfillment, we find, depends upon these very qualities of vulnerability, which allow us to love and be loved to the extent that we accept being simply human. Softening to our own fear and loneliness, we recognize more clearly the vulnerability of others and can share with them an openness to feeling.

Vulnerability is, by definition, dangerous. We are tempted, therefore, to fight against it with what resources we can muster, to resist, that is, ourselves. As modern psychology has taught us and as literature has always shown, many aspects of our personalities are defenses that enable us to make do in the world. When literature carries such tendencies to vivid extremes, we see such power typically as arrogance or as greed, greed for love or for prestige perhaps, as well as for money and other possessions. At the same time, colored by fear, resistance to ourselves erupts in violence toward others. This may be physical or emotional cruelty; often it is tyrannical treatment of those around us. On the other hand, when we have been carried into a sense of vulnerability, we may have some prospect of self-fulfillment, and the humility of self-knowledge can flow over into a sense of wonder. We find such an impact at the end of a Shakespearean comedy, as in fairy tales, myths, and the literature of devotion.[3]

In fiction and drama, a character is set within a predicament, the puzzling conflict that the story must resolve. If we emphasize the character's inner experience, however, we see that a character *is* a predicament. In real life, everyone's personality is a mesh of ongoing predicaments that get resolved (or not) to different degrees as one goes on living. The tension between any sort of desire and its inherent fear is itself a predicament that determines how we experience ourselves. What is more, each of us is the predicament of many impulses and many needs conflicting.

But also, simply to be human is in various ways a predicament: having a body and a mind at odds with each other, having a conscious mind with unconscious forces behind it, being caught between instinctive drives and social or moral prohibitions, feeling torn between the ambition for prestige and the natural desire for love and family, remaining continually dependent upon those nagging elemental needs that cost us money. As humans, we are not only mortal, we get to *know* that we will die, and that, as they say, is a whole new ball game. Being selves, immersed in this full experience of life's inherent conflicts, we must know ourselves *as selves*—but we find ourselves in the further predicament that we must need to see ourselves also as *others*, as other selves know us, as taxpayers like everybody else. As selves, we have

---

3. A major variation on this pattern occurs in stories of childhood or adolescence, where the young hero falls from a state of naive "innocence" into the disillusionment we call maturity. James Joyce's "Araby" is a well-known example. What I am calling "resistance" sometimes amounts to just the values and attitudes we are brought up with by rote or our customary but limiting social roles.

limitless desires and wish the world to suit us; as others, we follow the laws, suit our bosses, and learn to settle.

In other words, life is problematic, with "problem" built into the system. The problem isn't what you find yourself in, it's what you are. We can solve individual problems (sometimes), but the existence of "problem" itself we cannot. It comes with the organic cell, which lives by using itself up, as it prolongs itself in "desire," in order to eat, survive, and reproduce. And the trouble that is true of the cell is compounded drastically by consciousness. We cannot long escape the funniness and the furor of being conscious animals. To see a character as predicament, therefore, is to imagine the character's reality as a situation in consciousness that simply is. We can be amused as well as moved, as I think we are by Drayton's lover, whom we regard with the time-less wisdom of someone who is not in love at the moment. Essentially, how-ever, the way we relate to the character's experience is simply *realization*. We come up against it, and as we do so, we come up against what is problemati-cally human in our own nature.

We can see how this frame of mind arises when Goodman Brown, at the end of his story, cannot free himself from the predicament of despair. Another kind of example appears frequently in the work of Anton Chekhov, one of the greatest masters of both fiction and drama in this respect. His typical char-acters are conspicuously unremarkable people whose obsessions with them-selves are comically absurd. He portrays them, however, with acute sympathy, showing their obsessions as bewildered efforts to live. They are clearly people who discover that being oneself is a predicament one does not get out of.

In the story many consider Chekhov's best, "The Lady with the Pet Dog," he focuses upon Dmitry Dmitrich Gurov, who is restlessly drifting into middle age as something of a libertine.

> They had found a wife for him when he was very young, a student in his second year, and by now she seemed half as old again as he. She was a tall, erect woman with dark eyebrows, stately and dignified and, as she said of herself, intellectual. She read a great deal, used simplified spelling in her letters, called her husband, not Dmitry, but Dimitry, while he privately considered her of limited intelligence, narrow-minded, dowdy, was afraid of her, and did not like to be at home. He had begun being unfaithful to her often and, probably for that reason, almost al-ways spoke ill of women, and when they were talked of in his presence used to call them "the inferior race."[4]

---

4. Translated by Constance Garnett (New York: Macmillan, 1917, renewed 1945). Other translations call the story "Lady with a Lapdog," or simply "Lady with a Dog," which is how the original Russian has it.

Chekhov writes as though he were simply reporting facts, yet he is subtly preparing sympathy for his problematic character. His tone is sensitive objectivity. He notes simply as fact that Gurov had been married young to a woman chosen for him, yet the statement seems to imply that he was imposed upon. The wife lives within an image of herself that allows her some self-respect, but it *is* an image, defending her against vulnerability. She has style, but it is affected. Detached from her own feelings, therefore, she is not able to relate honestly to anyone else. In terms of character presentation, she is stylized as an *other* with whom we will not identify. She is a person, in fact, who has made an *other* of herself by living from the perspective of those she imagines she is impressing. We may or may not admire Gurov's faithlessness, but we can understand it. We can feel his predicament directly. When we hear, slipped in after his opinions of his wife, that she frightens him, we sense his deeper vulnerability. This opens him up to us as a complex person whom life can challenge. His image of himself is a fragile one, and that is fortunate, for it means he can change in the way characters usually change: by becoming more substantially themselves, by having a new relationship to their own experience.

When we are told Gurov's habitual opinion of women, it is explained curiously as a reflection of his own behavior. The opinion is clearly not admirable, but he seems at least half-aware that it is not a sincere judgment.

> It seemed to him that he had been sufficiently tutored by bitter experience to call them what he pleased, and yet he could not have lived without "the inferior race" for two days together. In the company of men he was bored and ill at ease, he was chilly and uncommunicative with them; but when he was among women he felt free, and knew what to speak to them about and how to comport himself; and even to be silent with them was no strain on him. In his appearance, in his character, in his whole makeup there was something attractive and elusive that disposed women in his favor and allured them. He knew that, and some force seemed to draw him to them too.

What draws him to women is his need to somehow be himself, and it is presumably his capacity and his need to do this that draws them to him as well. If he remains unsatisfied with his casual affairs, that too is not only understandable but even to his credit, for it conveys his longing for something more, something he gets neither from them nor from his marriage.

Not too surprisingly, Gurov meets a woman distinctly different from the others he has known and the contrary also of both his wife and his self-image. She too is unhappily married, but she is essentially virginal in character, and her naiveté undoes his sophistication. Her vulnerability is clear and open. When she yields to his seduction, she is torn with remorse, but she knows that she loves him and returns to her bleak homelife painfully. Gurov tries to dismiss her from his mind, as he has done with his other mistresses, but he cannot, and after putting up a struggle with himself, he finally pursues her to the village where she lives. There is no happy solution in 19th-century Russia, however. The result is most distinctly problematic:

> Then they spent a long time taking counsel together, they talked of how to avoid the necessity for secrecy, for deception, for living in different cities, and not seeing one another for long stretches of time. How could they free themselves from these intolerable fetters?
> "How? How?" he asked, clutching his head. "How?"
> And it seemed as though in a little while the solution would be found, and then a new and glorious life would begin; and it was clear to both of them that the end was still far off, and that what was to be most complicated and difficult for them was only just beginning.

In this state, Chekhov leaves them, with full respect for their situation. There is little basis for their hope, we know, but he lets us respect the courage with which they hold to it. Gurov has moved from a predicament that was meaningless to a predicament that is meaningful, one that is still frustrating but now has *value*. This, Chekhov suggests, is what life has to offer.

Sometimes, of course, characters, like us, retreat from feelings into defensive postures. But when they see the light, which is probably more common, they abandon resistance to accept the creative dangers of vulnerability. As Gurov's story shows, the process is likely to run through several stages. A character mired in a habitual lifestyle begins to feel dissatisfaction with it. The temptation arises to break out in a new and threatening direction. After resisting temptation, the character confronts the fact that something real has been aroused inside. A struggle ensues, until a choice is made between the alternatives or the state of inner conflict is honestly accepted. Then there is some reconciliation with a broader view of life, and this provides resolution. Life is to be lived more dangerously perhaps but more honestly. The meaning of the story lies squarely in this new state of mind and its relation to the past.

Tragedy Flawless

If what I have been saying in this chapter makes sense, it will be especially meaningful in the interpretation of **tragedy**. As it is applied to literature, especially to drama, this word has meant different things in different ages, and it is valuable to see what kind of plays have been called tragedies in the past. In his *Poetics*, Aristotle provides an invaluable analysis of what tragedy seemed to consist of as he looked at the plays of his day, but we do not need to insist that he saw all that was in them—or even what was most important—or that he saw all the possibilities in the concepts he worked with. We cannot fail to realize, moreover, that he had not read Shakespeare and quite a few other writers of and writers about tragic drama. While the modern view that I favor does not apply to all plays that have been called tragedies, it may, I believe, explain the special power those works we consider the great tragedies have made us feel.[5]

If we think of a tragedy as a symbolic form, its main service is to express what has been called "the tragic sense of life," or more simply, "the tragic." The tragic is a kind of grief about mortality. Many works of fiction have a tragic quality and engage our feelings with characters who attain a tragic vision or with narrators who regard their stories tragically. A tragic sense of things may also be conveyed through poems. In literary talk, however, we ordinarily reserve the term "*a tragedy*" for drama. Apparently, we feel something essential of the tragic sense comes to us in performance or at least in imagining life as an acting out. A critical factor about the tragic sense is that it comes to the self as the ultimate evidence of one's own vulnerability, and vulnerability is seen accordingly with dread. Objectively, we all know that we will die and that we may experience all sorts of hardship, but now the fact that great suffering is built into life *feels* utterly outrageous, especially because it is happening to *me* or to someone with whom I have identified.

Through the character we call a tragic hero, then, the playwright dramatizes the realization of selfhood in the face of mortality. The tragic hero comes to his knowledge of what life is through a powerful resistance to the facts, which makes the truth seem all the more dreadful.[6] We can see this resistance in what Aristotle calls the hero's **hubris,** which is commonly explained as a kind of arrogance or excessive pride. True tragedy does not give us, I think, the satisfaction of moral distance, by which we can judge the hero's character. Hubris seems to me simply a way that consciousness has about it, a quality that the hero takes up with a special commitment. When one faces as a *self* what mortality means, what one sees through one's naked consciousness has this special impact: *I* am going to die; *I* cannot control my unconscious mind, with all its dimly seen and troubling passions; *I* am utterly alone in my being;

---

5. This view, which follows, is akin to the philosophy of existentialism.

6. I will regard the tragic hero as masculine, because that's generally been the case. There are some tragic women in traditional drama, such as Shakespeare's Cleopatra and John Webster's two great heroines the Duchess of Malfi (in the play by that name) and Vittoria Corombona (in *The White Devil*); and there are certainly tragic women in modern fiction. For an explanation of why tragedy has seemed particularly masculine, you might consider a note in my book *The Art of Our Necessities: Form and Consciousness in Shakespeare* (Bern & New York: Peter Lang, 1989), p. 300. This book discusses Shakespeare's plays along the lines I have been sketching here. I have further discussion of tragic theory in a little book called *Tragedy and Innocence* (Washington, D.C.: United Press of America, 1983).

I feel devastated by the ordeal of humiliation. The hero has, therefore, a kind of integrity in his capacity to be horrified; this is the protest of hubris. He also has integrity in allowing himself to go through the ordeal in which he lives out what he has been horrified by. By imagining his ordeal, we feel for the moment reconciled to our nature, integrating it into a balanced sense of life.

What all this says about the famous "tragic flaw" is that it isn't. If tragic, not a flaw; if a flaw, not tragic. The idea flourishes in the classroom and in textbooks because, frankly, it is easy to explain. Translators and scholars have for the most part put it aside, taking Aristotle's own term *hamartia* to mean some sort of error. This is an improvement, since it is less judgmental, but it makes the tragic events seem like an accident. We can only shake our heads. If we do criticize the hero for being "flawed," we need to ask ourselves what an unflawed character would look like. God? Ourselves? The trouble with the hero—what makes him tragic—is that he is very, very human. His life falls apart because he is vulnerable. He is subject to imprudent desires, to frustrated rages, and dreams of glory. Being a king or prince or military commander, he gets to act out his passion without having to be psychopathic—where we would ordinarily compromise and settle for muddles. The hero is heroic precisely because he passes over the common sense that makes the rest of us so cautious.[7] Therefore, he gets to be more us than we are ourselves: "larger than life," we like to say. Each tragic hero allows himself to be absolutely vulnerable. This means he is subject to death and chaos a little more readily than the rest of us and a good deal more awesomely.

The tragic hero's job is to live out the dramatic process by which he makes his mortality clear to himself and to us. As he does so, he shows us that life is all the richer because it includes pain. Open to the anguish that vulnerability brings, the hero is also open to courage and to love. Like King Lear, he finds that his suffering permits him a vivid and unsentimental comprehension of others' pain. He finds that only the honestly vulnerable self can really see meaning in life; this is a self able now to recognize other selves and to know perhaps the difficult beauty of love.[8] Thus the hero is tragic not because of what is wrong about him but what is very importantly right.

Such a character's one primary characteristic is *emotional integrity,* an insistence that meaning must be found in his feelings—for example, Hamlet's "I know not seems"—and a willingness to follow where they lead him. He is, accordingly, eminently open to experiencing life. By exploring with us the far reaches of human *being* then, the author of tragedy is showing us why life

---

7. Hamlet may seem cautious about acting, but he is intensely passionate in his spiritual pain. It is for this that we are bonded to him, and it is for this that he dies and kills.

8. This last point barely figures among the Greeks, although there is something like it in the *Iliad.*

itself is the way it is, why it is difficult, crazy, full of contradictions and frustrations, elusive and endlessly fascinating. We should not expect to find out what to do or how to live safely. Perhaps we do get to see, however, how we can appreciate being what we are, in our selves and all together.

That tragic characters die at the end of their stories—like Romeo and Juliet or Hamlet or Edna Pontellier in Kate Chopin's novel *The Awakening*—does not mean they have been wrong or weak: They have heroically followed the tragic course. The important question is *how* they have died, in what state of mind, in what relation to themselves. We want to know what their deaths imply about the nature of the mortal person, not—something we all know well enough in principle—how to avoid the trouble that our feelings tempt us into.

Similarly, that Goodman Brown dies in despair does not mean he was weak of will; it shows, rather, the integrity with which one can be horrified by evil and the utter desolation the loss of faith must mean if one takes the word seriously at all—especially if we think of faith (as the story suggests we should) not only in the conventional religious sense but as faith in all the people one has respected and loved, in one's own perception, and in life itself. Like Hamlet, Brown is repelled because he cares, because life matters to him. Characters have inner conflicts because they are sensitive enough to be engrossed in living. Taken as a whole, therefore, the vision of tragedy is not simply bleak and pessimistic. Aristotle tells us that tragedy leads to **catharsis,** or "purgation," and that it gets us there through pity and fear. (Shakespeare's words—at the end of *Hamlet*—are "woe" and "wonder.") We can see now that catharsis is the acceptance of pain in the scheme of things, an acceptance that should be fully exhilarating because it yields to what is simply natural, a great relief from our anxious resistance. Through the open sensibility of the hero, we can take what life has to offer. Along with the playwright, we can imagine symbols of mortality that are sharply honest in their emotional challenge.

Generic Thinking

It is not, of course, a fact that life is tragic, nor is it an opinion, either of the playwright, the hero, or the critic. It is a function of consciousness, according to which we experience mortality as an impossible predicament, a situation that cannot work the agreeable way we all would like it to. There are too many contradictory factors, and they are all too powerful for each other. As conscious creatures we want to determine our virtues, our personalities, and our destinies. In tragedy we come up against something deeper than our conscious view of ourselves, something unmovable in life that shows our absolute limitations. This something is often experienced (and symbolized) as "fate" or the work of gods. It is commonly represented by death. Rather than being merely the account of an odd and messy or unfortunate life (which would be *pathetic* rather than tragic), tragedy is a statement that life in general is tragic and that it is tragic because it is mortal. The hero is only the most important image in the whole symbolic form that is the play. A tragedy may not even have a specific hero, any more than a tragic hero actually needs to die.

Comedy is also about our humanity, but it reveals that our mortal nature is wonderful. Being fallibly mortal, we are also very charming. This is a complementary perspective, and an equally important one. Each is a vision of life that comes to us through the stylization of its self-contained world. If the tragic world is characterized by its sense of dread, the comic is imbued with a hopeful feeling that culminates in delight. Each world makes sense while we are in it, seeing it in its own terms, because each projects clearly and "dramatically" a side of our overall truth.

If we accept the view of literature as symbolic form, then, we are not seeing characters as pseudo-people and stories as fake history. They are people-like and history-like, and we need to enjoy the fiction that they are really real. But it is more important to recognize that they are lively factors making up powerful image structures that communicate to us, each as a whole, as the play itself. In a tragedy or a comedy, we don't have the story of somebody with bad luck or good, with virtues deserving praise or faults deserving punishment. Rather, we have a genre expressing its intrinsic vision of life. Through that generic vision, Shakespeare, Sophocles, Molière, or Shaw shapes his own version of the tragic or the comic sense of things.[9]

Tragedy, then, is about an unstable structure falling apart—a structure that involves one's relation to other people and one's relation to oneself, which, of course, are closely interrelated. The world of tragedy is torn apart by tensions and frustrated forces trying to realize themselves, the forces of society and also the forces within. From both sides, within and without, the world is undermined by jealousy, arrogance, fear, and other self-inhibiting passions. These are drives that will always undermine the most polite and ordered society and hold back the most powerful personality from real human security: Macbeth's latent yearning for authority, Oedipus's anxiety about his identity, even Hamlet's tortured honesty. Such security comes only, as we have seen, from entering the storm, one of Shakespeare's favorite symbols. As Hamlet advises the players, "in the very torrent, tempest, and (as I may say)

---

9. In this and some other matters I am following Northrop Frye. His approach to literary study is developed most fully in his "bible," *The Anatomy of Criticism* (Princeton: Princeton UP, 1957). I am using the word "genre" loosely here. It usually distinguishes poetry, drama, and fiction as "kinds." Frye calls tragedy and comedy, and also romance and irony, "modes."

whirlwind of your passion, you must acquire and beget a temperance that may give it smoothness" (III, ii).

If tragedy is about disintegration, **comedy** is about a coherent structure emerging, one in which we can live joyfully. In comedy a vision of fulfillable life is projected for us to savor. It is life fulfilled socially and sociably. The fictional world is challenged by the same kind of disruptive force that erupts in tragedy—jealousy, guilt, and so forth—in the person now of the comic villain. This threat is, however, slighter than it is in tragedy, coming as it does from outside the norm group, the more-or-less unified society sharing a common understanding. A Malvolio, Shylock, or Don John would seem capable of destroying happiness, but we can tell from the start such characters are not to be taken too seriously. Their challenge can be met, because style and tone do not let it get all that threatening. By meeting it, the group sorts itself out, realizing the values that make society appropriately liveable as the lovers find together their blissfully just rewards. When society reasserts itself at the end of the play, it doesn't do so just out of narrow-minded and restrictive conventions but out of a spirit of geniality (or conviviality, to use Michael Polanyi's word). This is a warm feeling about life, good-natured and tolerant, which makes the society what a society should be, a genuine blend of persons. It is communally personal, so to speak. The values of comedy are not, therefore, moralistic, nor are they simply entertaining. They are naturally human, arising out of people's willingness to be vulnerable together.

Seeing the plays as symbolic forms allows us to appreciate them as expressions of our own nature, as human beings alone and together. As we read (or watch a performance), we imagine. As we imagine, we project our feelings into the fiction. As we project our feelings, we experience them sharply and clearly, insofar as the form itself is properly articulate. And at the same time we sort them out, recognizing their implications and the energies by which they work. Most importantly, we experience the resistance to feeling that keeps us from ourselves, then see how richly natural we become by following where feeling leads. Seeing such works as symbolic forms, finally, encourages us to read, as a rule, in the first-person plural. We, Will Shakespeare, Prince Hamlet, and the whole audience of our culture—*we* are in it together. Self is one, but it is also manifold. The symbolic form of forceful literature speaks for us all as we respond to its images, voices, and shapes of experience.

Chapter 6

A Formal View: How Literature Takes Shape

The Form of a Form

To appreciate the power of **form,** we should first question the common opinion that an artist imposes form upon life. All around us, life is already full of form. We immediately recognize the basic form of a tree that a child can draw, even though all real trees differ from one another even within one species. Or the form of an apple, an elephant, a man, a woman. Everything we can think about has form, from atoms to galaxies. Even when things are in flux, we still think of them as changing *in form* and *as form.* And not only things have form. There is form also in the recurrent cycles of day and night, in the four seasons, in the stages of life, in the succession of generations. Projects that we undertake have form: conceiving them, planning, altering plans, beginning, and carrying through to a resolution. Relationships have form: parents and children, teacher and students, lover and beloved, me and you.

There is also in the human mind a *sense* of form, which likes to perceive things as shapes and clusters, with symmetries and imbalances. That old human habit of naming things seems an extension of our need to give them identity, a wholeness in their own being, so that we can identify them. Language itself comes largely, perhaps, from this compulsion to make the world our own, to *own* it. Similarly, the mind needs stories—just as the body needs food. They are not just pastime, but a symbolic manifestation of our being, making us fully what we are as humans. Consciousness wants to know what it itself is, and story is a probe with which to find that out. Mythmaking and tribal storytelling were surely among the first social activities of humanity, following closely upon, or accompanying, dance and body ornament. Shared fiction and drama continue to carry our values and traditions, whether in the Bible, Shakespeare's plays, Charles Dickens's stories, Charlie Chaplin's films, or for that matter, soap operas and thrillers. But the drive for story goes still deeper. History is (quite literally) story, and that includes our personal histories (life stories), our family traditions, our childhood memories, as well as the voyages of Columbus, the Civil War, the Great Depression. We think of the past as time gone (whatever time is supposed to be), but what the past *is* is story still with us. It provides us a background that sustains us as we work to live in the present. And story hardly ends there, for the future is story too: fantasies and plans, desires and intentions, fears and hopes. Your college graduation, your career, your grandchildren, your last days, your job interview tomorrow: It is science fiction all, imaginatively projecting an unknown future. No wonder that culture has developed literature as a great good. In it, our story-ing drive attains recognition as a means of exploring our nature, making more real to us (through fictions) what we are.

Story is one clear way that the mind's sense of form addresses its environment—not to impose something on the impersonal truth, but to recognize a mental ecology, so to speak, an environment we have made human and personal by living in it actively—our world, which partakes of our nature. It is a world in which certain events have special importance to us and can be thought of therefore with some distinctness. There is form, in other words, in our relationship to our world, the form of our priorities. The events of our lives evolve from intentions into consequences; they have central characters with supporting casts (each of us within a world of others), themes and values, and conglomerations of appropriate images. What any artist is doing by making forms, therefore, is to *elicit* the form in life through the sense of form in the human mind, allowing this sense of form to "identify" life for us—to give it identity and confirm it as our own. Through this sense of form, we respond to rhythms, proportions, the self-containment of things. The artist elicits these formal qualities of perception and stylizes the world by stressing their presence. Whether creating an abstract painting, a song, or a novel, the artist forms a *seeing,* a vision, in life.

Relating to art requires, then, a responsiveness to form. Interpretation requires close attention to it. This means recognizing the structure of a sonnet or a Greek tragedy, but it also means appreciating the very particular beauty in what we perceive and enjoying the concrete world we are led to imagine.

For if the work and its elements *have* form, also they *are* forms. Is a circle its circumference or its area? Obviously both, nor can one exist without the other: a circle is not just a line chasing its tail. When we think of form in literature, we should try to think of it as area or substance, rather than outline or structure. The area is full of space: it is the space the form occupies that is our real concern. Think of a poem or story as a body with a given shape. It is a body of language, it is a body of image-world, it is a body of consciousness (or sense of self)—three dimensions of one whole. Thinking this way, we honor the concrete experience of literature rather than abstract principles of structure. It is customary to think of form as a container which holds some content of another nature, some abstract theme or some bits of reality that lie within it. Such a contrast between form and content can be useful if we know we are speaking very loosely, but the relation between *a* form and *its* form may be more appropriate and more fruitful. Obviously inextricable, they are only different perspectives on the same thing, like a substance and some features of the way it is: a body and its features of weight, height, strength, and so forth. We would not think of a rainbow merely as a curve in the sky, without seeing, if only in the mind's eye, that progression of lightly tinted air, just about to fade away, which does curve into existence and out of it again. In music we can enjoy form by itself, without emotional expression or objective reference, but it is not the abstract form of mathematics. It is full of rich sonorities that are organized in tensions, tensions that express the nature of sensibility itself, with its nuances, its qualities of awareness, its capacities for endless modulation. It is because of the fullness of form that in these chapters I have been emphasizing human presence in literature and the overall importance of sensibility in "the symbolic form."

Action as Form: Story

Life in Crisis

Poems tell stories; stories (including novels and plays) are often written in a style that we want to call poetic. There are narrative poems and there are verse dramas. There are even some verse novels (like Vikram Seth's *The Golden Gate*, published in 1986). All statements are actions; all stories come in words. Shakespeare's plays are stories and they are poems. Thus the sense of a form overlaps.

Emotion and imagery are two primary ways that experience assumes form, ways we have been discussing along the way so far. Now let us look at two other ways in which this occurs:

- Action as form, which we can watch most clearly in fiction; and
- Language as form, which we can watch most clearly in poems.

Much of the interest that a story has for us depends upon the fact that it brings us into a moment of crisis. This too is a principle of form. In a long work like a novel, an epic, or a five-act drama, our author will have orchestrated a sequence of crises that lead up to one grand crisis, the *climax*. This unravels into the *denouement* (literally, an "untying"), confirming triumph or disaster— or sometimes, as in Chekhov, an uneasy but clearly meaningful tension between the two. The moments of crisis may be turning points in personal development, like the onslaught of adolescence or the recognition of imminent death. They may be transitional times and transformational episodes, in which people find their lives revealing depths or heights they had not known before. They may be simply recognitions of natural things—in a flower, say, or a starry sky—but recognitions that make a difference:

> I wandered lonely as a cloud
>   That floats on high o'er vales and hills,
> When all at once I saw a crowd,
>   A host, of golden daffodils,
> Beside the lake, beneath the trees,
> Fluttering and dancing in the breeze.
>
> —*William Wordsworth,*
> "I Wandered Lonely as a Cloud"

They may be perceptions of symbolic significance, sparked by images seen, remembered, or fantasized:

> Ah, Sun-flower! weary of time,
> Who countest the steps of the Sun:
> Seeking after that sweet golden clime
> Where the traveller's journey is done.
>
> Where the Youth pined away with desire,
> And the pale Virgin shrouded in snow:
> Arise from their graves and aspire,
> Where my Sun-flower wishes to go.
>
> —*William Blake,* "Ah, Sun-Flower"

In a philosophical poem, these "crises" may be turning points in the development of an argument.

One way that a story carries meaning is through the *coherence* of its form ("cohering," holding together as something in itself). Having a distinct beginning, middle, and end—unlike most events in real life—it makes a statement. In a short story or a poem, a single crisis will inform (*in-form*) the whole. In a novel or full-length play, the many episodes building up the whole plot lead probably to an overriding sense of one grand transformation. This is all because narrative focuses upon life in crisis. Although in reality, life often seems to go on in tedious anticlimax, still in literature we come to see crisis as an underlying structure—in stresses and transitions, and in such crucial features of experience as love and death. Literature commonly represents these matters as cataclysms. All life revolves around the lovers, their gratification making all of life beautiful; the tragic hero's fall is devastation, his humiliation is torture, his death the end of a world. The crises in life come mixed with other events and life goes on; still they remain defining experiences that seem to tell us what our lives are about. In literature, therefore, they are made to stand out (projected), elevated through their coherent form. They have to be known, we feel, as a kind of total truth in order to be known for what they are. What I have said elsewhere about myth is true of literature in general: It makes reality "look like what it feels like." It is the nature of imagination to project emotional truths as literal ones.

Another way form conveys meaning in stories is through the pattern of relationship among characters. We do not, of course, encounter a random bunch of people who just happen to fall in together. Through the characters who make up the story's little world of people—its Elsinore, Salem, Dublin, or Chicago—the author sorts out various attitudes toward life. These are likely to present the central character with self-defining choices: various directions in which to go or different aspects of inner life to be lived out through choices at the point of crisis. In some narratives, subsidiary characters dramatize moral alternatives. These will be especially clear in an allegorical tale like "Young Goodman Brown." In this case, the hero has to choose between Faith and the Devil but is confounded when they seem not so far apart after all. We have in such fictions, then, a *critical structure*, which shows life's meaningful features in experiences of special stress. Typically, we see nurturing forces that support vulnerability against repressive forces that threaten it. In *Othello* we have the hero's devoted new wife Desdemona on one side of him, his malicious officer Iago on the other, a pattern very easy to compare—up to a point—with Hawthorne's tale. Other characters fill in the background of Othello's society. Each portrays an alternative "address to life," some way of compromising perhaps with the conflicting demands of inner and outer life, which may split the hero down the middle in his struggle to be a whole person. We can think of each character as an experiment in living, according to one attitude or another; some succeed, some fail, some are more valuable in failure than others in success. In a sample world as complex as Hamlet's, we can chart the complexity like this and talk about any of the relationships, one pair at a time:

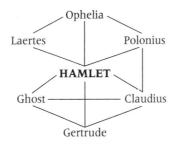

(You might also tuck in Horatio, Fortinbras, and Rosencrantz and Guildenstern to liven things up.)

Such patterns of character tension are sometimes regarded as spatial aspects of structure, which seem to stabilize in a diagram like the example on Hamlet. Actually, they become meaningful only as they play out their tensions through the process of the plot, in fictional time. Whether drama or lyric or satiric argument, the literary work is essentially temporal. Like a piece of music, it exists properly only as we go through it, allowing it to evolve—or to go through *us*. The voices have their say, the forces work out an ultimate vision of life in the way their assorted perspectives fall together or fall apart: who wins, who loses, what alliances are established, how our own allegiances and antipathies intensify through the course of the crisis. This evolution is implicit, we may notice, in the opening gambits. A plot is not a simple sequence of events, any more than a coherent argument is a simple sequence of points to be made. In the first paragraph or two of a short story, the first chapter of a novel, or first scene of a play, we find ourselves within a tense situation that must unfold its energies, fraught with the passion that needs to explode. *Othello* introduces its main characters through an ugly comedy reeking with danger:

IAGO: Zounds, sir, you are one of these that will not serve God if the devil bid you. Because we come to do you service, and you think we are ruffians, you'll have your daughter covered with a Barbary horse; you'll have your nephews neigh to you; you'll have coursers for cousins, and gennets for germans.

BRABANTIO: What profane wretch art thou?

IAGO: I am one, sir, that comes to tell you your daughter and the Moor are now making the beast with two backs.

BRABANTIO: Thou art a villain.

IAGO: You are a senator.[1]

---

1. Iago here pleasantly reveals Othello's elopement with Desdemona to the bride's father, whom he has awakened by calling out from the street. The Barbary horse refers to the fact that Othello is a Moor; "gennets" are Spanish horses, "germans" are relatives. Iago is apparently about to say something else when he substitutes the undeniable "senator."

A QUITE SHORT STORY; OR, FORM AS SELF, SELF AS FORM

Consider the following recitation:

> I woke up this morning, then had breakfast. I got in my car and went to school. I took a chemistry exam and after that I went to the cafeteria for a cup of coffee. My friend Joe came up to talk to me.

Now that may be the preparation for a story, but in itself it is just a sequence of events. They are *paratactic,* juxtaposed but not related. Let the muse transform these events into literature:

> I woke up this morning suspecting that I was making a mistake. My coffee tasted like it was three years old. On the freeway, I nearly smashed into a Porsche. Finally, I had to face my chemistry exam, and finally, it was over! I went to the caf, sat in the corner, and tried to comfort myself with coffee somebody else had made. My wounded mind cuddled with my girlfriend Janet. What is chemistry? Then I get to see Joe, my best friend, coming over with a nervous grin. "Sam," he tells me, "I'm in love with Janet and we're going to get married." When the earthquake subsided, I stood on the edge of the huge chasm that had opened up across the cafeteria floor. I was about to jump in: How lucky I was the floor had split completely. I caught myself just in time, however, and decided to push old Joe in instead.

One thing is leading up to another until we reach a grand climax: that is the **plot,** an organization of events. There is surprise, but a surprise that follows (as we can see after the fact) from our initial problem. Events expand or unravel with a freshness, a vivid pleasure, and that depends on a logic that relates them to each other.

The opening establishes the exciting element of suspense, and suspense can itself be a principle of form, as it calls forth the shape of a narrative structure. Often an author creates a kind of pseudo-suspense while letting it be clear enough what's going on and where it will lead. We enjoy a safe anxiety while following the plot's inevitable self-disclosure and the grace with which it is danced out. Of course the handsome, sincere boy will get the lovely and spirited girl. Of course if the tone is light enough, the hero will survive the threat of death. And of course he will die if foreboding signs demand a

The logic of events, however, depends upon the inescapable fact that our story is happening to somebody and that (the same) somebody is making it happen. It is a story *about* someone. Not only does one event lead to another, one state of feeling leads to another. It is a personal process, and this person's story takes place, furthermore, in relation to other persons. If we are moving through mounting frustration to some resolution, it is a character's frustration and his arrival at a stopping point. Through him and for him are we surprised and gratified.

Not only is the story *about* character, through its tone and its sense of style the story itself *has* character. It sets us in a frame of mind and develops our relation to the whole, through feelings and attitudes: a sense of the ridiculous, of recognition, sympathy, and satisfaction. Although the story is not philosophically profound, there is still some point to it. With a little imagination, we "get it." The structure has meaning in itself—a good example of what I am calling "fable" (see page 137).

There are several other features of literature that this compelling little work can demonstrate for us. Notice how much the specificity of detail contributes to the sense of character, but see also what we understand by innuendo, through what is not stated. What do we know to feel without being instructed on the matter—and how do we know that? Notice also an aspect of stylization: how imagination lets things be real and unrealistic at the same time, even how it actually makes things feel psychologically real through an unrealistic technique (that earthquake really is convenient!). Most of all, see how the story gives us the sense of *self in form*—and conversely, how the self is known though the form of its movement, as frustrations build until they work themselves out.

pathetic climax. We enjoy the fulfillment of what we expect along with the tension of uncertainty.

A coherent opening is, therefore, a set-up. We may understand what it contains only by hindsight, when we have watched the unfolding of its implications, but we are seeing then the resolution of energies that had been charged up for us at the start. We experience the dread, or the happy (but prolonged) anticipation, of what we know is more than probable. In either way, the whole plot works out the implications of the initial situation, revealing the meaning of its tensions as they work themselves out. In *Othello,* we can see that the opening is itself tragic—as, in other plays, it is comic. The self-confident malice of Iago will have to extinguish what he himself describes sneeringly as Othello's "free and open nature." The charming pathos with which Viola, the heroine of *Twelfth Night,* is shipwrecked will have to lead her toward a well-deserved fulfillment in love. A plot's movement in time can be thought of, therefore, as cyclical, the end leading back to its potentiality at the start. At the end of *Hamlet,* in fact, Horatio promises to tell the whole story to Fortinbras.

We can see all this a little differently if we go back to the idea of a character as predicament. A predicament is not in itself, of course, a story. The story must give us a *strategy* to cope with the predicament and bring it to some clarification.[2] When you are in a predicament, there is, of course, no clear solution. That is what makes it a predicament: Any way you go will seem wrong. A story's strategy is interesting, therefore, because it cannot be clearly safe or wholly desirable. It most likely relies upon a principle of sacrifice, giving up something that is felt as a need. In tragedy, it is usually life itself that must be given up. It comedy, it may be only the self-images that people have befuddled themselves with.

A story's strategy is likely to turn upon some form of *challenge* or temptation, which opens a new realm of experience. We evaluate a dynamic character by seeing how he or she faces a challenge, recognizing it for what it is. The challenge always presents a critical situation, where one draws, if one can, upon surprising resources latent within, perhaps an inner knowledge that is threatening to consciousness, a point of view that must be lived out. Ultimately, it must be either answered and invalidated or acknowledged and integrated. The challenge is often dramatized in the person of another character, someone who, for better or worse, has a radically different view of life, someone who upsets the hero's most basic values and assumptions. A hero's "heroism" lies in the capacity to respond. As we identify with the hero, through the bond of imagination, we take up the challenge ourselves: The work's meaning arises in *our* response, as we understand the impact the challenge makes upon our own view of life. A Shakespearean clown challenges us to take our common sense less seriously; a Shakespearean villain challenges us to enjoy our own selfish bitterness. The first proposition will, we hope, be sustained, the second soundly invalidated. We are challenged to understand characters we disapprove of; to appreciate, when we see it lived out, a philos-

---

2. At the start of his book *The Philosophy of Literary Form,* Kenneth Burke speaks of a literary work "as the adopting of various strategies for the encompassing of situations" (New York: Vintage, 1957), p. 3.

ophy that has made no sense to us; to follow out familiar assumptions to frightening consequences.

Temptation is the most obvious kind of challenge; it comes in positive and negative varieties. *Positive temptation* is towards something that feels very desirable. In comic forms, it leads to happiness ever after, but it can also lead to a way of life that is more honestly problematic (a state that can be fully tragic). Gurov's predicament in Chekhov's story "The Lady with a Pet Dog" (discussed on pages 120–122) finds him fixed in an unfulfilling marriage while he still has a powerful interest in women. The predicament that he *is* has to do with his sensitivity, intelligence, vulnerability, and charm on one side and his need on the other to live with self-respect in the worldly terms his society allows (which include a certain surreptitious manly liberty). The strategy he himself adopts is a life of casual affairs, giving in to easy temptations. The story's strategy for him is temptation of a new kind, the one woman who dissolves his pretense about himself.

Negative temptation is the spell of the devil. Goodman Brown manages to resist it, only to be left with deeper inner anguish. Macbeth's witches open to him the possibility of success, which turns into the inevitability of damnation. Iago's diabolic lies seduce Othello into killing his wife and destroying himself even more dreadfully. We are tempted "negatively" to solve problems through violence or, like Dr. Faustus, to give in to self-consuming gratification. Sometimes doing nothing is a very attractive way out. We can speak, therefore, of a subdivision here: *inverse temptation*, the lure of avoidance. We are tempted to clear out, succumb to madness, fall off a bridge, keep life simple by not thinking about it. Jonah tries to bypass Nineveh and winds up within the whale. One may think Hamlet is sorely tempted not to murder Claudius. (Some scholars, on the other hand, see his father's ghost as an evil spirit pointing him toward hell.) Usually, of course, neither negative nor inverse temptation proves a tenable strategy, since it doesn't solve the problem of living. Still, in either form, it leads a character into vulnerability—in fear, perhaps, rage, or helplessness—and that is where the story needs to go.

A conventional plot is a structure that turns on itself, like a melody. In this turning, we find meaning, in the story as it is shaped. When we think of a plot this way, we might call it the *fable*. The shape is usually one of symmetry that we read ironically, as in a set-up and reversal: the apparently weak are truly the strong, the self-righteous are the foolish, the sad become happy, the happy sad. The deserving and needy get either satisfaction or futility—either of which will be meaningful. It is "fable" that causes readers to oversimplify fiction by looking for the moral or message. This kind of interpretation works explicitly in stories that *are* fables, like Aesop's, when we refer to "fable" in its established sense as a specific genre. More broadly, however, as an element *in* fiction, fable should be taken qualitatively. Rather than being just a means to convey a message, it focuses on qualities of living and draws them forth to be seen, especially those qualities of tension with which we resist ourselves. In the midst of life's ambiguities and nagging vagueness, we still have capacities for transformations, through which we recognize something of what it is all about. Fable realizes these capacities; it expresses transformation. This does not mean, as a rule, that a character becomes a different sort of person: Rather, the character becomes more clearly himself or herself. An egg becomes a chicken or it becomes an omelet. The chicken does not become a cow. The ugly duckling was a swan all along, just needing to know it. One is transformed by becoming conscious of what was before unconscious, although sometimes (as with Katherine Mansfield's Miss Brill) one then retreats from more awareness than one can handle. At least momentarily, there is an opening to life, so it becomes clearer how life works, and if the character doesn't get it, still the reader does. Because the story is symbolic form, what matters is what it conveys as a whole, not just what the hero comes to know.

Mythic Form

Since ancient times classical **mythology** has provided authors with a special language, essentially metaphoric, that adds to their writing a richness (or as critics sometimes say, *a resonance*), for the myths of the Greeks and Romans are concise stories that represent the extremes of human passion in vivid images. They sum up the critical relations of life—between lover and beloved, between parents and children, between people and the forces of nature, between men and gods and demonic forces, between life and death. Mythic images and stories tend to be spectacularly unrealistic, although they follow a logic of their own and preserve their own kind of coherence as they portray such elemental forces. The images of myth are touching in a grotesque way that stirs in our imagination an uneasy fascination, revealing a weird beauty not only from times before time but from inner depths beyond clear knowledge.

Myths provide an important kind of literary **allusion** (a reference to another work or to some information the reader is presumed to know). Blake's sunflower poem quoted earlier in the chapter, for example, is based upon a myth from Ovid's *Metamorphoses,* the most important source of myths for European and English authors. Modern readers, no longer brought up with such a resource, usually need footnotes to understand such allusions. A note on the poem in one edition of Blake's works provides a handy explanation (but assumes we know that the Romans thought of Apollo as a sun god): "Clytie, in love with Apollo, was spurned by the god and pined away till she became a heliotrope, a flower fabled always to face the sun."[3] In modern

---

3. Mary Lynn Johnson and John E. Grant, *Blake's Poetry and Designs* (New York: Norton, 1979), p. 51.

literature, myths often provide the basis for complex works, which recreate something of the old myths' form and meaning, either closely or loosely. The author will naturally adopt a latter-day perspective, which may be ironic, romantic, or realistic, sometimes debunking and sometimes drawing upon the sense of mystery inherent in the ancient tales. The major authors of **modernism**—especially James Joyce, Thomas Mann, William Faulkner, T. S. Eliot, and Ezra Pound—drew upon the myths of various cultures to create in their novels and long poems a mythic sensibility that interprets modern life through the elemental patterns. For them, what was particularly modern was an ability to see the present in universal terms. Myth enabled them to relate their present world to the distant past in a way that conveyed something timeless about all life.

However, myth has a more pervasive importance in the study of literature, for it provides a strong sense of form in storytelling and some basic assumptions about how form has meaning. There are creation myths and flood myths and myths of the end of the world, but what most influenced the development of literature as we know it are hero myths. These portray a figure of more than normal capacities, with a talent for the impossible. His special stature, or charisma, is usually expressed by the fact that he has a divine parent. His story leads him on a journey to his culture's version of the underworld or home of the gods or to the lair of some choice monster. Symbolically, this journey follows a circular rhythm: The hero confronts death and, by confronting it, achieves a regeneration. This **archetype,** or fundamental image structure, writes large the movement from resistance to vulnerability that we have seen at the heart of most stories. In true myths, the colossal scale of things gives the movement an absolute force, as though to confirm it as a rule for all time.

In a book called *Myth and Mind,* I discuss this theme at exceedingly great length, basing my analysis on a "working definition" of archetypal myth: "A myth is a symbol in the form of a story, expressing (or producing) a confrontation between the limited perspective of the self and the unlimited context in which it exists."[4] This view is derived in part from the "depth psychology" of C. G. Jung, who saw mythology as a worldwide phenomenon projected from a *collective unconscious,* a level of the psyche that is basic to individual

---

4. *Myth and Mind,* p. 113. Archetypal criticism is often condemned for making everything sound alike. To be sure, every work is unique, but no more so than every person is. When archetypal criticism is helpful, we appreciate the theme to see how it is varied and appreciate the variation for its fresh view of the theme. Like any approach taken single-mindedly, myth analysis can easily become mechanical and self-justifying. It is always necessary to address a work with discretion, to see what kind of interpretation is appropriate to it. Its specific stylization, we recall, determines what it can "see"—as in the degree of its realism or the range of its self-consciousness. One must keep a sense of proportion and remember that perspectives are perspectives.

personality but common to all.[5] My definition centers upon the experience of a *radical confrontation,* in which the *self* (conveyed through the hero, as he is imagined by the reader) comes up against an absolute sense of the *other.* This other is the "unlimited context" in which, as selves, we exist. It can be seen as the world of nature, from which our human minds have separated us. It can be seen psychologically as the totality of the unconscious mind, which our consciousness comes up against. It can be seen as death, which the living mind confronts as something very strange indeed. Or it can be seen as the sheer danger of evil, which the well-meaning mind must cope with in horror. Or it can be seen as the mystery of existence itself, which strikes us with awe and wonder as our rational, practical thinking gives way before it. Or it can be seen as all of these at once. The utter different-ness of this *other* order of things (beyond conscious rationalism and objective fact) is expressed by images of the supernatural: gods and monsters, heavens and hells, magic weapons, superhuman powers, all-knowing animal helpers, and so forth.

The cyclical death-and-rebirth pattern of myth is closely associated with ritual, particularly the rituals of sacrifice and the rite of passage (or "transitional ritual") known as **initiation.** Initiation provides a common story pattern in fiction, reminding us of the ritual that entitles one to join a group through some transforming ordeal. (The word literally means "going into" or "beginning.") In tribal cultures, an adolescent undergoes an initiation process, often with real pain or deprivation, to join the world of men or women. Initiation stories in literature are usually about a young innocent who learns the problematic ways of the world by getting knocked about a bit. Once more, "Young Goodman Brown" is a helpful example. However, in a broader sense, all sorts of stories center upon what we can see as an initiating enlightenment about reality. In "The Lady with a Pet Dog," Gurov's early cynicism is, para-

---

5. In Jungian psychology, the hero's idealized beloved is a projection of the *anima* archetype in the "collective unconscious," the female side of the male psyche. The converse male side of a woman's psyche is called the *animus,* commonly expressed in the heroic lover. Another important Jungian archetype, the *shadow,* projects the repressed unconscious as one's own threatening opposite (usually in the same gender and generation). Monsters like Beowulf's Grendel and demonic villains like Iago manifest the "shadow." The *child* archetype, which embodies the wisdom of spiritual innocence, is apparent in many fairy tales, but also in Blake's "Songs." Shakespeare's versions of the *wise old man* archetype can be seen in Prospero and assorted friars; it is parodied in Polonius. Applying these concepts dogmatically can oversimplify literature, but remembering them should restrain the tendency to treat characters as people and go too far toward realism when one reads in genres that do derive from mythic style. For an accessible introduction to Jungian psychology and its relation to myth and literature, see C. G. Jung, *Man and His Symbols* (London: Aldus Books, 1964) and the various books (and videotapes) of Joseph Campbell.

doxically, a kind of innocence that gives way to a more difficult wisdom as he becomes more vulnerable. Perhaps this pattern is especially obvious in stories of a tragic cast, as a process of humiliation in which the hero's sense of reality is squashed. However, there is comic humiliation also, as when in *Much Ado About Nothing* those staunch enemies of love Beatrice and Benedick are faced separately with the unsettling fact (which we have realized from the start, of course) that they are in love with each other. There is one type of comic humiliation, we have seen, in which a killjoy like *Twelfth Night*'s Malvolio is merrily ridiculed as a scapegoat, but there is also the central type, in which basically amiable people are allowed to function more humanly when they are laughed out of their egoism.

As myth, derived from oral tradition, gave way to literature, *letters,* it left its spirit behind in tragedy, romance, and epic, which are the major traditional genres.[6] This was partly a matter of subject, as in the Greek epics and tragedies, but beyond that it was a matter of form, as new story types evolved out of old concepts of what stories and characters were like. To understand most of the great literature before the rise of the novel (and a good deal of it afterwards), it is necessary, therefore, to expect archetypal form, to recognize what it can accomplish that a realistic style cannot, and to appreciate the kinds of meaning appropriate to it.

Tragedy has often been considered a kind of sacrificial ritual. The hero's death does not exactly bring us salvation, but he suffers his ordeal in such a way that it clarifies the common limits of our consciousness. His suffering is the psychological equivalent of descent into the underworld or combat with demons. We join an imaginative communion with him, which lets us integrate vulnerable mortality into our sense of ourselves, and in catharsis we experience a kind of "rebirth." Equally important in the history of European literature is the stylized form of storytelling known as **romance.** The fiction of **realism** portrays characters more objectively, as we recognize people within the factual limits of life as we know it, limits governed by economics, social mores, the predominance of other people, and the ambiguities of ordinary minds. We see such forces controlling characters' lives and setting the terms by which they may succeed. Stylistically, realism pretends to report on actual events as one might see them happening to others. To apply a helpful word we used in an earlier chapter, realism is essentially *mimetic,* or imitative.

In contrast, romance projects a symbolic world subjectively, somewhat as our dreams do. Some characters specialize in goodness, some in badness, some in foolishness, some in mischief, all isolating aspects of life in themselves. Life is seen in absolute terms, therefore: The beloved is utterly beautiful (a *cynosure,*

---

6. A fourth, satire, may derive from rituals of public license or ridicule.

or focus of universal attention), the hero remarkably doughty, the enemy unutterable. Through the hero's story, we move into an imaginative realm, a symbolic space where personal forces are played out. Like the mythic hero from whom he has descended, the hero of romance undertakes a journey into this space, where (psychologically speaking) he confronts the symbols that manifest unconscious forces. "Goodman Brown" serves as an example once more, the symbolism of his trip to the forest made all the clearer by allegory. His *quest* emerges from some mysterious compulsion. In myth and romance, motivation does not follow from specific causes but erupts from the heroic need for integrity, a finding out impelled always from within.

In medieval tales of knights in armor, we have a pure form of romance. As the novel developed in the 18th century, it followed some features of romance, such as the initiation ritual, which we see elaborated in the **Bildungsroman** (German for "education novel"), the "history" of a young chap who eventually matures after experiencing the dangerous, devious ways of the world and coping with its temptations. Good examples are Henry Fielding's *Tom Jones* and, later, Charles Dickens's *Great Expectations* and *David Copperfield*. An extension of this form can be seen in autobiographical first novels, in which a young hero who takes himself very seriously becomes at the end, oddly enough, a novelist. James Joyce's *Portrait of the Artist as a Young Man* is probably the most famous instance.

As the novel evolved further toward realism, however, it still often leaned back toward romance. In Hawthorne and Melville, in Joseph Conrad and William Faulkner, we are to greater or lesser degrees in the realm of romance. Sea adventures like *Moby Dick* and Conrad's *The Secret Sharer* sail us over the dangerous ocean of the unknown as we join the hero's quest for some essential clarification of life or a root sense of identity. A book like Jane Austen's *Pride and Prejudice*, on the other hand, overlays shrewd social satire, psychological realism, and an extraordinary amount of irony upon the old fairy tale theme of an ideal young lady being carried off by an ideal young man to an ideal place far from her nice but essentially helpless father and her unpleasant mother.

Although we usually think of romance as a synonym for love—and many great works of romance literature, like *Romeo and Juliet*, are indeed love stories—still romance may focus upon its other great motif, *adventure*, or a combination of both—adventure (literally "a going forth") being the exposure to danger which allows the hero to evolve through vulnerability. As we can see in works like *Moby Dick* (and the popularized descendents of romance, like science fiction, spy stories, and detective mysteries), love is not essential to it, although it fits in well, especially as an expression of the hero's fulfillment.[7]

---

7. We should distinguish, I believe, between mythic literature and fantasy. Fantasy is, as we frequently say, escape. It is trying to get somewhere else; myth is a coming home. Fantasy is based upon sensation and gratification (and in the case of science

Nevertheless, in the Middle Ages (with antecedents among the Greeks) the form of romance developed our great tradition of love literature, which continues to influence not only our popular entertainment, like "romance" novels and soap opera, but our modern expectations about courtship and marriage as well. In the tradition of literary romance, love is an absolute force that has both spiritual and aesthetic power. It is the pinnacle of human experience, it makes the lovers better people, and it is preeminently beautiful. Lovers are artists, refining their capacity for experience; and art, conversely, is the appropriate expression of love.

Considering its full range, therefore, romance is not just a sense of form; it is also a vision of life and a form of stylization. As vision, it comprehends life through a sense of wonder or innocence. As stylization, it fosters lyrical language, heightened characters, spiritual contrasts, cataclysmic plots. It minimizes motivation and intensifies subjective experience—emphasizing experience, in fact, as the essence of life. We can see all this underlying the stylization of Shakespeare's plays and leading to the quality of wonder that his plays induce. (The usual Elizabethan word was "admiration," although Horatio describes the proper impact of Hamlet's tragic story as "woe or wonder.") While there can be a fundamental quality of romance in tragedy, we find it more clearly, of course, in the comedies, like Shakespeare's, that we know as **romantic comedy.** Here we find fulfilled the ultimate drive that romance exerts: to integrate mortality as a perfectly natural phenomenon. The threats of death and shame, the sense of a tragic potential, are transcended. Vulnerability makes love possible, love transcends life's ills, life so known is intrinsically meaningful, and the proper response to all this is delight in the sheer beauty of it.

The *Odyssey* has sometimes been considered a romance rather than an epic, and in some sense the two forms here overlap. Along his way Odysseus (aka Ulysses) meets with many marvels, as romance heroes do: otherworldly encounters male and female, combats and enticements, and guidance from some sources of miraculous wisdom. He triumphs through hardships to confirm his heroic stature. An **epic** is distinguished by its cultural scope and its tone of inspired dignity. Not just the hero but the entire poem feels heroic, a monumental achievement. Crucial, often cataclysmic, events center around larger-than-life figures who suffer stalwartly amid their people. (The typical hero of romance, by contrast, goes alone from his familiar world into one of adventure.) The epic is said to embody cultural ideals and a kind of cultural memory.

---

fiction, speculation); mythic literature, upon sensibility and confrontation with what is radically problematic in life. What is called fantasy literature can sometimes have a mythic quality, but that usually occurs when it takes in a genuinely tragic awareness, from which serious wonder can emerge. When studying mythic form, it is especially important to remember that form is the area of the circle, not the circumference or structure.

Both epic and romance originate before writing. If Homer was indeed writing or dictating his own compositions, his material still draws together many generations of hand-me-downs. C. S. Lewis distinguished helpfully between what he called *primary epics,* whose origins seem to have been in this way anonymous if not communal, and *secondary epics,* like the *Aeneid* and *Paradise Lost,* which are literary compositions clearly by individual poets, who, in fact, are staking their claim for greatness through these works.[8] They write in the tradition of the masters and emulate the aura of cultural authority that surrounds their legacy. Sometimes, large novels are called epics, when, like *Moby Dick,* they seem to capture the "soul of a nation" or an elemental struggle with cosmic forces; or when, like *War and Peace,* they portray a whole society changing amid great historical events. In the epic, at any rate, the sense of self is solemnly communal. It dramatizes the past, usually the legendary past, as a world in which "we" know ourselves together, with a sense of importance in our shared destiny.

Unform

In a museum we see paintings set off within their frames, which emphasize the integrity of form, the way form encloses itself into a self-contained whole. Similarly, the form of a sonnet, a romance, or a tragedy holds the literary experience in a stylized world of meaning. As in a museum or a concert hall, we go to the work of art in a spirit of respect, if not a little awe, for the special reality that has been created for us. As we enter this world, we learn to adapt ourselves to its requirements, so we can hear the music its voices have shaped and see the vision its distinct style has molded.

If meaning can be conveyed through the fulfillment of form, however, it can also be found in the violation of form. If form does exist in life, and if we do have an innate sense of form, still there is that side of the mind that keeps saying chaos is at least as real. Form all too easily rigidifies, and creative conventions have a way of becoming "conventional." Dead form is all too oppressive, in both senses of the word: "dreary" and "tyrannical." Not only does each generation grow suspicious of the forms it has inherited, but from time to time, we see a need to challenge the validity of form itself, insisting on the priority of immediate sensation and free-flowing consciousness. There is a catch, however. In the **free verse** of much modern poetry, the poet may intend complete freedom from form but actually does something more interesting, creating new conceptions of form as part of his or her personal style,

---

8. C. S. Lewis, *A Preface to Paradise Lost* (London: Oxford, 1942).

creating a new form, perhaps, for each poem, according to the theme and feelings emerging in it.

There is within literature a broader "anti-literary" tradition, going back to the classical "unform," *menippean satire* (after the Greek author Menippus), an energetic mélange of humor and philosophy, poetry and narrative. Blake's *Marriage of Heaven and Hell* is an example of this. Sometimes there is, even in the early stages of a form, a kind of embarrassment about its artificiality that wants to be exorcised. The first "official" English novel, Samuel Richardson's *Pamela* (1740), began a vogue for the **epistolary novel,** clearly fictitious yet composed entirely in letters, as though to say, this is not just a story, it's somebody's real life—as you can see for yourself. (Trust me: I made it up so I should know.) Henry Fielding, who began writing fiction in order to satirize Richardson, composed his *Joseph Andrews* (1742) and *Tom Jones* (1749) as self-proclaimed "histories," promoting the long-lived convention of fiction that insists it is true, though we know perfectly well it is not. We come to a most definite example of "unform," however, in fact its masterpiece, with Laurence Sterne's *Tristram Shandy,* published in installments during the 1760s. This novel is a monument of gleeful distractions and interruptions, containing a black page, a marble page, blank pages, a chapter of asterisks, a style of sly innuendos, characters who are touchingly fuddled, and a story that progresses, when it does, with perverse reluctance. The following is a complete chapter (XIII, from Volume II) in the midst of a conversation on begetting children:

> My brother does it, quoth my uncle *Toby,* out of *principle.*—In a family way, I suppose, quoth Dr. *Slop.*—Pshaw!—said my father,—'tis not worth talking of.

In a "chapter on chapters," Sterne explains his method of chapter-division, conversing with himself as the perturbed reader:

> Is it not a shame to make two chapters of what passed in going down one pair of stairs? for we are got no farther yet than to the first landing, and there are fifteen more steps down to the bottom; and for aught I know, as my father and my uncle *Toby* are in a talking humour, there may be as many chapters as steps;—let that be as it will, Sir, I can no more help it than my destiny:—A sudden impulse comes across me— drop the curtain, Shandy—I drop it—Strike a line here across the paper, *Tristram*—I strike it—and hey for a new chapter!
>
> The duce [deuce, *the devil*] of any other rule have I to govern myself by in this affair—and if I had one—as I do all things out of all rule—I would twist it and tear it to pieces, and throw it into the fire when I had done—Am I warm: I am, and the cause demands it—a pretty story! is a man to follow rules—or rules to follow him?
>
> —Volume IV, Chapter X

In its merry irreverence, Sterne's novel is comic in the highest sense, as a celebration of living.

Modern culture has recorded in many ways the breakdown of traditions and the pervasive sense that civilization has needed virtually to reinvent itself. In many ways, therefore, the disruption of literary form has inevitably created a radical new sense of style. The typical hero becomes an **antihero** (a conspicuously ordinary person), "plots" often seem to go nowhere, poems strive to achieve a more subjective language, and the world in which a story is set loses any impression of solidity. The conscious view of an ordered reality has yielded to the fluid psychology of the unconscious and the physics of relativity. The most important literary convention has always been artistic integrity, the illusion that the framed world of an art work has a special wholeness to it. Now this is repeatedly exposed as pretense.

In Chekhov's plays, written at the turn of the 20th century, very unheroic characters talk past each other about trivial matters, while the life they cannot quite get their hands on continues to elude them. The effect is simultaneously pathetic and comic, as we are deprived of the satisfaction of either tragic or comic clarity. In the fiction of Franz Kafka, written mostly in the early 1920s, personality, society, action, and thought seem to have lost their solidity altogether. We are caught with Kafka's vague characters in something like a comic bad dream. When, in *The Metamorphosis,* Gregor Samsa awakens as a giant insect, all he can worry about is the fact that he is late for work and the inconvenience he will cause his family.

The **epic theater** of Bertolt Brecht was an attempt to bring the spirit of revolutionary politics into the theater by breaking down the distance between stage and audience, overflowing the frame, as it were. Inspired by existential philosophy and the revelation of absolute evil in World War II, what has been called the **theater of the absurd** distorted all aspects of dramatic form by doing violence to both our aesthetic and emotional standards. In the works of Samuel Beckett, Eugène Ionesco, Harold Pinter, and other absurdists, pain and glee mingle grotesquely in a language that often seems to have lost either its ability or its will to communicate. Ionesco called his first production, *The Bald Soprano,* an "anti-play" and another, *The Chairs,* a "tragic farce." In *Jack, or the Submission,* a supposedly "naturalistic comedy," our rebellious hero Jack rejects a prospective bride named Roberta because she has only two noses and isn't ugly enough, so he is presented with another woman named Roberta (played by the same actress), who has three. Jack's parents and grandparents are all named Jack. Roberta's mother and father are named Robert. The play leaves its blessed lovers amid strange romantic endeavors that are actually meant to embarrass the audience, destroying any idea of an elevated aesthetic impact.

This is one way in which unform attacks aesthetic integrity, breaking down the traditional relationship of author, work, and reader. Conventionally, the author offers his fiction as an artifact, then stands out of the way to let us admire his achievement. The best-known play by the Italian dramatist Luigi Pirandello is *Six Characters in Search of an Author* (1921), his title making the point for us. The Irish novelist Flann O'Brien went several steps further with his wacky novel *At Swim-Two-Birds* (1951), about a student who is writing a novel about a novelist who insists that all his characters live at his own hotel. He seduces one of them and has by her a (full-grown) child. The "child" joins the other characters in an uprising against their creator, whom they put on trial and punish mercilessly.

The current style of **postmodernism** carries these trends further yet. Aspects of postmodernism originated in authors like Kafka and Beckett, but it rejects the kind of intensity we find in their work, even though that may have been an intensity of desolation. One main characteristic of these more recent authors, such as Thomas Pynchon, Donald Barthelme, and John Barth, is a leveling of style. For them, the persistent ordinariness of life, which can be depressing, can also seem a relief from the artifice of "literary" language or "literary" themes, characters, and stories. They cultivate, therefore, a studious banality, with inspiration sometimes from comic books and other popular media. In Barthelme's first book, one story ("The Joker's Greatest Triumph") is about Batman, who at the beginning is drinking tomato juice and vodka—and trying not to share it with his guest. Batman reads literary criticism. Robin is away at prep school. The Joker easily unmasks the great crime-fighter, but it is no big deal.

Through its many permutations, unform reveals the flip side of form, its undoubted limitations and restrictions; still, the first side remains. If unform inverts form, still it must continually remind us of the form it is inverting. It is, in technical terms, parodic, and like all parody, it clearly has meaning in relation to the work it targets. An inverted form, moreover, is necessarily a kind of form in itself, not random chaos. For as long as such authors are involved in symbolic processes, stylizing their visions of the world, it is symbolic form that they will be evolving. And no matter how insistently they proclaim life's resistance to form, still form will reassert itself. As long as spring follows winter and children their parents, as long as lovers come in pairs and bodies age in one direction, as long as hunger leads to food, ambitions lead toward goals, and tears can lead to relief, the human imagination will recall its sense of form to confirm its own nature.

Language as Form: Verse

In the symbolic forms of literature, as we have been seeing, the sense of self arises through the sense of form. A character's predicament is a *structure* in experience. A crisis is meaningful as we imagine living through it. Voice is inextricable from style and tone. Figures of speech, which are officially rhetorical formulas, are in fact perceptions of a special kind of world (as shown in Chapter 3), a world defined subjectively and created uniquely in each instance. If we think of the form of a poem as its "area" rather than its "circumference," it is a form composed of sensibility in language. The painter has character emerge through shapes of pigment, the poet through shapes of wording. We can define a poem, in fact, as *a structured and highly crafted piece of language that exploits the features of language to convey significant experience, emphasizing the nuances of sensibility.*

A Question of Rhetoric

The structural nature of style is perhaps clearest when we think about the form of sentences and their organization into movements of thought. And this is clearest when we consider stylization through *rhetoric.* All good writing takes advantage of rhetorical principles, which means simply that it is designed to be effective. But sometimes writing is conspicuously rhetorical as a matter of stylistic convention, with a deliberately patterned sentence style meant to be intensely dramatic. We expect such a style in much of our earlier literature, especially tragedies and epics, where language often seems to be (and sometimes was) declaimed rather than merely spoken. The speaker is passionate, but the passion seems to be held at arm's length, to be looked at with awe and an awareness of the speech as a formed whole. In the poetry and drama of Renaissance writers including Shakespeare, it was a way of claiming the formal stature of Roman classics. To modern readers, such a self-conscious style may seem cold and false, but when it flourished, its artificiality was felt to have a kind of heroic dignity—an elevation of thought and experience above the level of ordinary affairs—and we can still enter the spirit of the style by reading responsively.

The main features of the rhetorical style are:

- Parallelism, which repeats a specific expression or formula, often building up to a climax through the rhythm of repetition.

- Symmetry that sets one side of a thought in balance with or contrast (*antithesis*) to another.

- A pattern of wordplay, often winding meanings together ingeniously, playing them against one another.

- The elaboration of thoughts through accumulated figures of speech.

- Inversion of ordinary word order to produce a deliberately unusual, often ceremonial, effect.

- Especially complex sentences that move steadily toward a grand finale, interweaving subordinate clauses along the way.

- A weighty vocabulary that in earlier writers includes words with Latin origins, sometimes newly minted for the occasion.

- Dramatic use of exclamation, questions, and answers (including the famous "rhetorical question" that wants no answer), as well as much apostrophe (formal speeches meant to be overheard—by us—rather than heard—by whomever or whatever they are aimed at).

These (and many more) stylistic devices have impressive Greek names that you and I can do without. Shakespeare and company knew them well. What is important, however, is to realize that we all pick up some sense of them as we let our language work for us. Like all principles of form, they arise from inner impulses as much as they do from subtle learning. Although they become self-consciously stylized, they respond to the drives of the mind.

Originally, among the Greeks and Romans, rhetorical style was a technique of speechmaking, meant to stir up listeners' emotions and impress them with the importance of the speaker's argument. It was the method of public speaking taught to lawyers. In its literary form it is equally stirring, especially in speechifying. The most famous example is Mark Antony's speech beginning "Friends, Romans, countrymen" from *Julius Caesar.* At the end of *Richard III* (to give another), the monstrous monarch is finally challenged on the battlefield by the Earl of Richmond, who is about to become Henry VII. Before the fight, Richmond rallies his troops by impressing upon them the king's depravity and his followers' lack of enthusiasm:

> For what is he they follow? Truly, gentlemen,
> A bloody tyrant and a homicide;
> One raised in blood and one in blood established;
> One that made means to come by what he hath,
> And slaughtered those that were the means to
>   help him;
> A base foul stone, made precious by the foil°   *gold backing on which*
> Of England's chair, where he is falsely set;   *a jewel is set*
> One that hath ever been God's enemy.
> Then if you fight against God's enemy,
> God will in justice ward° you as his soldiers;   *guard*
> If you do sweat to put a tyrant down,
> You sleep in peace, the tyrant being slain;
> If you do fight against your country's foes,
> Your country's fat° shall pay your pains in hire°;   *wealth; repay you*
> If you do fight in safeguard of your wives,
> Your wives shall welcome home the conquerors;
> If you do free your children from the sword,
> Your children's children quits° it in your age.   *will requite*

Moments later we hear Richard exhort his own army in a nasty tone that confirms Richmond's portrait of him, as he maligns the soldiers ("gentlemen") we have just admired.

Remember whom you are to cope withal°—	*deal with*
A sort of° vagabonds, rascals, and runaways,	*a band of*
A scum of Britains° and base lackey peasants,	*Bretons*
Whom their o'ercloyed country vomits forth	
To desperate adventures and assured destruction.	
You sleeping safe, they bring to you unrest;	
You having lands, and blessed with beauteous wives,	
They would restrain° the one, distain° the other.	*take away; dishonor*
· ·	
Let's whip these stragglers o'er the seas again,	
Lash hence these overweening rags of France,	
These famished beggars, weary of their lives,	
Who (but for dreaming on this fond° exploit)	*foolish*
For want of means (poor rats) had hanged themselves.	

The patterned speeches are clearly designed to work up the soldiers' enthusiasm for bloodshed. The audience recognizes this immediately, understanding the style. Aside from the speakers' rhetoric, however, there is the play's structural rhetoric. The symmetry and contrast between the speeches has in itself a rhetorical effect, highlighting the dramatic difference between the king who has been and the king to come.

Rhetorical repetition can also have a ritual effect, particularly appropriate for celebrations and for mourning. Edmund Spenser rejoices in his own marriage:

Now all is done; bring home the bride again,
Bring home the triumph of our victory,
Bring home with you the glory of her gain,
With joyance bring her and with jollity.

—"Epithalamion"

To begin his lament for a dead friend, John Milton summons in apostrophe the trees that obviously cannot hear him:

Yet once more, O ye Laurels, and once more
Ye Myrtles brown, with ivy never-sear,
I come to pluck your berries harsh and crude,
And with forc'd fingers rude,
Shatter your leaves before the mellowing year.
Bitter constraint, and sad occasion dear,
Compels me to disturb your season due:

For Lycidas is dead, dead ere his prime,
Young Lycidas, and hath not left his peer:
Who would not sing for Lycidas? he well knew
Himself to sing, and build the lofty rhyme.

—"Lycidas"

The dead young poet is mourned appropriately in a self-consciously poetic style. The language is solemn and formally passionate, as a funeral would be.

Rhetorical effects can also be playful. They are very important in satire. In *The Rape of the Lock* Alexander Pope interrupts the wit of high teasing (full of such techniques) to admit a strain of hard reality in the form of a lecture to his heroine:

Oh! if to dance all night, and dress all day,
Charm'd the Small-pox, or chas'd old Age away;
Who would not scorn what Housewife's Cares produce,
Or who would learn one earthly Thing of Use?
To patch, nay ogle, might become° a Saint,   *be becoming to*
Nor could it sure be such a Sin to paint.°   *use cosmetics*
But since, alas! frail Beauty must decay,
Curl'd or uncurl'd, since Locks will turn to gray,
Since painted or unpainted, all should fade,
And she who scorns a Man, must die a Maid;
What then remains but well our Pow'r to use,
And keep good Humor still whate'er we lose?

Line-by-line, Pope plays upon delicate antitheses, paradoxical word play, and inversions of word order, all reinforced by the steady movement of rhyme and the varied proportions of phrasing.

Nor have modern writers been averse to such formality, with its emphatic patterning. Here Yeats and Wallace Stevens make fine music through rhythms of repetition and balance:

Labour is blossoming or dancing where
The body is not bruised to pleasure soul,
Nor beauty born out of its own despair,
Nor blear-eyed wisdom out of midnight oil.
O chestnut-tree, great-rooted blossomer,
Are you the leaf, the blossom or the bole?
O body, swayed to music, O brightening glance,
How can we know the dancer from the dance?

—*W. B. Yeats,* "Among School Children"

The body dies; the body's beauty lives.
So evenings die, in their green going,

A wave, interminably flowing.
So gardens die, their meek breath scenting
The cowl of winter, done repenting.
So maidens die, to the auroral
Celebration of a maiden's choral.

—*Wallace Stevens,* "Peter Quince at the Clavier"

Even the "natural" Robert Frost may structure language for an intense effect:

I have been one acquainted with the night.
I have walked out in rain—and back in rain.
I have outwalked the furthest city light.

I have looked down the saddest city lane.
I have passed by the watchman on his beat
And dropped my eyes, unwilling to explain.

—"Acquainted with the Night"

When she chooses to be burned rather than endure life in prison, George Bernard Shaw's Joan of Arc echoes Biblical rhythms but builds upon them in her own indignant ecstasy:

You think that life is nothing but not being stone dead. It is not the bread and water I fear: I can live on bread: when have I asked for more? It is no hardship to drink water if the water be clean. Bread has no sorrow for me, and water no affliction. But to shut me from the light of the sky and the sight of the fields and flowers; to chain my feet so that I can never again ride with the soldiers nor climb the hills; to make me breathe foul damp darkness, and keep from me everything that brings me back to the love of God when your wickedness and foolishness tempt me to hate Him: all this is worse than the furnace in the Bible that was heated seven times. I could do without my war-horse; I could drag about in a skirt; I could let the banners and the trumpets and the knights and soldiers pass me and leave me behind as they leave the other women, if only I could still hear the wind in the trees, the larks in the sunshine, the young lambs crying through the healthy frost, and the blessed blessed church bells that send my angel voices floating to me on the wind. But without these things I cannot live; and by your wanting to take them away from me, or from any human creature, I know that your counsel is of the devil, and that mine is of God.

—*Saint Joan*

And Shaw's Don Juan denounces Lucifer's modern "friends" in a breathless flow of ironic antitheses:

> They are not loyal, they are only servile; not dutiful, only sheepish; not public spirited, only patriotic; not courageous, only quarrelsome; not determined, only obstinate; not masterful, only domineering; not self-controlled, only obtuse; not self-respecting, only vain; not kind, only sentimental; not social, only gregarious; not considerate, only polite; not intelligent, only opinionated; not progressive, only factious; not imaginative, only superstitious; not just, only vindictive; not generous, only propitiatory; not disciplined, only cowed; and not truthful at all: liars every one of them, to the very backbone of their souls.[9]
>
> —*Man and Superman*

In each such passage, older or newer, the patterning of thought joins rhyme, rhythm, line length, word sound, and proportionate phrasing to establish *the self in form* with graceful presence.

Verse Structures

A well-made **sonnet** offers a good model for the principles of form in literature, since it is a short, self-contained whole that relies clearly upon its shape. It also shows well how creative the conventions of form can be. Fourteen lines of (usually) iambic pentameter, each sonnet is rhymed according to a set pattern that gives it an internal as well as an overall structure. The poet willingly adopts these limitations for the tension their constraint provides, the walls of outline that the form comes up against; or for the pleasure of mastery that comes in faceting jewels; or for the special punch that comes from the quick emotional insight a sonnet can convey so well. (We don't know of anyone being forced to write sonnets.)

In earlier chapters, I quoted separately the two parts of a sonnet by Michael Drayton. Now let's put them together.

> Since there's no help, come let us kiss and part;
> Nay, I have done, you get no more of me,
> And I am glad, yea, glad with all my heart
> That thus so cleanly I myself can free;
> Shake hands forever, cancel all our vows,
> And when we meet at any time again,
> Be it not seen in either of our brows

---

9. I have omitted ten more contrasts, listed in separate sentences before these.

That we one jot of former love retain.
Now at the last gasp of Love's latest° breath,   *final*
When, his pulse failing, Passion speechless lies,
When Faith is kneeling by his bed of death,
And Innocence is closing up his eyes,
Now if thou wouldst, when all have given him over,
From death to life thou mightst him yet recover.

The poem combines features of the two primary types of sonnet, the *Italian* (or Petrarchan) and the *English* (or Shakespearean). The Italian sonnet falls into two parts: first the *octave* (eight lines), then the *sestet* (six). The English sonnet runs through three quatrains (four-line stanzas), then caps them off with a concluding couplet (a rhymed pair of lines).[10] The dramatic movement of Drayton's lively piece falls neatly into the Italian two-part form, each part carrying a distinctive quality of voice. In the octet the lover is talking himself into a capacity for "resistance," into a future of happy detachment (without, however, being very convincing about it). In tone this movement is touching but amusing. In the sestet the lover drops his pretense, allowing himself to be vulnerable, and the amusement diminishes. We get the nicely proportioned balance of the Italian pattern, therefore, in which the shorter second part carries more weight than the longer first because it delivers the counter punch. However, the rhyme scheme of the sonnet follows the English style, with three fours and a two. In the first quatrain, the lover summons his determination to leave, in the second he paints an image of the future without his lady when his struggle is completely over, in the third he reverses himself into pathos with the allegorical scene at Love's deathbed, and then, in the closing couplet set against the rest of the poem, he finally reaches out to his lady far enough to ask her to reach out to him.

Thus, we see already three features of poetic form: the overall sonnet whole, compactly holding the drama within its balanced shape; the internal divisions, moving the speaker through stages of his discourse; and the rhyme pattern, providing melodious circuits through which the mind revolves, heightening the sensuality of the experience. Although we think of **rhyme** as a matter of line endings, with individual words rhyming, we get a clearer sense of form as *area* if we think of one whole line as rhyming with another—

---

10. Each part of the Italian sonnet is tied together by just two rhyme endings, the sestet being allowed more variations, so the poem may run: *abbaabba cdcdcd.* In the English, each quatrain and the couplet have a different rhyme set, the most common form of the whole being: *abab cdcd efef gg.* (For clarity, I've put spacing between the parts, but ordinarily one does that only when there are stanza breaks.) Italian is an easier language to rhyme in than English, hence the difference.

or of phrases and clauses rhyming together upon the sound that rounds off the line. Thus, the whole thought "let us kiss and part" chimes nicely with "glad with all my heart," as "you get no more of me" does with "I myself can free."[11] All aspects of this poem's form and style—but especially the transformation of feeling from octave to sestet—illustrate well the point I made earlier about the dramatic nature of language (and of symbolic forms in general): the poem's meaning comes not only from what it says but at least as much from what it does.

Another form that poets have liked to make *do* something is the **ballad** stanza. Strictly speaking, it alternates first four- then three-beat lines and rhymes them *abab,* with the alternating lines rhyming together, or *abcb,* with just one rhyme between the second and fourth lines.[12] Originally set to music, the old ballads have, when read, a regular beat and swing that would often seem at odds with their tragic themes. The effect, however, is often a poignant combination of passion and austerity.

> "O where have you been, my long, long love,
>   This long seven years and more?"
> "O I'm come to seek my former vows
>   Ye granted me before."
>
> "O hold your tongue of your former vows,
>   For they will breed sad strife;
> O hold your tongue of your former vows
>   For I am become a wife."
>
>   —"The Demon Lover"

Emotions turn around and around as the drama moves on in short, precise steps. Form drives the feelings, and the feelings call for form in which to lament. This effect is achieved not only through the stanza structure itself but, along with it, through the technique of *incremental repetition.* A line is repeated and then repeated again, with expansion each time, reaching to a climax. Emotion builds as the picture intensifies.

---

11. Rhyme between the end of one line and another is *end rhyme;* there is also *internal rhyme,* as in "the sound that pounds" or "She is the best who took the test." While we're at it, you should know the distinction between *masculine rhyme,* ending on a stressed syllable ("between," "unseen"; "this rhyme will climb") and *feminine rhyme* ("ending," "bending"; "feminine," "put lemon in"), and you should recognize what is called either *off-rhyme* or *slant rhyme* ("rhyme," "fine"; flow," "through"; "masculine," "the rascal's thin"), which is properly used to exploit its effect of dissonance, for humor or for pathos.

12. A similar stanza form is *common meter,* with four beats to each line. Made familiar by Protestant hymns, it was favored by Blake, as in "The Tyger" and "London."

Modern poets have imitated the ballad to achieve similar effects. Some, like Coleridge writing *The Rime of the Ancient Mariner*, have wanted to sound old-fashioned. Others, like Emily Dickinson and Thomas Hardy, have found its simplicity appropriate to meditative themes. Here is a complete poem of Hardy's, "In Time of 'The Breaking of Nations.'" The poem is an answer to Jeremiah, 51: 20–23, and the title alludes specifically to Jeremiah, 51:20.

I

Only a man harrowing clods
   In a slow silent walk
With an old horse that stumbles and nods
   Half asleep as they stalk.

II

Only thin smoke without flame
   From the heaps of couch-grass;
Yet this will go onward the same
   Though Dynasties pass.

III

Yonder a maid and her wight°   *man*
   Come whispering by:
War's annals will cloud into night
   Ere their story die.

In the following two excerpts Hardy varies the stanza, giving four beats to only the third line:

   "Had he and I but met
     By some old ancient inn,
We should have sat us down to wet
     Right many a nipperkin°!   *mug of beer*

   "But ranged as infantry,
     And staring face to face,
I shot at him as he at me,
     And killed him in his place. . . ."
         —"The Man He Killed"

What curious things we said,
What curious things we did
Up there in the world we walked till dead,
Our kith and kin amid!

How we played at love,
And its wildness, weakness, woe;
Yes, played therat for more than enough
As it turned out, I trow°!   *I believe*

    —"Intra Sepulchrum°"   *within the grave*

As in many of the old ballads, the brief stanza helps dramatize the awesome gulf between life and death: There is little to say, so much to feel. Hardy adds to this structural effect different kinds of sound dissonance—in the rhyme between "infantry" and "at me" in the first example (placing an archaic accent on the last syllable of "infantry," which music would have called for in an old ballad); and in the second example the off-rhyme between "love" and "enough."

A good deal more complex than the ballad form and much less common are the **villanelle** and the **sestina**. The villanelle repeats not just rhyme sound but entire lines. It starts with a triplet (a three-line stanza), then its first and third lines become the third line of the succeeding four stanzas, more or less intact. The sixth and final stanza is a quatrain, using both of the repeat lines. Examples include Dylan Thomas's familiar appeal to his dying father, "Do Not Go Gentle into That Good Night," and Elizabeth Bishop's "One Art."

The sestina does not actually rhyme. The words that end the six lines of the first stanza, however, are repeated at the ends of the lines in each stanza following. They are woven into the sense with a fixed pattern: The word that ends the first line ends the second line of the next stanza,

then second moves to the fourth line,
the third moves to the sixth line,
the fourth moves to the fifth line,
the fifth moves to the third line,
and the sixth moves to the first.

The poem ends with three lines that repeat all six words, in their original order, two per line. In "Ye Goatherd Gods" Sir Philip Sidney gave us a lovely double-sestina, which runs through the routine twice with the same six ending words. Here are the first three stanzas and the conclusion. This poem is also an excellent illustration of the pastoral lyric; in it two Greek-named goatherds (instead of the usual shepherds) exchange verses lamenting a departed goatherdess.

STREPHON

You goatherd gods, that love the grassy mountains,
You nymphs that haunt the springs in pleasant vallies,
You satyrs joyed with free and quiet forests,
Vouchsafe your silent ears to plaining° music,   *lamenting*
Which to my woes gives still° an early morning: *always*
And draws the dolor on till weary evening.

KLAIUS

O Mercury, foregoer to the evening,
O heavenly huntress of the savage mountains,
O lovely star, entitled° of the morning,   *called*
While that my voice doth fill these woefull vallies,
Vouchsafe your silent ears to plaining music,
Which oft hath Echo° tired in secret forests.   *a nymph*

STREPHON

I that was once free-burgess° of the forests,   *citizen*
Where shade from sun and sports I sought at evening,
I that was once esteemed for pleasant music,
Am banished now among the monstrous mountains
Of huge despair and foul affliction's vallies,
Am grown a screech-owl to my self each morning.
· ·

STREPHON AND KLAIUS

These mountains witness shall, so shall these valleys,
These forests eke,° made wretched by our music,   *also*
Our morning hymn is this, and song at evening.

In good sestinas and villanelles, poets demonstrate their virtuosity, but if
the form is justified, it provides a basis for the poem's impact. In Sidney's
poem, the repetitions feel delicately mournful—with "plaining music"—and
they demonstrate the quaint kind of aesthetic refinement typical of the pastoral convention. The line ends are more than just endings: They control the
thought of the whole, and they blend into many ingenious musical effects that
weave through the single sentence of each stanza.

Words in Tune: Sound

The features of language that the poet draws upon include the possibilities of meaning and the expressiveness of sentence form, but they include also
the various sound qualities of words, what we can loosely call its music. The
primary "stuff" of language is the material of vowels and consonants, out of
which the music can be made. (A poem need not be set to music to *have*
music.) Consider this little song that some have considered the quintessential

English poem, which was recorded with its melody around 1500:

> Western wind, when will thou blow,
> The small rain down can rain?
> Christ, that my love were in my arms,
> And I in my bed again!

If one is alert to the language, one senses the repeated *w*'s in the first line, the *r*'s in the second and third, the short *e* sounds in the first and last lines. In that first line, every word includes a *w* sound, although "thou" doesn't include the letter. As the rain keeps raining, the lines establish a frustrating consistency, which is broken up by the strong words "blow" and "Christ."

The poetic features of sound depend on the way that consonants and vowels are arranged. **Alliteration** repeats consonants; **assonance** repeats vowels. But beyond noticing such simple repetitions, we should take in the passage of verse as a tight web of sound qualities moving in and out of each other, running in overlapping sequences, modulating a particular type of sound, balancing and giving way. Try reading just the vowels in a passage, then sound the consonants. Notice which vowels you make in the front of your mouth, which in the back, which are "short" (*i* as in *wind; e* as in *western*), which "long" (*i* as in *I; o* as in *blow*). What we call the "sound" of language, you will see, is not just what you hear but what you feel, quite sensually, in your mouth as you move your lips and tongue and press the breath along. Notice the different qualities of *nasal* sounds (*m* and *n*), *liquids (l, r), sibilant* consonants (like *s*) and other *fricatives* (sounded by air coming through your partly closed teeth and lips: *f, h, sh*), and the obvious *dentals* (*d* and *t*) and other *plosives* (sounded by letting out little bursts of air: *p, b, g, k*). See the effect of particular sounds coming together (we*stern*, wi*ll th*ou, *bl*ow, *Chr*ist *th*at), the kind of effort you have to make to say them.

In *Antony and Cleopatra*, Shakespeare describes Cleopatra's first appearance before Mark Antony in language that is as vivid and voluptuous as she is and as intensely concentrated as his response to her. Antony's captain, Enobarbus, is speaking:

> The barge she sat in, like a burnished throne,
> Burned in the water: the poop was beaten gold;
> Purple the sails, and so perfumèd that
> The winds were lovesick with them; the oars were silver,
> Which to the tune of flutes kept stroke, and made
> The water which they beat to follow faster,
> As amorous of their strokes.

This begins an extended rhapsody, but Shakespeare never describes Cleopatra's face or body. He recreates the effect that she has upon others, and this effect takes place, necessarily, in the language. Beautiful words *are*, for us, the experience of *her* beauty. The effect is accomplished through mythmaking imagery: lovesick winds, the erotic stroking of silver oars in panting water. It is accomplished through the wit and the magic of overstatement. But also, it is accomplished through the sensuous feeling of words as we sound them—or imagine sounding them—in our mouths. The six-and-a-half lines I have quoted contain every consonant sound in English (including the *th* in both *the* and *throne*). The first two lines include almost every vowel sound (although in Shakespeare's day they would have been spoken differently). Many of the consonants cluster together, so that we have to say them without a break: *rge-sh, nd, shdth, nb, rnd, nth, tr-th, pw, sb, n-g, ldp, rpl-th, ls, nds, rf, dth, th-th* (voiced and unvoiced), to cover just the first half of the passage. Yet in spite of this variety of sound qualities (the passage leads up to an account of Cleopatra's own "infinite variety"), we remain aware of conspicuous repetitions: the *b*'s and *r*'s, then the *p*'s, then the *f*'s and *s*'s. The opening movement "barge—burnished—throne—burned" is only the most dramatic instance. The consonants weave among each other like the instruments of an orchestra, called upon at different times in changing combinations. The vowels, meanwhile, establish their own movement from one to another and combine simultaneously with the range of consonants to produce the sensual whole. All the sounds play against each other while also they merge in continuing transformations. (And we are ignoring, for the moment, that equally important musical feature *rhythm*.)

The effect of pleasantly smooth sounds, melodious liltings, is *euphony*. The strident clash of harshness is *cacophany*. Naturally, each effect should suit the meaning of the passage. And naturally, most language will move between the extremes, picking up the special effects from time to time. Such sound qualities are exploited most heavily by poets with an emphatically *rich* style, who are of a primarily romantic cast, such as Marlowe and Shakespeare, Keats and Shelley, Hopkins and Swinburne, and Dylan Thomas. I like to think of this as a "gloppy" style, because it suggests the way sculptors enjoy getting their hands into a mound of wet clay, revelling in the feel of it. Such poets seem to glory in the voluptuousness of their language. They also love complex, even convoluted, sentence structure, strong rhythms, and a potent vocabulary. Take the best-known (and much parodied) passage from Algernon Charles Swinburne:

> When the hounds of spring are on winter's traces,
> > The mother of months in meadow or plain
> Fills the shadows and windy places
> > With lisp of leaves and ripple of rain;
> And the brown bright nightingale amorous
> Is half assuaged for Itylus,
> For the Thracian ships and the foreign faces,
> > The tongueless vigil, and all the pain.

> —"Chorus" from *Atalanta in Calydon*

We can contrast this richness to the *firm* style, which is crisper in its sound and more precise in its telling. Favored by writers of a classical persuasion writing a poetry more likely to make statements or tell stories, it is sometimes compared to stone cutting (the word "lapidary" is used). Generally, short words are placed together in strong statements, with occasional longer words of Latin origin. Here the great master is Alexander Pope (notice that, in context, the first line is not the optimistic bromide it is usually taken to be):

Hope springs eternal in the human breast:
Man never Is, but always To be blest:
The soul, uneasy and confin'd from home,
Rests and expatiates in a life to come.

—An Essay on Man

I quoted earlier this famous passage from A. E. Housman, who was in fact a professor of Latin:

With rue my heart is laden
    For golden friends I had,
For many a rose-lipt maiden,
    And many a lightfoot lad.

—"With Rue My Heart Is Laden"

We should not expect to categorize all English poetry according to these two kinds of style, however; from the 19th century on, most poetry probably falls between them. A third way of writing we can call the *plain* style. It avoids the self-consciousness of the two traditional poles of style by maintaining the casual effect of colloquial speech. You will find it easily in Wordsworth. It is most common, of course, among moderns, such as Frost, although you will find it in Chaucer. It also occurs in lighter verse, such as limericks and epigrams. Still, all good poets are unique and some cannot be described in these terms at all.

Words in Tune: Phrasing

As we speak or as we write, words blend into phrases of expression that make up more complex pieces of thought. Often these phrases follow an idiomatic tendency to think thoughts along a certain line. This is largely a matter of how our feelings—such as desire, fear, or anger—combine with thoughts and facts in grammatical units. It is also a matter of how we ask a question, how we exclaim, how we complain, lament, or sigh, with different kinds of emphasis and different swings of rise and fall. As phrases combine, they make patterns as they go, with different kinds of movement and different proportions of length. If we focus upon the phrases of "Western Wind," we feel the rhythm with which they move along, balancing shorter and longer expressions as they accumulate:

> Western wind—when will thou blow—The small rain—down can rain?
> —Christ—that my love were in my arms—And I in my bed again!

The segments of thought reach toward the line end and carry themselves into full meaning as they advance through the stanza. The shift from question to exclamation carries an impulse that moves the feeling along dramatically. The forceful opening of each sentence—"Western wind" and "Christ that"— gives way to the more melodic expression of longing—"when will thou blow" and "that my love were in my arms."

Running through this rhythm *of* phrases, one to another, is the rhythm *within* phrases. If we look back at the example from Housman, we can feel in the movement of the lines a division that may run like this:

> With rue   my heart is laden
> For golden friends   I had,
> For many a   rose-lipt maiden,
> And many   a lightfoot lad.

Within each phrase we can feel a rhythmic lift and drop as the syllables combine into meaning:

With rue   my heart is laden

For golden friends   I had,

For many a   rose-lipt maiden,

And many a   lightfoot lad.

Phrases build sentences; sentences build the flow of thought, feeling, and action. Poets and other good writers cultivate such rhythmic effects with sharp attention and loving care. Poetry is thoughts and images, but it is also molded language as surely as sculpture is molded clay or music "molded" sound. "Language music" is the molding of phrases and sentences out of words. A poem doesn't have to be set to music to be musical. There is a flow, a beat, a melody to all well-written language and to fluent speech as well. Sometimes the effects are primarily graceful, sometimes primarily forceful, sometimes primarily rough and conflicted. Commonly, the poet lets us feel a particular flow but then changes it on us, frequently to drive home a thought or dramatize a feeling. The grace and the forcefulness of rhythm provide sensual pleasure but they also support meaning—in both the regularity of a beat and in the surprises that keep altering it.

Words in Tune: Rhythm

In language, rhythm has to do with the relative emphasis or stress among syllables.[13] In English any word of more than one syllable has its natural-born rhythm, which any dictionary will show.

happy **ex**tra **fi**nal **sal**ad **dark**ness

in**tense** ex**treme** ful**fill** pol**lute** pro**pel**

happily **in**terview **sac**rilege **av**enue **cri**ticism

fa**nat**ical po**lit**ical in**ten**tional ex**cru**ciate

absolutely **ex**halation rever**ber**ation recon**sid**eration

ex**hib**it exhi**bi**tion re**volt** **rev**olution pro**claim** **proc**lamation

When **words** of **one** syl**lable** are **run** into a **thought,** they **join** the **rhythm** of the **phrasing.** You can even tell the stress-shape of many fine words no one has ever seen before: *argophilous, alicopastinate, sardolamp, concardifer, paradicanival, astilusian,* and many more of your own invention.

It is customary to study the rhythm of verse with the system of **scansion** derived from classical **metrics,**[14] by marking off accented and unaccented syllables in units called "feet." The most common metrical feet are the **iamb** (*Jŏánne, ĭnténse*), the **trochee** (*Árnŏld, jólly̆*), the **anapest** (*Mărgŭeríte, ŭndĭstúrbed*), the **dactyl** (*Éleănŏr, ágĭtăte*), and the **spondee** (*Jóhn Pául, Góod Gód!*). We usually mark them off with little lines between each foot, and we place a double line to mark the *caesura,* a strong pause, if there is one (or two), in the middle of the line.

Ĭámbĭcs should bĕ cleár ĕnoúgh.

Yŏu sée thĕm évery̆whére yŏu loók.

---

13. Stress (which is force) should not be confused with pitch (which is elevation of tone).

14. The Romans and Greeks counted the length of syllables rather than their emphasis, however. Their method is called *qualitative* (rather than *accentual*) meter.

But whole lines of verse, and sometimes whole poems, come in one of the other meters. We can call them "gallopers":

trochee: **What** is **love**? the **tur**tle **asked** me.

            When I **saw** her **I** went **crazy.**

anapest: In the **eyes** of the **law** we are **all** very **strange.**

            On the **day** of my **birth** I dis**cov**ered my **des**tiny.

dactyl: **Het**erose**x**ual **pas**times en**light**ened him.

            Carpenters **al**ways in**sist** on their **vege**tables.

spondee: **Four huge mice dance gay jigs.**[15]

            Come quick, please! Help! Ed Smith's shot! Oh, oh, oh!

You will notice that the strong beat of a galloper can attract stress where you do not need to put it in ordinary speech. Also, a line often has an extra syllable or two at the beginning or the end (*destiny*).

Now from the frivolous to the sublime:

    To be or not to be: that is the question.

This gives us five feet of iambic pentameter,[16] known as **blank verse** when it is unrhymed, the standard verse form of Elizabethan drama, or *heroic couplets* when the lines are rhymed in pairs. However, there is an extra syllable at the end of the line, and "that is" is not iambic at all but trochaic. We have then a trochee substituted for an iamb. Why? Because it provides a dramatic emphasis. *What* is the question? *That* is the question! (If Shakespeare has contracted "that is" to "that's," as we do in common speech, then he had two trochees: "that's the question.") Emphasis on some syllables allows us to express emphatic thoughts or, like Hamlet, to answer a question with a punch. (Do you? I do. — Who does? I do.) The art of metrical composition, which Shakespeare developed with such grace and power, is based first of all upon the adaptation of natural English to a regular flow, regularizing the rhythmic tendencies already there in English words and phrases. But it is based also upon the knack for adroit variations along the way, as sense and feeling call them forth.

---

15. Obviously, "dance" would be unstressed if this line followed that metrically interesting expression "Eight elegant elephants dance minuets."

16. "Pentameter" denotes the line with 5 feet. Other lengths are *dimeter* (2), *trimeter* (3), *tetrameter* (4), *hexameter* (6), and *heptameter* (7).

To watch the expressiveness of metric variations in something a little more complex, consider these two quatrains from Shakespeare's Sonnet 8 and notice the effects that are not simply iambic. Here Shakespeare discusses music with extraordinary music of his own, combining the richness of sound qualities with some twists of rhythm:

Music to hear, why hear'st thou music sadly?

Sweets with sweets war not, joy delights in joy:

Why lov'st thou that which thou receiv'st not gladly,

Or else receiv'st with pleasure thine annoy?
. . . .

Mark how one string, sweet husband to another,

Strikes each in each by mutual ordering;

Resembling sire and child and happy mother,

Who all in one, one pleasing note do sing . . .

Music must be a trochee: The word simply *is* stressed on its first syllable. But if you read each line as straight iambics after that, you no longer have a natural voice and the music that Shakespeare is talking about is drastically reduced:

Mark how one string, sweet husband to another

And lost is the drama of voice asking, exclaiming, urging, balancing thoughts, and emphasizing. We wouldn't feel how jarring the "war" might be, the "annoy" wouldn't be quite as annoying, the "*one* string" and the "*one* pleasing note" would not be as singularly single, the "husband" would not be as "sweet." The lovely simile of family harmony would not be quite as lovely.

If we look back at "To be or not to be" (to move ahead with a simpler example), we see that conventional metrics can quickly become complicated. Maybe you weren't satisfied about that strong stress on "be." Do you really want to say the second "be" as strongly as the first? I don't. The "not" seems to me stronger than either "be," since it registers a very striking contrast to the basic affirmative proposition, "to be." In fact, distinguishing only two kinds of stress (some and none) seems to me unnecessarily artificial. It is right for nursery rhymes, where the contrast between two strongly differentiated levels makes us feel mindlessly happy: all the way up and all the way down. But if we read most good poetry this way, we don't recognize the sensuous power rhythm can have in its flexibility. We want nursery rhymes to feel simpler than spoken language and completely regular. In serious poetry we want to feel the modulations of voice that carry our tensions of feeling and our complexities of awareness. Can we improve on the method that works so well for nursery rhymes? We can, I believe, by simplifying a system that certain linguists have proposed, working with four natural levels of stress.[17] This seems closer to the way our voices and our ears do work. To mark the four degrees, I use these notations: *unstress* (ˇ), *intermediate stress* (ˇ), *stress* (ʹ), and *extra* (or *super-*) *stress* (x). Thus, although I can see other possibilities, I would read:

> To bě or nŏt tŏ bě: thăt iš thě quěstiŏn.

and

> Márk hŏw ŏne strĭng, swěet hŭsbănd tŏ ănŏthěr,
>
> Strĭkes ěach ĭn ěach b̆y mŭtŭal ŏrděring;
>
> Rěsěmblĭng sĭre ănd chĭld ănd hăppy mŏthěr,
>
> Whŏ all ĭn ŏne, ŏne plěasĭng nŏte dŏ sĭng . . .

A good reading responds simultaneously to the regular meter that runs through the whole passage but also to the emphasis of natural speech. The formal meter we can call the "underrhythm":

> Tŏ bě or nŏt tŏ bě: thăt iš [*or* thăt's] thĕ quěstiŏn.

If Prince Hamlet's noble thought were to occur to you spontaneously, you might put all the emphasis on "not" and "that," with the other words trailing in contrast. Here my intermediate stress shows that some syllables don't deserve the full stress that a straight metric reading would give them. We can see this in polysyllabic words (*nătiŏnálitý, ŏbfŭscátiŏn*) and in phrases, where "little words" fall in a stressed position (*nŏt tŏ bě*) or get minimized in a galloper (*lĭttle crŏcŏdĭles*). Observing the intermediate level allows us to keep the tune at the back of our minds, nodding to the meter, while giving priority to the dramatic voice which carries the meaning. When we can't quite make up our minds whether a syllable should be stressed or not, intermediate stress lets us evade the decision by moving to the middle, allowing the claim of each possibility.

Traditional metrics, it seems to me, gives us an unreal contrast between syllables that are stressed and those that are not. But also, I think, it worries us unnecessarily about the artificial units called feet. If we overemphasize them, we can miss many of the more interesting musical qualities of verse. Like the feet we walk on, metrical feet impede the flow when we pay them

---

17. George L. Trager and Henry Lee Smith, Jr. I have their concept from John Thompson, *The Founding of English Metre* (New York: Columbia University Press, 1961), 6–14, although I treat it rather differently.

too much mind. Simply put, regular scansion breaks up phrases and polysyllabic words into unnatural units. Iambic and dactylic meter, for example, are usually described as rising, trochaic and dactylic as falling; but it is quite possible to have a falling rhythm in a line that is technically iambic:

Ă póem lóvelў aś ă treé.

Ŏn Súndăy Hárrў cáme tŏ lúnch.

In the standard book on English metrics, Paul Fussell shows (among many other examples) how effectively Housman substitutes a trochee for an iamb in this passage about a nice young murderer about to be hanged:[18]

Hĕ stóod, ănd heárd thĕ steéplĕ

Sprínklĕ thĕ quártĕrs ón thĕ mórnĭng tówn.

The little "sprinkle" does "animate the clock," as Fussell claims, making a dramatic opening for the line, but this is the second of four closely placed trochaic words that make up a kind of "metrical rhyme": *steéplĕ, sprínklĕ, quártĕrs, mórnĭng*. Breaking down the lines into feet, I think, spoils the natural and simple rhythm that such words have in their own right. Furthermore, the movement from "steeple" at the end of one line to "sprinkle" at the start of the next intensifies the "animation"—especially since it is enjambed.[19] If we think of the phrase "sprinkle the quarters" as one unit, instead of breaking it into a trochee and an iamb, we can appreciate not only its strong start, but the contrasting effect of the two unstressed syllables that follow it together: *sprínklĕ thĕ quártĕrs* (which we could also see as a dactyl and a trochee). This leads into a sequence of three unstresses: *-tĕrs ŏn thĕ*. All of which stays with a two-level reading. If we want to try all four, we might hear it this way:

Hĕ stóod, ănd heárd thĕ steéplĕ

Sprínklĕ thĕ quártĕrs ón thĕ mórnĭng tówn.

Certain poems invite a jog-trot reading, especially if they are based on ballad form. Or incantation:

Týgĕr, týgĕr, búrnĭng bríght,

Ín thĕ fórests óf thĕ níght;

---

18. *Poetic Meter and Poetic Form,* rev. ed. (New York: Random House, 1949), 52. Housman's poem is "Eight O'Clock." I have filled in the scansion.

19. *Enjambment* is the movement of thought at the end of one line directly on to the next, without an end stop.

What immortal hand or eye,

Could frame thy fearful symmetry?

But see how much we can gain by working against that tendency, especially if, at the same time, we note phrase grouping rather than feet:

Tyger, tyger, burning bright,

In the forests of the night;

What immortal hand or eye,

Could frame thy fearful symmetry?

Hearing the natural voice, we respond to the drama of its modulations, but we still feel that strong underrhythm. Fighting the metronome, as it were, we have the intensified drama of push and pull. In this case, it is, most appropriately, like staring at something that horrifies us.

Scanning closely helps us appreciate a particular poem's music, and that is an aspect of form contributing a great deal to its beauty. It trains us, therefore, to be better language-listeners in general, more appreciative of the contours in English and the nuances of the human voice. As listeners, we have more sensitive equipment with which to make our recordings and to play them back. However, scansion can also help us interpret what we are reading. In fact, the close attention that scansion requires virtually forces us to determine meanings. As you sense what the most important words are in a line or phrase, you are responding to what the passage means. You should be aware of the line or phrase as part of the whole movement of thought through the sentence, growing out of the previous sentence and leading to the next. Don't just read line by line. Notice what points are being balanced or contrasted against each other, which are building up to a climax, what is most urgently on the speaker's mind. Pay attention to the voice, and take in what it needs to emphasize to make its point and express its feeling. Try to scan quickly and spontaneously, without thinking too much, as you would tap your finger or foot to music. Your body may catch on more quickly than your mind. You can train yourself by noticing how you and others pronounce words when you talk. Think of long words and personal names and scan them quickly: *excommunicate, exhilaration, indubitably; William Shakespeare, Christina Rossetti, Pablo Picasso, Luciano Pavarotti, John Fitzgerald Kennedy, Anonymous.* Scan sentences of prose. Notice how you pronounce things that you say. Go to the dictionary and compare its reading with your own.

Since scanning is partly a matter of interpretation, there is not always a correct reading. I may read a line differently at different times, changing my mind or wanting to bring out other possibilities. However, as in any aspect of criticism, there is likely to be a legitimate range of possibilities (and then there is left field), with an optimal reading one decides upon for a very good reason.

There are several principles that limit what we can do:

- Every syllable must count. You have to hear each one and determine its force. In older poetry there may be contractions that don't show up in print and other adjustments accepted by convention, often blending vowels that come next to each other for example. Also in older poetry (including Shakespeare), suffixes like *-ious, -ient,* and *-ion* were commonly two syllables instead of one (*pássiŏn, pátiĕnt, pĕrsúasiŏn*). No one will blame you if you don't observe these niceties, but knowing about them does help you hear the lovely music better.

- Words of more than one syllable come with built-in rhythm, and you are not to violate that. You won't want to say *élephănt,* except for a moment of strange pleasure. In most polysyllabic words emphasis is likely to fall on the root, which carries the basis of the word's meaning, rather than on the prefixes and suffixes, which modify it. You need to watch out for words that mean something different when the emphasis changes, like *cóntĕnt* ("what is in the box") and *cŏntént* ("how you feel when you've got what you want"). British pronunciation often produces different stress than American: *lăbórăt'rў* instead of *láb'rătorў.*

- Articles (*the, a, an*) and one-syllable prepositions (*in, on, of,* and so forth) ordinarily do not want stress, although meaning in some cases does emphasize them ("I am going *in,* not *out*"). Remember what we must do to the national anthem, which was set to an old drinking song: *thĕ bómbs búrstíng ĭn áir.*

- Vivid words are chosen to make a strong point and are therefore likely to be especially emphatic. So are words in important grammatical positions. Some people, when scanning, like first to mark the clearly stressed syllables in a line or sentence and then sort out the rest.

- Terms of contrast, as we saw in *to bé or nŏt to be,* are usually emphatic, since they must be made clearly parallel to each other (again, "I am going *ín,* not *óut*" or structures like "on one hand *thís,* on the other *thát*"). Like Hamlet, we want to make our answers dramatic.

Look now at "Western Wind" and try out my reading of it:

Wéstĕrn wínd, | whĕn wíll thŏu blów,

Thĕ smáll ráin dówn căn ráin?

Chríst, | thăt mў lóve wĕre ín mў árms,

Ănd Í ĭn mў béd ăgáin!

What dramatic effects are achieved (or helped along) by the rhythm and other sound qualities? Notice how effective the pauses are in setting off word groupings of different length. Notice the strong stresses coming one after another in the second line, together with the repetition of "rain." What is the underrhythm of that line? How is the last line different from the rest and to what effect? A strict metrical scansion would see the third line opening with a trochee followed by an iamb. Would there be an advantage in seeing "that my love" as an anapest?

Here are two revisions of the poem. How many aspects of poetic style are changed? To what effect? How is our poet attempting to "improve" the original? Scan each. What do sound qualities, including rhythm, contribute to the changes?

> When will spring bring
> Drizzling weather?
> I wish my girlfriend and I
> Were sleeping together.

> Oh, when will the spring breezes return
> With their gently refreshing showers?
> I would that my fair love and I
> Were entwined on beds of sweet flowers!

When is clarity not necessarily a virtue?

Here is my scansion of the Drayton sonnet (for this week). First do your own, and then compare your version with mine. Which of my readings seem to work for you and which don't? Can you see why I made the choices I did? Where is my scansion related to my interpretation of the poem? What did I miss? Which of your readings do you want to defend? What do you now see that rhythm contributes to voice and drama in a poem like this one? What effect does the dramatic rhythm have in contrast to the regularly end-stopped lines?

> Since there's no help, come let us kiss and part;
> Nay, I have done, you get no more of me,
> And I am glad, yea, glad with all my heart
> That thus so cleanly I myself can free;
> Shake hands forever, cancel all our vows,
> And when we meet at any time again,
> Be it not seen in either of our brows
> That we one jot of former love retain.
> Now at the last gasp of Love's latest breath,
> When, his pulse failing, Passion speechless lies,

When Faith is kneeling by his bed of death,

And Innocence is closing up his eyes,

Now if thou wouldst, when all have given him over,

From death to life thou mightst him yet recover.[20]

It is not necessary that a line of verse have any super-stresses or inter-mediates. That this poem shows so many supers underscores the sense of urgency we feel in the voice as we read it. They reflect the mind's insistence on what is most important. The strongest effects come in stresses (or supers) close together, of which there are quite a few here: *no more, one jot, last gasp, glad yea glad,* and possibly *come let* and *shake hands.* (I've simplified my readings to make the point.) Another kind of strong effect, more sensuous in a way, comes from following a strong syllable with two or more clearly weaker ones: *kneeling by his, Innocence is.* As you do a scansion, you should note what it shows about your reading of the poem and also what features of the poem you may not have taken in before but may now be able to explain.

The four-level view of rhythm may seem to make matters more dread-fully difficult than they are already, to be, in a word, simply too subtle. If it remains frustrating for you, by all means stick to two. In metrics, as in all areas of interpretation, however, the advantage of subtlety is that it is more realistic. A subtle reading may actually be easier to produce and to comprehend be-cause it accounts more readily for one's actual experience of the work. When we realize that, subtlety becomes less intimidating, more inviting. We meet a sensitive text with a sensitive response. This four-level view of rhythm, I suggest, is therefore more natural and less "technical" than conventional scan-sion. However, it is not the analytic technique that is really important. So much of the beauty of English verse comes from the flexibility of voice that it allows. The point is to hear and enjoy the part this flexibility plays in the whole.

---

20. You will notice that, in the last lines, "wouldest" and "mightest" have already been contracted to "wouldst" and "mightst." In the previous line, I decided that "given" is also one syllable, since I know that would have been an option for the poet. It is possible that "over" was just one also (in older poetry sometimes spelled o'er), but then "recover" would have to be two. Drayton may have pronounced "Love's" as two syllables; the Elizabethans sometimes spelled such possessives as "Love his." However, I have kept the poet to the ten-syllable line that was customary in that period, except for the final couplet. This would also make ten if "over" and "recover" are contracted. Do you see a dramatic advantage to having the extra syllables at the end?

PART FOUR
A Happy Style

Chapter 7

The Critical Essay
as a Literary Form

A Concise Dictionary Lesson by Way of Prelude

The huge Oxford English Dictionary, or **OED,** is the great treasure house of our language. It shows meticulously, with examples from writers throughout the centuries, where our words have been in the past and how they have got here. If you want to know what a word meant to Shakespeare or John Donne or Shelley, you can look it up in the OED. In the title of this section, the old but still usable expression, "a happy style," *happy* means "felicitous," "appropriate," or "fitting." Tracing the word from its original meaning of "lucky," the OED offers as definition for this usage "characterized by fitness for the circumstance or occasion." However—like *felicitous,* which the OED gives as a synonym—a "happy" style suggests to us a *delight* in finding the right word and carrying out the flow of a sentence. This is the comfortable feeling of being at home in what we have written, knowing it serves to convey what we had intended, or just about. If you look up *felicity,* in the OED you will discover that its history is the opposite of *happy*'s. It originally meant what it most commonly means today, "bliss" or "extreme happiness" (from the Latin word *felix*), but by 1605 it came to mean "a happy faculty in art or speech; admirable appropriateness or grace of invention or expression." In that year, we read, Francis Bacon dedicated a book to his King, James I, praising His Majesty's own style for both its "facility and felicity," felicitously letting these two like-sounding words define each other, *facility* being an "easy, or apparently natural, manner" that thereby produces felicity.

First word of advice about writing: Cite dictionary definitions only when you think they are really interesting, giving information that is not reasonably obvious. When you need to explain a word, try to define it yourself—and then, if you aren't sure of yourself, check a dictionary to see how the editors put it. (You might keep in mind that dictionaries are compiled by pretty smart people—Mr. Webster no longer being one of them—but not by God.) Let your writing be by you almost entirely.

Second word of advice: Work (and it may very well *be* work) toward a critical style that gives you pleasure: pleasure because it serves well to achieve your purpose, capturing accurately your reading experience, and pleasure because it feels natural to you (after working at it), giving a sense of you at your intellectually charming best. If you enjoy writing it, there's half a chance your reader will enjoy reading it. One reason to write well, certainly, is to communicate your ideas clearly. Another, however, is to use yourself as well as you deserve, so that you can enjoy your mind in fluent action—just as in sports or in love you may have the pleasure of feeling the fluency of your body. As in sports and in love, so in writing too, the pleasure is infectious: One wants to participate. As the undertaker told his new helper, "No one said you can't have fun working."

Writing as a Reader

Developing one's style is an ongoing process, a lifetime process maybe, so you may not get as far along as you want to be in the very near future, but you can make it a meaningful project for yourself from wherever you are. How can you develop a happy style? There's a definite limit to what anyone can teach you about writing. Let's take a roundabout approach.

A literary work is a complex field of energy: characters and causes, ideas and feelings, fears and hopes, perceptions and frustrations, all in both tension and harmony with each other. They are in tension and harmony also with the writer's aesthetic techniques, such as sentence rhythm, plot pacing, arrangement of events, narrative point of view, and even chapter or scene divisions. We have suspense and we have gratification. Most clearly, we have desire and anxiety—from the characters inside the story and from ourselves as readers— desire that things "work out well," perhaps, and anxiety that they will not. And there is the energy of the author's creative intensity encompassing all the rest.

As we read, we take in this energy. We plug into it, so to speak, and our imagination is stimulated. As we get access to the work's power, we may find that it can generate our own. The critical writer has no more valuable resource for inspiration than this stimulus. We should be moved to write about a poem or story by the same feelings that moved us as we read it. If we follow out the poem or the story's impact into our own desire to communicate about it, our work is largely cut out for us.

Let's say you have just read *Romeo and Juliet*. You may wish to develop your interpretation out of a real desire to bear witness to your experience, very likely because you feel that other people (teacher, classmates, critics) aren't getting it right. Remembering the work's impact on you, you may feel that you want to take a stand about its vision of life. Or you are grieved by the deaths of the lovers and impressed with Shakespeare's ability to make them so beautifully moving. Follow *the intelligence of your feelings* into a discussion of how that happens. Stay moved and let yourself sound moved, but look clearly at what Shakespeare is doing and think clearly about what it all adds up to. Show how he has involved us in the lovers' lyricism, built up the sense of danger in their dedication to each other, laid around them a frustrating society of other people with other feelings and motivations, and whatever else you notice. Discuss, perhaps, the combination of violence and luxury, and show how it leads to the lovely sadness of it all. See what terms of the play's tension *you* are responding to, and look carefully at how they work upon each other.

In Chapter 1, I recommended that you stay grounded in your essay by "representing" the text solidly and clearly. Doing so keeps the energy flowing from the author's inspiration to yours so that you have sufficient impulse not only to start but to keep going until you have resolved your own insights into your own conclusion. Stay in contact with the work and with your responses to it, and you should have plenty to talk about. Stay true to what the text says literally. Keep checking your "data": what characters have really done and what they have really said to each other, and what the author really seems to have implied about it all. But also, stay true to your feelings when you interpret what you have read, probing your experience in such a way that you can convey that too with fair precision.

Learning by Muscle

If you think of yourself as composing an *essay* rather than just knocking out a paper, you are yourself engaged in literary effort. Although you are not producing a poem or a play and you aren't Shakespeare, you can benefit from the fact that you are writing about literature by drawing on some of the virtues of literature in its more imaginative forms. Doing so can improve all of your writing by helping you develop your own sense of form and your sense of style. It is doubtful that anyone can do this simply by following rules, however, or taking advice; but you can do it, I think, by *kinesthetic* (or *mimetic*) learning.

Any kind of learning is a response to pressures from inside and from outside. From without you probably get reasons why you need to do something, and you get materials to work with and rules to follow. But from within you get the capacity to do the job. For our purposes you get an assignment from outside; you also get the English language and the principles of modern American style, and you get Shakespeare. To do the job well, of course, everything else needs to come from within. How do you learn from within? By the principle of participation, *alias* imagination. This is a way of "learning by osmosis," but *deliberate* osmosis, like going abroad to learn the language.

If you are an athlete, when you watch the pros, you probably feel your body participating with theirs as they maneuver themselves in action: pitching, diving, blocking a ball, lifting a skating partner, making the last push to the finish line. Similarly, if you are a dancer, you dance with every member of the corps de ballet, not as a partner but from inside the dancer's legs, arms, and torso. If you play any kind of music or sing, you have your masters, and you sense in yourself the ability to perform through them, along the impulse of their genius. In all such instances, you expand your own conception of what can do as you feel yourself doing it. You learn what mastery is by participating kinesthetically—bodily—in the self-assured skill of the master to whom, for the moment, you are apprenticing yourself. You learn the pleasure of fluency, in which all the aspects of one's skills merge appropriately according to the needs of performance. You learn nuance, the slight adjustments of technique that have such telling effect, vibrating with sensitivity.

Fortunately, we can read kinesthetically too, metaphorically speaking. You learned to talk this way once upon a time, and you continue to develop your mind by thinking along with lively thinkers—and by sensing when something seems fishy in what you're hearing, when a movement of thought just doesn't seem to be coming along naturally. A good reader recreates an author's style *in reading*. That is, you think the words you read and work out the development of sentences. In the process, you can discover mind-muscles you didn't know you had—ways that you can express yourself in your own writing and effects of all sorts that you can achieve, from sentence rhythms to the building up of phrases and clauses to the integration of quotes to the resolution of triumphant conclusions. You see what works well for you as a reader, and you imagine yourself pulling it off.

For now we are concerned primarily with essay style, and more specifically style in critical essays, but from poets and playwrights you also expand your intuitive sense of what the English language can do when it's stroked or tickled, pinched and pressed along the impulses toward self-expression. You learn how the language likes to think and how it likes to talk, how qualities of idiomatic phrasing convey a natural voice, how sense flows from thought to thought, how simplicity and complexity each has its own place, how freshly the right word sparkles even (or especially) when it is a very familiar word, how graceful can be a particular reversal of phrasing. In this way you get the point of all the rhetoric you learned in comp classes. Kinesthetic learning, then, is not a process of just imitating others, although for practice that's not a bad idea. Becoming used to a greater range of stylistic possibilities and following them out time and again, you should find them becoming more intimately part of *your* language.

Being of Two Minds: Writing and Revising

The good writer is at home in two places: author's mind and editor's mind. Often they seem like separate countries, and not very friendly ones. Your loyalties may need to shift back and forth between them, and at times you can watch them negotiate in a kind of diplomatic dialogue. It's important to listen to each and maybe also not to trust either too far. They can both be rather arrogant. For the real pro, they probably work side by side, at least part of the time.

Author, of course, is a creative genius, eager to show off and take chances, eager to experiment with sudden inspirations. In this mode all one's feelings and all one's ideas are terribly important and will have to be appreciated by the world at large. When things go well, one enjoys being oneself, dancing in one's mind as one writes. Inspirations can be intoxicating, when they come, and they can be encouraged by trusting one's impulses, giving them a chance, being a little crazy. Author is no fool, however. Evidence is needed to help clinch one's point and provide some self-defense. When hunches come along, they need to be nurtured carefully, or discarded if they start to wither. The most satisfying pleasure comes from achieving illumination about one's subject that feels truly fitting, from finding the right word or phrase, from building up a climactic sentence, and from watching ideas evolve their own shape as they are worked out into paragraphs and finally into the form of the essay.

The author's chief enemy, as we all know, is fear or self-doubt in the form of that notorious demon the writer's block. This is a genuine problem. The best ways to get around it are casual or even playful ones that let you sneak into seriousness behind your own back. If you can't begin with a strong opening, sketch out whatever ideas you will want to see flowering later on. Doodle scattered thoughts knowing they may not lead to anything. Try free association of words and phrases that the topic brings to mind, as many as you can think of quickly for a while. You need to accumulate enough rough material so you won't feel empty. Above all, don't defeat yourself by condemning ideas before you've given them half a chance. Let your mind wander off distractedly, then surprise yourself when you've relaxed and see what thoughts come up when you get back to the topic. Jot down a few quotations from the text

that strike your fancy or a few phrases that evoke your feelings about a character. Then ask these phrases and words what they imply; ask in turn what
the implications imply and what assumptions lie behind any points that
you've made. Write some straight "representation," as I described it in the first
chapter, trying to stick to a simple description of the work, and grab hold of
any thoughts that lead you into interpretation. It may help if you realize that
writing can be creative for the same reason that we fear it: Thinking and using
language are involved closely in our sense of our selves. Of course writing will
reveal our vulnerability, but that must become an opportunity more than it is
an obstacle.

When you find yourself getting all twisted up in a sentence that's going
nowhere, when you feel you are being so stuffy you can't stand yourself,
when you are laying down one brick after another and not knowing what
they have to do with each other, or when you know you aren't really saying
what you mean or meaning what you say—stop and *talk it out*. Say what you
mean in a relaxed tone, after a deep breath. Say it to yourself or to someone
who loves you (well enough). But let it come out naturally and it has a better
chance of coming out in English. Then, before you lose it, write it down and
see if you can keep going with your new-found rhythm.

Editor is a tough cookie, whom you may need to keep at bay while you
write your first draft. Author is hot (properly impulsive, attached to great
ideas); editor is cool (detached, calm, and critical). Author wants to see what
one can get away with; editor says, "Nice try, but really . . ." As editor you are
suspicious about whatever doesn't sound right either in style or in thought.
You ask, "What do you mean? So what?" You screen for misspellings and
punctuation errors systematically and scrupulously, and wonder whether certain words are being used correctly—then check the dictionary to find out.
You claim the right to make judicious cuts, with a sharp eye for utter nonsense. You bring to your draft not just a list of rules, though, but a feeling for
clear, natural-sounding language. You like to hear ideas growing out of previous ideas and leading smoothly to what follows. From time to time, you add
one of the **transitional expressions** that I call "pivots" because they allow
your thoughts to swing along from one sentence or clause to another, showing
more clearly and gracefully how the logic of your thinking moves along. (You
might want to photocopy the boxed list of pivots I've provided here and keep
it handy when you write.) As editor, you listen as though you were your
reader, pointing out what isn't clear, where one wants more information,
what doesn't really sound like the poem or story that you remember reading,
and what simply doesn't seem smooth and graceful in expression. The editor
isn't sentimental about the author's genius but can respect the difficulty of the
project and does appreciate real gems. When editor is both humane and constructive, that is a happy critic working for you. On the other hand, if editor is
tough, author needs to learn toughness too, to be able to take it without

PIVOTS

Not this but that

Not exactly this but really that

Not only this but that as well

This and even that

Apparently this but actually that

Although one might think . . . one finds (sees) that . . .

Rather than merely . . .

In reality, . . . Actually, . . . As a matter of fact, . . . For that matter, . . . In fact, . . .

Generally speaking, . . .

For example, . . . To put it more specifically, . . . One might say, in fact . . .

Therefore, . . . As a result, . . . Consequently, . . . For that reason, . . . Accordingly, . . .

Nevertheless, . . . Nonetheless, . . . Otherwise, . . . Instead, . . .

On the other hand, . . . Conversely, . . . In contrast, . . . As opposed to this, . . .

More (or most) importantly (or significantly), . . . What is more, . . . What is even more important, . . . Most emphatically, . . .

Furthermore, . . . What is more to the point (more interesting, fortunate, surprising, disturbing, . . .) . . .

It is obvious that . . . Clearly, . . . Surely, . . . Certainly, . . . Obviously, . . .

It goes without saying that . . . Needless to say, . . .

One could say (conclude, argue) that, . . . Arguably, . . .

It is reasonable to say that . . . Thus we can see that . . .

In other words, . . . that is to say, . . . so to speak, . . . in a manner of speaking, . . . as it were, . . . at the same time, . . . in short, . . .

crumbling when editor starts laying it on. And if you can see that this editor is not really on your side, stand up for yourself and get another.

The editor is the master of **revision,** in short, capable of being constructive as well as tough, with a good sense of what *works.* Revision is by no means merely *correction,* the catching of mechanical errors. It may call for some basic changes of approach, some reorganizing, trying out new beginnings or endings, filling out paragraphs so that their ideas are developed with a sense of sufficiency. At its best, perhaps, revision is a kind of remolding. The most important skill the editor can encourage in the author is the ability to let a sentence or phrase dissolve back into the impulse that brought it forth and reemerge in a wholly (or partially) new guise. Often you try to change just one word at a time, and things still don't sound right. That can go on for hours. As author, you don't want to sacrifice the sentence you bought so dearly, but as editor you let it go, you let it go. Then author goes back to the previous sentences, picks up the train of thought once more, and behold, you have a new strategy to express the pesky concept or elusive memory, new words but also a different kind of sentence, a different order of phrases and organization of logic. You remember how many different ways there may be to say essentially the same thing. (Concepts, you see again, can be expressed in different forms. There is not a fixed form, you note, that an idea must fall into. The possibilities for formulating a particular notion are various, one realizes. Whatever you want to say, as you know, you can say in any number of ways. Etc., etc., etc.) Different formulations are likely to have different implications and different effects, but that's the point. You now have options; you can choose the version that best suits your context and your style and that conveys most closely what you have in mind. Author and editor are friendly partners once more.

Essaying the Essay

What distinguishes a critical essay, properly speaking, from a mere English paper? A "paper" is all too often a mechanical exercise satisfying a checklist of requirements. It works out formulas, from the opening "In this paper, I am going to show . . ." to the concluding "In conclusion, I have shown . . . ," or something of the sort. It speaks straight to the professor, who presumably knows what you are going to say already, or to no one at all, or to your notebook. The essay, on the other hand, is distinguished by its sense of form, its tone, and its relation to the reader.

In form the essay, like any literary work, is a self-contained whole, bringing you into its world. The **opening** paragraph establishes this mental world through the intellectual equivalent of dramatic gestures, which (ideally) sweep the reader up into its mindset. We are confronted with a proposition that is intriguing so that, as in a short story, some suspense is established: Can our author demonstrate such a devastating thesis? We are eager to see the masterstroke pulled off but anxious lest the world fall apart in the process. The paragraph may open with the debonaire gesture of a question, a strikingly apt quotation (from the text or otherwise), a description of an incident from the work, a bold affirmation of thesis, or an even bolder affirmation of a broader point that leads up to the thesis. And we take off.

In the **conclusion** we do not get a mere repetition of what we have just read. Rather, we land after our flight with our two feet on the ground. We have made it: *the end.* Discussion is rounded off, perhaps by reaffirming the main point in much more solid terms than were possible at the start because of all we have gone through together in the meantime: the closely argued and specifically demonstrated treatment which has grounded the proposition vividly in the work you are discussing. Between the opening and the closing, each paragraph has progressed from the previous one, leading forward from the opening proposition, just as (ideally) within each paragraph, every sentence grows out of the one before it, spelling out what it has not quite managed to say and suggesting still some further development, until the ending, when we have arrived and one need say no more. We are ready for a graceful exit. (In the box on pages 187–89, I have provided samples of lively opening and concluding paragraphs from a few student essays.)

Like a plot the essay's argument has cast a spell over us, an intellectual one, and has absorbed our minds into its logic. The essay's style, therefore, is politely seductive. Like a story or a poem, it has, most importantly, the quality of *presence,* a sense there is somebody home. In **tone,** an essay is usually genial or friendly, and its style is personable. There are certainly angry essays, written sometimes in a revolutionary spirit, but in them also we are brought to feel the presence of a thoughtful and sincere person who earns the right to be heard. You write an essay, therefore, as a self who wishes to say something that matters. A true essay has a sense of purpose about it. The author is consciously exploring a realm of experience, trying out some understanding of it. (The primary meaning of *essay* is "attempt"; Michel de Montaigne began our literary usage in his French "essaies.") As a critic, the immediate experience you are writing from is, of course, a reading experience, but you are bringing to it the depth and complexity of your personality and your experience up to now in living. It is essential to your case as a critic, therefore, that you *be there,* in your tone and through your style, as the interesting and sensible person that you are. (And if you don't think you are interesting, you might consider this: Interesting people are *interested;* they are curious and concerned.)

As a student, of course, you are likely to be writing, really, just for your instructor. Perhaps a friend or two will read your paper also, but the practical

REVISION, AN EXAMPLE

1. In Eudora Welty's story, "Death of a Traveling Salesman," the writer employs characterization in such a way that the people of the story personify certain elements of human nature. The story illustrates how opposing tendencies, specifically the natural human bent toward independent self-sufficiency and the inherent need for intimate identification with others, may be either reconciled, with constructive results, or allowed to remain imbalanced, with destructive results. This use of characterization is essential to the story line and is accomplished mainly through the use of indirect presentation. Welty succeeds in making us understand what kind of people the characters of the story are by dramatizing what they do.

The main character, R. J. Bowman, a traveling salesman, is apparently meant to be a living example of what can occur when the desire for self-sufficiency is not balanced with the need for intimacy, warmth, and love. Initially, we see only his autonomous side; the very fact of his occupation indicates a personality accustomed to functioning independently and this impression is enhanced when we realize that he has left the hotel room, where he had been recovering from a serious illness, before his convalescence is complete.

2. In ~~Eudora Welty's~~ story, "Death of a Traveling Salesman," ~~the~~ *her*
Endora Welty
~~writer employs~~ characteriza~~tion in such a way that the~~ people *es*
~~of the story personify certain~~ elements ~~of~~ human nature. The *as personifications of different in*

story illustrates how opposing tendencies, [specifically the natu-
[describe in another sent?]
ral human bent toward independen~~t self-sufficiency~~ and the ~~in-~~ */ ce*
~~herent~~ need for ~~intimate~~ identification with others,] may be

reality of the matter is that they will just be looking in. As an essayist, however, you write for a community of readers who are just as gracious and intelligent as you are. They are interested in learning from you and have no intention of giving you a grade. This is a fiction, no doubt, but it is one that allows you to practice literary criticism as a sociable activity. It allows you to develop a sense of style that is humane, drawing upon your awareness of

either reconciled ~~with~~ constructive ~~results,~~ *ly* or allowed to remain imbalanced, with destructive results. This ~~use~~ *Style, mode?* of characterization ~~is~~ essential to the story line ~~and~~ is accomplished
mainly through ~~the use of~~ *a technique of* indirect presentation. Welty ~~suc-~~
~~ceeds in making~~ *lets* us understand what kind of people the characters ~~of the story~~ are by dramatizing what they do.

   The main character, R. J. Bowman, a traveling salesman,
is ~~apparently meant to be a living example of~~ *exemplifies* what can occur
when ~~the desire for~~ self-sufficiency is not balanced with ~~the~~
~~need for intimacy, warmth, and~~ love. Initially, we see only his
~~autonomous~~ *independent* side ~~the very fact of~~ his occupation ~~indicates a per-~~ *suggests*
~~sonality accustomed to functioning~~ independently *ce* and this im-
pression is enhanced when we realize that he has left the hotel
room, where he had been ~~recovering from a~~ serious ~~illness,~~ *ly* before ~~his convalescence is complete.~~ *he had completely recovered.*

3. Characters in fiction often personify elements [*forces, factors?*]
of human nature. In Eudora Welty's "The Death of a Traveling
Salesman," the main character, R. J. Bowman, is torn between a
natural human bent towards self-sufficiency and a need for relationship with others. Such a conflict, we see, can either be
resolved constructively or left in destructive imbalance. By indirect presentation—dramatizing what they do—Welty shows

Continued

yourself as a person among persons. It allows you to develop your intellectual
ability as a natural part of your full personality.
   Who then is your **audience?** To whom are you speaking when you
write? If you address your instructor, your work may sound like an exercise,
answering questions that are set to you. Because you expect your instructor
to know the work you are discussing rather well, you may not stay grounded

what forces Bowman and her other characters represent. He demonstrates what can happen when this conflict, between independence and intimacy, become apparent in a person's life.

At first, we see only Bowman's autonomous side: his occupation suggests an independent life-style. His independence [determination to be independent, to live on his own resources?] is even clearer when we realize that he has left his hotel room before he has recovered from a serious illness.

4. R. J. Bowman, a traveling salesman, has been living in a hotel room recovering from a serious illness. He is not yet well when he goes back on the road, determined to pick up again his life of independence. When he discovers, however, the limitations of self-sufficiency, it becomes impossible for him to go on living at all.

The natural drive toward independence and the need for intimacy present a basic conflict in human nature. Bowman's life has been seriously imbalanced; by the time he realizes this, it is too late for a resolution. By dramatizing such a conflict in the lives (and deaths) of characters, an author often explores the effect it can have upon our own lives. In this story, "The Death of a Traveling Salesman," the author, Eudora Welty, shows us the power and meaning of the conflict without discussing it directly. She simply follows out what Bowman thinks and what he does. We see for ourselves just how destructive the conflict can be.

in your "representation" of it. On the other hand, if you write for your roommate, the chemistry major, you may have to do too much explaining and filling in. What I suggest is that you imagine yourself writing for people who read the work some time in the past. You are then able to count on some familiarity with your subject; but as you focus specifically on the aspects of the work that concern you, you will also sketch in representative details from the work, reminding readers what it was like.

And what are *you* like as you address this audience? You should expect your readers to be skeptical, so you need to make a cogent case and not take too much for granted. You can also expect that your readers are quite willing to be convinced, to be glad to join your company, so you can reach out in a spirit of welcome, as a host who is proud of his or her domain and pleased to have visitors. What you have to say *in* the way you say it should make your reader as (extremely) interested as you are yourself. You can afford to extend your best self confidently, with charm and wit, discrimination and curiosity,

SOME OPENINGS AND CONCLUSIONS FROM STUDENTS' ESSAYS

Openings

Learn to Die, Learn to Live

"The Country Husband" by John Cheever reveals that preparation for death is preparation for life. In the story, Francis Weed—almost killed in a plane crash—must grapple with mortality. Weed will either grow to accept death or stagnate in mediocrity.—*Jill Root*

"The Lottery": Jackson's Symbolism and Irony

Shirley Jackson's "The Lottery" takes place in a seemingly typical small American town in which the townspeople appear to relate to one another in much the same way as we the readers do when we congregate with friends and acquaintances. From the beginning Jackson gives us no reason to suspect anything out of the ordinary is about to occur as the villagers gather in their town square to perform an annual lottery. In fact, the very title of the story suggests that somebody is about to be a winner, to gain something.—*Karen Dempsey*

The Security of Superficiality

There is a certain security found in monotony, a repetitive familiarity that offers constant comfort. Monotony and repetition offer freedom from change that may be stressful. Yet change is a necessary factor of life, and without change life becomes shallow, eventually degenerating to mere existence. In John Cheever's "The Country Husband," the community of Blenhollow is sharing such an existence. The superficiality of the town is revealed as the story's events unfold, mainly through strong contrasts provided by the main character's increasing awareness of life's depths and the constantly shallow attitude of the social order. The townspeople struggle successfully to maintain their superficiality and, through this, their security and sense of safety.—*Wendy Schutz*

Honor: A Comparison between Two Poems

In times of relative peace, the world tends to romanticize war. The movie screens today are still filled with post–World War II epics on the same theme—"Johnny comes marching home" after fighting for his country to find his loved ones waiting at the doorstep with open arms and dinner on the table. At these times we want to forget the realities of war. Even when we remember those who have died in a war, we do so as if they had lived in a dreamy world of valor, honor, and glory. We can live with the memories of heroes; death and destruction are somewhat easier to accept when there is some semblance of an underlying purpose or reason for their existence. A poem which typifies this dreamlike romanticism of war is Richard Lovelace's "To Lucasta." In sharp contrast, even in opposition, to this type of idealism is Wilfred Owen's "Dulce et Decorum Est." The tone of the two poems could not be more opposite. While Lovelace's speaker expresses an eagerness for war, the speaker in Owen's poem is embittered and angered by even the most "honorable" aspects of it. That both poems are as effective as they are is a tribute to each poet's ability to use tone to make his ideas come to life for the reader.—*Monica Ochoa*

Conclusions

Toby Out of Oats

Chekhov's play is satisfying because in spite of their comic histrionics Mrs. Popov and Smirnov are real people reaching for love, for a force more powerful than money, land, and status. They have had all that, and it did not bring them happiness. Love is the only thing in the world that cannot be bought, bartered, or forced; it has to be won in its own terms. And so, in the end when Mrs. Popov cuts off Toby's oats, we, the audience, know that she is moving on to a real life at last; we know that both of them are no longer children playing at life, but grown up adults obeying their natural impulses, shedding their preposterous attitudes towards life, and we see them going confidently forward into the future with love binding them together.—*Virginia O'Brien*

On Kafka's "The Hunger Artist"

Being part of the animal world of the circus has finally brought his chance. Now he is able to satisfy his hunger for endless fasting; and he begins to fast, and fasts on and on. Nobody counts the days anymore, even the artist himself has stopped counting. He is finally satisfied with his fasting and feels on his way to everlasting bliss. Nobody stops his fast. The artist's body grows weaker and weaker. He lies in the dirty straw and all his physical energy is consumed. With his last breath, like a kiss to the world, he answers the question about his endless fast. He whispers his revelation, "because I could not find the food I liked," then he ceases to exist; he is dead. Death opens the door to eternity for the hunger artist, as it does for all men.

This earth does not contain food to still man's eternal hunger; this need remains unfulfilled as long as we are alive. This longing for eternal existence is part of our humanness, and man must love and embrace his humanness to live. It is this humanness which differentiates us from the higher being, God. Man, like the hunger artist, destroys himself when he does not accept this paradox of our existence.—*Erika Scherer*

Is **The Cherry Orchard** *a Comedy?*

If the economic failure of Lyubov and Gayev is viewed as the death blow to a better way of life, then *The Cherry Orchard* is not a comedy. If their failure is just a correction in the direction of social development, then the play is indeed a comedy as Chekhov claimed. But, regardless of how the economic failure is viewed, the blow to human dignity is painful; we feel this particularly when we are nearly forced to view Lyubov's refusal to destroy something of beauty for the sake of her future as just another in a string of manifest errors in judgment.

The exuberant spirit of Anya and Trofimov at the end of the play is a positive sign, a sign of the possibility of redemption from this failure. However, Anya and Trofimov are too young to be trusted fully with our hopes. The closing words of the play, mumbled by Firs, who was not forgotten but lost in the shuffle, include a hint of caution, "When they're young, they're green." Following Firs's last words, this sound of a "snapped string" challenges us with its intriguing and discordant qualities.—*Don Mason*

On Camus' "The Guest"

That Daru should die because of his honorable action points out another existential quality, the absurdity of life. Just as the prisoner's murder of his cousin is senseless, so too will be the murder of Daru, a good and useful man. Camus wisely chose a setting that reflects this philosophy (and the story's theme) and used it to achieve a profound effect. In the Algerian desert were, as Camus writes, "outcroppings of rock that gave the landscape a chaotic look." Like the earth we inhabit, life is often just as confused, just as absurd, and all too often even more so.—*Dennis Alioto* compassion and sincerity—for you do have all of these qualities, when you trust yourself and expect to be appreciated. They are all appropriate qualities for a critical style. At least the Happy Critic thinks so.

Words

As emerging essayist, you will want to develop two obviously basic resources: a vocabulary that is both well-stocked and readily accessible and a flexible sense of sentence style. To survive well simply as a reader of literature, of course, you will find that a good vocabulary is essential. You've been accumulating words almost all your life. A little effort now, though, can make your word stock much fuller and much more precise. Many words you pick up as you go along. Do notice how often you can wisely guess what a word means from its context, especially if it's a word you know you have heard but never have been comfortable with. Yet you cannot wait for new words to arrive with their meanings perfectly clear. Your dictionary is simply one of your best friends. It would probably be a good idea for you to list the new words you look up and to check in on your list now and again. Since we comprehend words best in context, let the dictionary show you possibilities of meaning while you think of what the word seems to mean as it is being used *in vivo*— while, that is, you are reading.

As you examine dictionary entries, try to absorb a feeling for how words work in general. Remember that dictionaries distinguish the meanings that words take on as they are used in different ways. Meanings shade off from each other, often extending their applicability by metaphor. Notice how meanings derive ultimately from foreign terms (or Anglo Saxon); how their history may reflect some feature or fashion of life in the past; how they may be built up of recognizable segments of meaning, such as roots, prefixes, and suffixes, that relate them to other words you know. Notice also the level of usage, the degree of formality or informality in which particular words may sit most comfortably. Note (with pleasure) their sound qualities or "texture," what they feel like to say and to hold in your mouth. Appreciate their connotations, their associations and implications as they are used.

One of the most important features of words is their capacity to detect specific nuances and tonalities of meaning, giving us just the right touch to capture an elusive point. For this reason, a good vocabulary doesn't just help you express your thoughts better, it helps you *think* better, making precise discriminations. When we consult a thesaurus, we can see how words that are close in meaning still differ from one another, for it lists together related words, moving us further afield as the list goes on. You undervalue a thesaurus if you just mine it for impressive nuggets. It is a more useful resource if you just let it remind you of those words you have "on the tip of your tongue." If it calls to mind words you aren't quite comfortable with, you know where to go to check out their meaning.

For Grace and Drama

Words, naturally, come alive in **phrasing,** and phrases in sentences. You may think of writing as laying one word ponderously after another like bricks. You should find that the language works better for you, however, if you habituate yourself to think in terms of phrases. *You should find that—the language works better—better for you—if you habituate yourself—habituate yourself to think—to think of meaning—meaning in terms of—in terms of phrases.* Phrases overlap and they grow out of one another. They have various lengths, rhythms, and textures. They have movement. They can balance one another, a few little fellows bracing against a hefty one. They can gracefully rise to a climax of clarity and emphasis. As you read kinesthetically, notice above all how sentence rhythms grow as they flow. Notice this in how you yourself speak when you are expressing yourself with feeling and urgency, how, for example, you hold back words you want to emphasize, leading up to them with an introductory phrase (or two): "When I opened the door, there before me *was a terrifying spectacle."* Notice how one's voice naturally rises and falls as one speaks meaningfully, how phrases and subordinate clauses are held down in an undertone (as when we read something in parentheses) and how climactic points ascend in their stress. When you read and when you write, watch how the same qualities of *voice* are built into the structure of flexible sentences.

Tedious writing plods along word by word, sentence by sentence. An energetic style looks forward to a goal, continually reaching for it until it is achieved. The goal is the fulfillment of an engagement, when a thesis has been substantiated, its implications made fully clear. This "thesis" may be the point of your whole essay; it may also be the point of a sentence. In either case, you work it out until it is happily realized. Then you have carried out your engagement. The sentence is firm. The thought is manifest. The essay has rounded itself to a thumping conclusion. And you need not be writing very complex sentences to say so. You should also know how to condense in order to be accurate and energetic at the same time.

Taking in the way style works well for others, then, you notice things that you can do in your own writing. What specific features of style can you draw upon to make your writing more fluent (which means, incidentally, "flowing") and more lively? Sometimes by asking a question, and then answering it. Sometimes with a "rhetorical" (I prefer to say "dramatic") sentence fragment. Sometimes by interjecting a more personal comment parenthetically.

In freshman composition you were taught to avoid faulty parallelism. Now indulge in some dramatic parallel movement (without overdoing it): reexamining a point that you've made, bringing out new aspects of it, and building up to a smashing conclusion. It is a kind of caress of your thought: such metaphors and analogies as this one adding another kind of vitality. Encourage your word-hoard to supply you with vivid but familiar words: Reach especially for dramatically expressive verbs and specific nouns. Realize how large your reading vocabulary already is; draw upon more of those words that you recognize but don't ordinarily think of using. Let the operative word be "drama." These distinctions are not very realistic (all three genres have all three qualities), but from poetry get rhythm and nuance, from fiction get suspense and the movement to a concluding revelation, and from drama get (you guessed it) *drama*. In a dramatic style there is living presence, there is conflict of interests, there is vivid action, and there is flourish. Vivid words, active sentences, energetic movement to firm conclusions, strict economy of effect, pleasure in elegant touches—these are specific qualities of dramatic style in critical essays as they are on the stage.

Most of all, respect the qualities of your own voice, the rhythms in which you speak, molded now to a presentable degree of (relative) formality. Listen to rhythms and the idiomatic phrasing with which other people talk, in order to broaden your feeling for natural English. Enjoy writing, however, with the qualities of your own temperament. And trust your own intelligence—both your capacity to see clearly and your capacity to make inferences from what you see. Trust also your ability to judge what is effective in your own writing—judging, for example, when it is effective and when it is lame to start an occasional sentence with "And" or "But." Wanting a touch of grace in your sentence movement, you can precede your main clause with a participial phrase ("Wanting a touch of . . ."). When you have just done that, you can start with a subordinate clause ("When you have . . ."). Both of these openers allow you to hold back for a little suspense, so that your main thought then comes along for the climax.

An explanatory clause or phrase after your main clause ("so that . . .") can round off your thinking with a sense of careful precision. One of the easiest kinds of revision you can make, in fact, is to spot at the start of sentences subjects that might better be set after a preparatory phrase or clause. In your first draft, for example, you may find yourself wanting to get the subject of your sentence down on paper right away. You write, "Hamlet, when he passes Claudius kneeling at prayer, refrains from killing him," which sounds a bit wooden. If you change it very simply to "When he passes Claudius kneeling at prayer, Hamlet refrains from killing him," you have an introductory clause that allows you to swing upwards to the main clause. Keeping the main clause whole (with the subject and verb together) lets it sit more solidly, which is helpful in a sentence like that one, when a rather short clause is making the main point.[1] Instead of "Shakespeare, in his great tragedy *Hamlet* . . . ," go for "In his great tragedy *Hamlet*, Shakespeare . . ." It may be that the first version will work better in some particular context, but try the difference and find out. An isolated sentence of this sort is not terrible, but a number of them near each other can sound deadly. With a little adjustment of just one such sentence, you can add a touch of grace and emphasis. A graceful style is built of such touches.

When you are making a point about some matter that requires information, you might find yourself blurting out too much at once and getting into a jumble. An ambitious student of mine was discussing Peter Brook's powerful but exceptionally pessimistic film of *King Lear:*

> Knowing that he would not live up to the fullness of *King Lear,* he pioneered a new path regardless of his 1962 stage production. Not long after, he began work on his film version. . . .

The effect is like tripping over your own feet. Try *backtracking:*

> Brook's 1962 stage production was relatively conventional. When, not long after, he began work on his film version, he realized he could not live up to the fullness of the play as he had staged it. He pioneered, therefore, a new path.

First things first: Consider what you ought to have said before you can say what you want to now. In laying out the facts, you can see, I was also able to sharpen the contrasts: stage vs. film, conventional vs. new. Discussion could now go on to still another contrast, which I think is implied here, between the "fullness of the play" and the selective focus of the film. Through these contrasts and through this build-up, the movement of thought is made clearer as it is also being made more dramatic. Avoid, therefore, *blurt,* the tendency to say it all at once. You can develop an essay smoothly (and to a sufficient "fullness") by first preparing and then by following through. In doing so, you also make it more interesting and more informative. Here is a professional horror to make us all feel a little better. It opens an essay published in 1951 (*Secunda Pastorum* is *The Second Shepherd's Play,* a masterpiece of medieval drama):

> To interpret the "Three brefes to a long" passage in the *Secunda Pastorum* (c. 1450–60) as a reference to a musical figure anticipating Beethoven's immortal phrase ("Fate knocking at the door") as well as our own Morse code symbol for the letter V—an interpretation which has

---

1. You may be tempted to write, "When Hamlet sees Claudius . . . , he refrains. . . ." Better, however, that the proper name go in the main clause and the pronoun in the subordinate element.

had at least one public expression [footnote supplied]—is pleasant and facile but as truly fallacious as would be any interpretation arrived at by superimposing musical ideas and practices of a later time upon this bit of medieval criticism.[2]

Another way to heighten your grace and emphasis, one which makes a great difference for some writers, is to catch a tendency you may have (as I do) to churn out "preposition strings." Preposition strings are sequences *of* phrases *with* prepositions *before* them *in* a sentence; they are wooden *in* effect and they often go *with* a tendency *toward* verbs vague *in* meaning and abstractions *without* justification, which *in* combination can be hypnotic *to* the extreme *in* this form. Whoops! Let's try again. Preposition strings are sequences of prepositional phrases; they sound particularly wooden, and often they crop up when we are thinking in unnecessarily abstract terms and relying on weak verbs, a combination that can be extremely hypnotic. A little better, anyway, I hope. Here is another professional example, a sentence that appeared in "a higher education journal." The editor tried to entice me into reading the whole piece by printing this extract on the cover. I am happy to report that I resisted successfully.

> Conservative attempts to represent national standards as an insidious attempt by politically correct elites to impose their counter-culture values on America reduce the importance of uniformly raising education standards in secondary schools and improving the entering classes moving into higher education institutions.

Prepositional phrases are a basic part of our language, and combinations of them can be effective when they are sorted out. Abstractions may be very appropriate, especially when you are running in a philosophical vein. If we can't use abstractions—like *abstraction*—our ability to think is limited indeed. But both prepositional phrases and abstract language can be hypnotic; try alternatives and see. Whenever you find yourself caught in states of being, see if you cannot transpose your language, more dramatically, into an account of *people doing things* (instead of "Entrapment in states of being finds improvement in accounts of personal action," a preposition string that comes along again with the abstraction). The passive voice can be quite appropriate and helpful. It can be used unobtrusively. Properly, of course, it should express passivity or, more dramatically, victimization: "She was run over by a car." "The country was devastated by war." A passive subject should clearly be what it is that we want to talk about: "It can be used unobtrusively." The passive becomes deadly, however, when it encourages us to be inappropriately

---

2. This is a decent time not to cite the author.

abstract—especially when it becomes employed in that category of prose by which it feels that impressive and intellectual writing is being produced by the author (like that). Be active, be dramatic.

All these pointers about stylistic grace apply to any kind of prose. One clumsy-making habit of style undermines lively critical style in particular. In his anthologies, the poet X. J. Kennedy speaks of avoiding a mechanical style.[3] Don't let authors sound like mechanics *using* tools or cooks *putting in* ingredients. Processes of imagination are more organic than that. You can avoid saying "Shelley uses a lot of metaphors in the poem" simply by getting inside the work and letting the metaphors speak for themselves: "Metaphors occur frequently in the poem." Instead of "Shelley includes the image of the West Wind because he wants to express spiritual freedom," try "The West Wind expresses. . . ." Readers are probably well aware that you're talking about Shelley by now, and the specific features of the poem have their own effects whether or not the poet intended them consciously. (And don't make matters worse with expletives: "*It is* in this poem that Shelley. . . .") Kennedy's examples show that a mechanical view of how poetry works leads to a static and mechanical essay style, a style weighted down by repetitive sentence structures and unnecessary abstractions. If this approach is mechanical, the alternative is presumably an "organic" one. It would open more possibilities of graceful rhythms and a sense of lively feelings. You would dramatize the metaphors, showing them in action, let the words of the poem do the work of the poet.

Throughout this section, I have been both describing and prescribing some features of effective writing. They are principles of technique, but for the most part they can't be "applied" by rule. By reading kinesthetically, a good writer becomes more aware of them as possibilities available for use. They become internalized. Then, as ideas and feelings come along, dying to express themselves with grace and force, they find out such means, naturally, through which to flow. You can help this process along. Let the memory of your reading experience come forth with the kind of energy you experienced *in* your reading; and *be there* yourself, in your lively mind, having specific and lively experience as you think with pleasure about what you have enjoyed reading.

Toward a Philosophy of Punctuation

The connection between grace and emphasis leads to a basic point about the "philosophy of sentence structure." Grace is aesthetic delight, which is

---

3. "How to Quote a Poem," in *An Introduction to Poetry,* 8th ed. (New York: Harper Collins).

very nice in itself. There is a lilt in graceful sentences, as their phrases rise and fall. Grace also carries along a general flow of feelings and thoughts as we follow out the development of ideas, and that perhaps is even nicer. But grace is also in itself related to meaning. In large measure it comes from variety among sentences and from the web of phrases and clauses within sentences, and in both ways, it leads to emphasis, an important aspect of what we mean, certainly, since it conveys what is important about our point. It does this in sentences both simple and complex. Giving our thoughts parallel structure channels them according to their logical similarity. Subordinating contributory factors to main (independent) clauses sorts out the elements of our experience and interprets the logical relations among them: what causes what, what follows what, what occurs in spite of what, what must be noted in passing to fully appreciate what, and so forth. A complex sentence portrays a complex world by reaching for it with a complex thought, one in which contributing thoughts feed into the mainstream at appropriate places. As we express through sentence structure the relationships we perceive in reality, our writing is more accurate, more realistic. The point of "sentence variety" should be that it follows naturally from the movement of our thought, when we are writing smoothly and clearly, just as it does when we speak fluently—in both cases allowing various points of our thinking to take on the shape, movement, and stress that they call up for themselves as they come along. Then grace arises in the feeling that life works naturally.

If there is a philosophy of sentence structure, there is a "philosophy of punctuation" also. Instead of wondering where to "stick in" the commas, colons, or semicolons, think of them as markers that help organize and clarify your thoughts. As you relate the elements of your experience into sentence structure, you sort them out with these little squiggles. There are, mercifully, only a very small number of them. With your old composition handbook, you can learn systematically and once and for all the principles of what they can do for us (the "rules," that is), but more importantly, you can train your eye to watch how they work when you are reading kinesthetically. They set off certain phrases and indicate (sometimes by their significant absence) the logical relationship between clauses. They organize items in series and so forth. Especially important, and especially common, is the use of commas (for more emphasis dashes—for less, parentheses) to interrupt a primary thought or to set off phrases and clauses that lead up to one. If you need still to learn how to use commas, it helps to realize, at any rate, that they are there to help us structure our thoughts and to communicate them. There are some arbitrary conventions involved (and some differences between American and British usage), but by and large they make sense and help us make sense. When you get them wrong, you look inept for a reason that you can easily learn to deal with. When you get them right, you show one more way in which you understand how the English language works and how you can get it to work best for you.

One punctuation dilemma you may well face in your essay's opening line is whether or not you should use a comma before a title. It is not a very important issue in itself but it illustrates my larger point that punctuation usually supports meaning. Notice this difference and see the logic behind it:

> In Shirley Jackson's story "The Lottery," a group of villagers are casually preparing to perform a human sacrifice.

> In a story by Shirley Jackson, "The Lottery," a group of villagers are casually preparing to perform a human sacrifice.

You may think you put the comma in the second time but not the first because in the second your voice stops before the title; in truth, however, you pause *for the same reason that* you use the comma. In the first, the title is necessary to identify the story; it fills out the single unit of meaning "Shirley Jackson's story 'The Lottery.'" In the second version, "*a* story by Shirley Jackson" is a unit of meaning that can stand by itself; the title is additional information parallel to it. If you lift the title out of the sentence, the sentence will remain just as coherent. The first example is similar to what grammar books call a *restrictive* element, because the title "The Lottery" restricts the possibilities of what "story" can mean; the second example is *nonrestrictive*, because it doesn't.[4]

If this problem is utterly befuddling, think about the following distinction in a nonliterary example:

> His son Edward is in college but his son Harry has graduated.

> His son, Edward, is in college but his daughter, Harriet, has graduated.

And now compare these:

> Do you refer to Samuel Butler the poet [who lived in the 17th century] or Samuel Butler the novelist [who lived in the 19th]?

> The poet William Blake was also a distinguished painter and engraver.

> My favorite poet, William Blake, was also a distinguished painter and engraver.

In the last, you will notice, the parallel (or *appositional*) terms "favorite poet" and "William Blake" receive equal emphasis as you say them. Keep in mind, however: context can change meaning and usage.

---

4. In the last sentence, I used commas before the two "because" clauses because the main point of the sentence is the *terms*, not the *explanations* for them. *Ergo*, the "because" clauses are nonrestrictive. I am answering "What are they called?" not "Why are they called it?"

I have just read a story that has left me in a state of shock. In the story, "The Lottery," a human sacrifice is performed casually in a modern American town.

Without that first sentence, the commas around the title might very well be wrong.

Searching and Researching

Think of research as playing with the big kids. You watch them to see how they do it, and, after being overawed, you start to feel you can do at least some of it yourself. Your first attempt doesn't come off brilliantly, but gradually you begin to get the hang of it. The adrenalin rushes as you feel your daring. You discover you can survive in their company. Even if you're no star, you can pull off what you try more and more frequently. You have good reason to feel pleased with yourself.

One thing you learn about big kids is that they're not always such hot stuff. Maybe they've mastered some tricks and routines. They've been around a while and have picked up useful information. But they don't know everything and they don't always see straight. They are fallible like you, which means you have some legitimate abilities like them. The more you get in there and play, the better you'll get at it. You will pick up the tricks (and some of the knowledge) as you go. In the process you learn to appreciate those tricks, the know-how, seeing the kinds of agility they take and seeing also what they can do for you. You get savvy.

In literary study, the big kids got their Ph.D.s ages ago and have been poring for decades over the poems of Emily Dickinson or the plays of Shakespeare, scrutinizing not only the works themselves but what legions of others have had to say about them. They've learned the hard way that each bit of knowledge is connected to billions of others. Yet they also developed some idea—and it was probably early in the game—about the limits of what they needed to know in order to have their say. They learned that, as they studied, they came into certain patterns of information which allowed them to develop viewpoints, viewpoints with a cogency almost demanding that someone proclaim and argue their merits. In other words they didn't need, thank God, to know everything. They learned, furthermore, to think about literature in terms of certain theories or methodologies, the philosophic foundations for their work. They could have their say, therefore, both because different information struck them as significant and because different approaches seemed to them compelling. But this account still oversimplifies the matter. They responded to many different specific influences—philosophical, scholarly, and political, in their lives and in their training—and they had different temperaments. Most important of all (though maybe for all these reasons and more), when they read and reread the works they loved, the impact of the reading experience struck them with a particular emphasis and flavor.

It is good to be able to write critical essays directly from your response to what you've read (and perhaps talked about in class). You learn to trust your judgment, taking your own thoughts and feelings seriously without being overwhelmed by impressions of what you should think because the experts say so. It is especially good to do this as you are learning better how literature works. There are two main reasons, however, why, as a student, you should do scholarly and critical research for some of your essays—substantial research for a proper "research paper" project and occasional briefer forays for shorter jobs. First of all, research provides valuable contextual information about the author as well as about the author's times, influences, and other writings, all information that helps you understand where he or she "is coming from." Secondly, research lets you into the "community of discourse" around an author's works, so that you can expand your own immediate impressions. You enter a room, as it were, where clever folks (and some of the other kind) have already been arguing for a while. You pick up the thread and some basic assumptions, then start to realize you want to have your say also.

Following out the way critics argue, you see the point of interpretations that would not have occurred to you and you notice features of the works that you had not appreciated before: the integrity perhaps of a character you had thought of simply as a weakling, a strain of imagery that suggests sexual domination, or a view of God that may lead to despair. What is more, you get general conceptions that you can try out yourself, from different sources you get partial insights that you can combine into grand new truths, and just as important, you see in specific ways how wrong other people can be (even when they are experts) so you can argue against them. We read critics in part in order to disagree, so that we can develop our own viewpoints. Seeing how others have argued, we also learn what features of a work we had better take into account and what kinds of argument we need to advance in order to protect ourselves from counterattack. We read criticism, then, in order to think—not simply to find out what a work means. (The more critics you read sometimes, the scarcer any final answers seem anyway, since they all write, more or less as we do, in order to disagree!) In other words, we get to sling it out with the big kids, getting to feel bigger all the time.

The most difficult part about doing research may be incorporating it into your writing. You may be asked to do a factual scholarly paper, for which you select and assemble information. You are probably expected in a case like this to show how fair and detached you can be. In a more creative mode of work, you may be asked for scholarly-critical essays, in which the scholarship serves the purposes of criticism. You present, in Northrop Frye's expression, "the educated imagination." As a critic, you are developing your own point of view, which provides a focus for the essay, but you also draw upon both scholarly information and especially perceptive critical argument to develop and substantiate your case and explore its implications.

Using research in this way means you must integrate into your own essay the material that you have gleaned. Do not settle for a pastiche of what other people have said. You are clearly the author now speaking, the resident critic. As such, you are responsible for the worthiness of the authorities you cite, the guest experts you present to us. You must judge who seems reliable and who does not. You are not to assume that anything you find in print is sound. You may actually cite some folks in order to disagree with them. Very likely, you will have to negotiate among your sources, to sort out your own picture of what makes sense. If you do enough research, you will be able to consider what some of your sources say about each other. You may find them doing this explicitly or you may see that they represent points of view that counter each other, leaving you to see where you stand. You may stand on one side or the other, in the middle, or in an eclectic position that extracts some kind of truth in one argument and some kind in the other. Often, the most convincing case you can make shows how other people's partial vision contributes to your new overview.

Using the results of your research raises a few technical problems. As in most matters, watch closely how the pros do it. For documentation, English instructors will probably expect you to follow the Modern Language Association (MLA) stylesheet, now standard usage in the profession. You should learn it properly. (I usually give my students a choice, since I dislike this newer method myself. Inserting bibliographic information in your text rudely interrupts your voice and breaks up the flow of your prose. Besides, some of us enjoy making footnotes, and major wordprocessing systems make them easy.) Whatever system you follow, however, it is necessary, alas, to be consistently systematic and utterly finicky. You need to know where to use commas, where colons, and where parentheses; where last names first and where only last names; when to say "bibliography" and when "works cited;" how to cite books, how to cite chapters, and how to cite articles. Follow a guide closely and, once more, pick up what you can as you go along: watch how your sources note their sources. (On page 202–203 I've listed separately the main features of both MLA style and traditional style according to the *Chicago Manual of Style,* which various publishers follow.)[5] At least, not many people expect

---

5. For a detailed guide to MLA style, get Joseph Gibaldi, *MLA Handbook for Writers of Research Papers,* 4th ed. (New York: Modern Language Assn., 1995). A good coverage of the University of Chicago style is included in Kate L. Turabian's book *A Manual for Writers of Term Papers, Theses, and Dissertations,* 6th ed., revised by John Grossman and Alice Bennett (Chicago: University of Chicago Press, 1987).

Latin abbreviations anymore, the *ibids* and *op cits* of yesteryear. To help you understand the notes in older texts, however, you should still know the big three: *ibid.* (short for "the same") refers to the same author and title cited in the previous note and is followed by a different page number; *loc. cit.* (for "place cited") refers to author, title, and page cited in the note just before; *op. cit.* (for "work cited") refers back to a text cited in an earlier note and substitutes for just the title, requiring the author's last name and a page number.

For some people the biggest problem with integrating research is working quotations into their writing. Here are several rules:

- Quote less than you want to. Paraphrase and summarize your sources (accurately and precisely) except for pithy expressions and succinctly stated main points.

- Lead up to your quotations just as logically as you lead up to any point you are making for yourself, and, of course, lead away from them just as naturally. Often a paraphrase of the quotation helps lead to or from, showing what you see in the passage that you want your reader to recognize.

- Be sure that whatever you quote is grammatically coherent with the setting you provide for it. If you quote an incomplete sentence, the phrase(s) with which you lead up to it (or in some cases, follow it) must make it both grammatically and logically complete. Thus:

According to Alfred Kazin, Hawthorne "makes ancient 'rotting' Rome the most detailed item" in *The Marble Faun.*

Notice, incidentally, that this example avoids an automatic tag, like "Kazin says . . . ," "Romeo says . . . ," and so forth. Try for more specific verbs: An author or a character can *exclaim, declare, announce, interject, suggest, inform us, insist, argue, emphasize, demonstrate, speculate, ask, inquire,* and on and on. (You don't have to go as far as *asseverates.*) Often, as in the Kazin example, phrases help integrate the quotation dramatically. You have often seen expressions like these: "Kazin raises an important point in this regard." ". . . raises a challenging objection." ". . . implies as much when he says . . ." ". . . sums up this viewpoint perfectly." Just remember the range of options always available to help you express yourself in a lively way. Like all your writing, researched papers too can be graceful and gracious, happy criticism in a happy style.

On That Most Unhappy Topic Plagiarism

There are two kinds of plagiarism: stupid and dumb. You are being stupid if you deliberately violate your own integrity, asking to be heard and judged

DOCUMENTATION STYLES: A SUMMARY
MLA (Modern Language Associaton) Style

BIBLIOGRAPHY Title it Works Cited. List works alphabetically by author's last name (or by title if no author is given). Place a period after each main element. Double-space, indenting second and subsequent lines five letter spaces or ½ inch.

1. *Book*

```
Busybody, Mortimer, and Jack Spratt. Our Opinions on the Subject of This Book. New
     York: Publisher, 1952.
```

If you list more than one work with the same authorship, use three hyphens for author(s) after the first entry.

```
Busybody, Mortimer, and Jack Spratt. Our Opinions on the Subject of This Book. 2nd ed.
     New York: Publisher, 1952.
---. More Opinions on the Subject of This Book. New York: Publisher, 1953.
```

For second and later editions add "2nd ed." ("3rd ed.," etc.) one space after the period following the title.

2. *Book translated and edited*

```
Busybodov, Pierre Heinrich. An International Masterpiece. 3rd ed. Trans. A. Native
     Speaker. Ed. Clever Fellow. Strange City: Publisher, 1996.
```

3. *Article in journal*   Give volume number and date of journal, plus page numbers of article.

```
Thornwhistle, Laura. "This Essay and I." Journal of Interesting Topics 67 (1952):
     80-93.
```

4. *Article in book*   List by article author. Give volume editor, if any, plus page numbers of article.

```
Spindrift, Sam. "My Definitive Contribution." Perverse Views of a Trivial Subject.
     Ed. Claire Cuttedge. Grosstown: Gravy State UP, 1936. 5-63.
```

5. *Foreword (Introduction, etc.) to book written or edited by author*

```
Ripper, Jacques de. Foreword. Studies in Technocriticism. By Fred Sosorry. New York:
     Publisher, 1952.
```

CITATIONS IN TEXT Quotation or restatement of someone else's idea requires citing the author's last name (or shortened title if no author is given) and page number. In-text citations refer to entries in Works Cited.

1. Place the last name of the author (or the shortened title) and specific page(s) in parentheses after the closing quotation mark and before punctuation at the end of your sentence: (Busybody 310). Set off and indent quotations longer than four lines ten letter spaces or 1 inch and place the parenthetical citation one space after the final punctuation.

2. If the name of the author is given in your text, give only the page number(s) in the parentheses.

```
As Busybody and Spratt argue, "What we think cannot be disputed" (310).
```

3. If you cite more than one work with the same authorship, add a short title before the page number.

```
As Busybody and Spratt argue, "What we think cannot be disputed (Our Opinions 310).

As one confident pair of authors has claimed, "What we think cannot be disputed"
(Busybody and Spratt, Our Opinions 310).
```

4. You may provide comments or incidental information in a numbered endnote. Endnotes appear on a separate page before Works Cited. Mark what the note refers to with a superscript (raised) number.[1]

University of Chicago Press Humanities Style

BIBLIOGRAPHY Title it Bibliography, Selected Bibliography, Works Cited, or Sources Consulted, depending on what it includes. Since notes provide all information, a bibliography usually is included only in books or long papers. List works alphabetically by last name of author (or by title if no author is given). Place a period after each main element. Single-space within and double-space between entries. Indent the second and subsequent lines five letter spaces. Compare the entries below with those on the facing page.

```
Busybody, Mortimer, and Jack Spratt. Our Opinions on the Subject of This Book. 2nd ed.
    New York: Publisher, 1952.
```

If you list more than one work with same authorship, use the underscore key struck eight times for author(s) after the first entry.

```
Busybody, Mortimer, and Jack Spratt. Our Opinions on the Subject of This Book. 2nd ed.
    New York: Publisher, 1952.

_____. More Opinions on the Subject of This Book. New York: Publisher, 1953.
```

CITATIONS IN TEXT Follow what is being cited with a superscript (raised) number at the end of a sentence or clause;[1] use a corresponding number for a note either at the bottom of the same page (footnote) or on a separate page at the end of the text of the paper (endnote). Note in the following examples that authors' names are not reversed since entries are not in alphabetical order. Commas are used between the elements. Place of publication, publisher, and date are in parentheses. Page references are to the specific pages being cited. Set off quotations of two or more sentences that run longer than eight lines, and type them single-spaced indented four letter spaces.

1. *Article*

In text:

```
As Laura Thornwhistle says, "I know I'm right."[1]
```

Endnote or footnote (first reference to the article):

```
    1. Laura Thornwhistle, "This Essay and I," Journal of Interesting Topics 67
(1952): 84.
```

Subsequent reference:

```
    2. Thornwhistle, 89.
```

2. *Book*

```
Busybodov remarks on this as well: "I never saw anything like it!"[3]
```

Endnote or footnote (first reference to the book):

```
    3. Pierre Heinrich Busybodov, An International Masterpiece, 3rd ed., trans. A.
Native Speaker, ed. Clever Fellow (Strange City: Publisher, 1996), 180.
```

Subsequent reference:

```
    6. Busybodov, 247.
```

Subsequent references to more than one work with the same authorship:

```
    8. Busybody and Spratt, Our Opinions, 157.

    9. Busybody and Spratt, More Opinions, 86.
```

3. *Informative note.* You may use footnotes for incidental information and comments. If you need to include a reference, you may work it into your discussion.[12]

```
    12. In My Opinions on the Subject of this Book (New York: Publisher, 1952),
M. S. Busybody.
```

without being there. You invite someone else to communicate with you while you send in your place a substitute, someone you think is more valuable than yourself. And, of course, you are wasting somebody's money, not getting what you can from your education.

Dumb plagiarism, the garden variety, is easy to fall into. It is not conscious and deliberate—but it may well earn you a failing grade just the same. The dumb plagiarist simply does not appreciate what it means to put one's name on a piece of writing. Producing an essay in your name means that the writing is yours, and your writing includes both what you are saying and how you say it. It is a matter of expression (phrasing, sentence form, and so forth) and structural strategy (opening, development, conclusion, transitions, and the like), but also of thought and information.

Now, you may very well have got your information from research, and your thoughts may well have been influenced by critics you have read. One of the facts you know may be what Kazin said about Rome in *The Marble Faun.* On the one hand, when you have learned something, it is your knowledge, and when you have pondered possible opinions and accepted some, they become your opinions as well. In both ways, you have a right and a need to speak for yourself in your own voice. But on the other hand, it is both courtesy and truth in merchandising to clearly acknowledge your help. Clear truths and generally accepted facts need not be documented, but the specific results of a scholar's research must be. Also, it keeps your head clear if you note where you have gleaned your main information on, say, Shakespeare's early life or the Brontë family relationships. The vague sort of opinion that a book is a good one need not be documented, but a viewpoint or conclusion that is peculiar to another writer's argument should be. Of course, you need to recognize the difference between information and opinion in order to integrate either one meaningfully into your discussion.

Many people fall heedlessly into plagiarism by taking sloppy notes during research. It is essential to make clear to your later self what you are taking down verbatim and what you are summarizing or paraphrasing. You may think, when you are writing, that a phrase or sentence is your own when it isn't. An understandable error by your later self, but at least one of these selves is guilty of plagiarism.

A little trickier is the problem of presentation: how to write up material from sources so it is yours *and* you are being honest. The rule is simple: *Really* paraphrase or *really* quote—or combine the two while keeping the difference clear. And remember paraphrase means speaking in your terms in your way. You are not even to follow the sentence structure of the original. You do not change words one by one.

Here is a fairly difficult example. In a book on *Beowulf,* the scholar Edward B. Irving, Jr., introduces a topic that he calls "embedding":

The socially embedded character is all matrix, a locked together package, at the appropriate points wired into essential relationships and identifying connections.

One thing you can do is what I just did. State simply and truthfully what you know to be so: "In a book on *Beowulf,* Irving writes . . . ," and supply the quote. It is a pithy sentence, with a couple of nice metaphors, and it is worth quoting—though because it is so technical it should be followed by explanation and by illustration. If you quote too much, however, you will not be writing an essay yourself. You will be stitching together a patchwork quilt. You should be able to restate the concept in your own way, something like this:

In one style of characterization, the characters are portrayed predominantly within the conventions of their society.

You can precede this with "As Irving argues . . ." or "To follow Edward Irving's distinction . . . ," not letting yourself repeat over and again the basic "Irving says . . ." After the paraphrase you might add, "Irving calls this form of stylization 'embedding'"(65)—if your citations follow MLA style. To paraphrase like this, it may help if you forget about the passage for a while, once you have read it carefully, then write out freshly what it meant to you, finally checking to make sure you are not too close to the original. It's all right to lose some aspect of the thought, just so you are conveying what Professor Irving actually meant. However, to integrate his thinking more closely, you can lift a key phrase or two and "embed" them into your own sentence (using quotation marks, of course):

One kind of character, whom Irving calls "socially embedded," is, in his words, "all matrix," coming to us as an individualized picture of the society (65).

Edward Irving describes one kind of character as "all matrix." We see such a character strictly in the terms of his culture, "wired into essential relationships and identifying connections" that typify the society he represents. This manner of characterization Irving calls "embedding" (65).

What you are not to do is this:

The "embedded" person is entirely connections, an interlocked whole, connected in the right places to necessary connections that identify him.

This may take some intelligence, but it is a word game, not writing. It switches around some words and substitutes one expression directly for another. Even if you attribute the thought to Irving with a clear and correct citation, the expression is not yet yours. Technically, you are still perpetrating plagiarism. Notice, furthermore, how hard it is to make such a sentence nicely readable without redoing it altogether—and how many options you have to do things differently.

In Conclusion: The Perfect Beginning

I want to end with a tip. I am reluctant to mention it, because it sounds suspiciously like a formula and shouldn't. You should discover it as a focus, I suppose, after you have thought your subject through. Looking at the sample openings earlier in this chapter, I see happily that some of my students were working this way even though I wasn't explicit on the theme in those days. Nevertheless, the point may drive home much of what I've been trying to convey in this book. It is about the most important aspect of critical writing—what the essay is saying—but it is also a matter of how you work out your thoughts according to your insight. And it does seem to make a good finale for me that can be a good overture for you. So here goes.

The best thesis is a paradox. Why? Because, first of all, good literature commonly expresses a paradoxical view of life, and, secondly, because the techniques of literature are in themselves interestingly paradoxical. You are likely to want a thesis that grasps the story or poem's viewpoint or some feature of the way it works artistically.[6] You want to articulate your insight into the work's insight and into the way that the work conveys it.

And why, you may well ask, does literature gravitate toward paradoxical insights? Because life is itself paradoxical (a *predicament,* as I put it in Chapter 5), and significant literature usually concerns itself with the ways that this is so. We live by dying: That is the nature of mortality. We become more conscious by acknowledging our unconsciousness: That is the nature of the mind. We achieve wisdom by knowing our foolishness, strength by accepting vulnerability, courage by admitting fear. By trying too hard to tell the truth, we may deceive ourselves. Good and evil we often find, alas, inextricable, as

---

6. Your instructor may require an explicit thesis sentence for your essay. At any rate, if you have difficulty focusing your discussion, it is a very good idea to have one. As you probably learned in freshman composition, there are several ways you can present a thesis. You can start your essay with it, although that may seem too blunt. You can usually lead up to it by the middle or the end of the first paragraph or even at the start of the second. Often, it is enough if your thesis is implicit in the essay, just so it is clearly implicit. Your reader needs to get the point one way or another. A good thesis statement cannot be self-evident; it is controversial and risky, crying out for defense. That is why paradoxical theses can be especially strong: They sound tantalizingly illogical and need to be justified. Earlier in this chapter, I included some sample openings from student essays: You might look back at them now.

well as love and hate, desire and revulsion. Also male and female, the human
and the divine, rationality and the irrational. All such oppositions that civilization commonly teaches us to expect, literary vision blends back into their
primeval unity. We see such insights dramatized forcefully in Shakespeare's
great tragedies—most clearly in *King Lear*—but they emerge in lyric poetry
of all ages, in comedies and satires, in modern short stories and ancient epics.

And how does literature tell us such truth? It tells truth *paradoxically* by
telling lies: the lies of made-up stories, the lies of metaphor, the lies of dramatic overstatement. It gives us the vivid and urgent mélange of life, moreover, in little bits of vocal movement strung together and in lifeless marks
recorded on a page. It gives great passions in little sonnets, the arduous comprehension of dying in "plays." What is more, like all other forms of communication and all other social institutions, by shaping its particular truth
literature distorts some other truth, ignoring some aspect of life's paradoxes
that will strike another author in another age.

When, in the opening of a critical essay, you wish to focus upon a central
implication of *King Lear,* you might well develop such a thesis as this:

> Ultimately, Cordelia saves Lear by starting the course that leads to his
> complete disintegration.

For other essays you might write something of this sort:

> In *Death of a Salesman,* Willy Loman follows his lofty ideals to the point
> of death, showing us their utter meaninglessness.

> In his efforts to transcend all human knowledge, Dr. Faustus becomes a
> master of parlor tricks.

> Through simple words and childlike rhythms, Blake composes a bitter
> and sophisticated criticism of social institutions.

> The power of Marvell's great poem derives from the paradox that flesh is
> sensual for the same reason that it decays.

A variation on this kind of paradox thesis occurs in contrasts between appearance and revelation, or reversals of expectation: "Although such and such
seems to be the case, it eventually becomes clear that the truth is exactly the
opposite." Our hero must realize, very likely, the truth that he or she would
have been most dead set against.

> Young Goodman Brown's ordinary New England village, full of friendly
> Christian citizens, is the last place we would expect to find the Devil's
> playground.

> Young Goodman Brown, newly married to a pretty wife named Faith,
> has every reason to believe his trip into the forest of his soul will be a
> pleasant one.

Such expectation leads us inevitably to a "but in reality . . ." or "but in fact . . ." Reversals of this sort underlie the common pattern of narration in which a customary view of life is transformed, when resistance, in particular, yields to vulnerability. The change is the growth of insight that the author leads us through. It occurs typically as a transformation of consciousness in the main character, or sometimes in the narrator. The example of "Goodman" Brown reminds us that this pattern is a potent kind of irony.

As thesis sentences such paradoxes can actually structure your essay for you, because they tell you where you need to go and what you need to say. A paradox wants to be explained. In itself it raises all the questions your essay will answer. As you formulate the thesis, therefore, you may realize that it suggests how you will in fact organize your commentary upon it, giving you the basis for an outline. Very simply, you can first explain and demonstrate one side of the paradox, then the second, then the combination that is the logic of the paradox itself—and you have your conclusion, clinching your case.

Such theses have the obvious advantage of getting to the heart of a work's impact. Also, like the work itself, they are full of suggestive implications, waiting for you to develop them through concrete examples and explanations of their relevance. Since paradoxes are apparent self-contradictions, they are fraught with tension. The natural response to them is a kind of frustration: How can this be? Because these paradoxes are about the deepest themes and creative techniques of the work, they pick up the deepest power within it and allow you to carry some of that energy into your own writing. Just as the work is doing, you are grappling with essential mysteries of our lives. Like your author, you can write with some sense of urgency. So the happy critic is engaged in criticism with that strength of personality where intelligence and passion are, not so paradoxically, one.

A Postlude: Nietzsche on Style

The philosopher Friedrich Nietzsche was one of the greatest German prose stylists. In 1882 he composed the following principles of writing for Lou Salomé, a brilliant young woman who was an intimate friend.[7]

---

7. In Lou Salomé, *Nietzsche,* translated by Siegfried Mandel (Redding Ridge, CT: Black Swan Books, 1988), pp. 77f.

Toward the Teaching of Style

1

Of prime necessity is life: a style should *live*.

2

Style should be suited to the specific person with whom you wish to communicate. (The Law of *mutual relation*.)

3

First, one must determine precisely "what-and-what do I wish to say and *present*," before you may write. Writing must be mimicry.

4

Since the writer *lacks* many of the speaker's *means*, he must in general have for his model a *very expressive* kind of presentation; of necessity, the written copy will appear much paler.

5

The richness of life reveals itself through a *richness of gestures*. One must *learn* to feel everything—the length and retarding of sentences, inter-punctuations, the choice of words, the pausing, the sequence of arguments—like gestures.

6

Be careful with periods! [Meaning long complex sentences, which can be exceptionally ponderous in German.] Only those who have long duration of breath while speaking are entitled to periods. With most people, the period is a matter of affectation.

7

Style ought to prove that one *believes* in an idea; not only thinks it but also *feels* it.

8

The more abstract a truth which one wishes to teach, the more one must first *entice* the senses.

9

Strategy on the part of the good writer of prose consists of choosing his means for stepping close to poetry but *never* stepping into it.

10

It is not good manners or clever to deprive one's reader of the most obvious objections. It is very good manners and *very clever* to leave it to one's reader alone to pronounce the ultimate quintessence of our wisdom.

SOME POINTERS, REMINDERS, SUGGESTIONS, AND RULES
OF THUMB ON WRITING AND REVISING CRITICAL (AND
OTHER) ESSAYS

1. Speak for yourself. Your essay is your statement. You will have
to find your way to appropriate effectiveness in spite of all the
rules, formulas, and pointers. Use the first person as it makes
sense to do so and feels natural, but don't keep saying your
opinions are only your opinions. State them boldly: False modesty is occasionally tactful, but it is usually as impertinent as
arrogance.

2. Maintain an appropriate and consistent tone. For essay style it
will probably be balanced between the formal and the informal,
the personal and the impersonal. Essay style is a public style,
but it should be the personal "you" who is going public.

3. Colloquialism and slang are likely to break the tone that you
have set for such a subject. Find words that accurately "fit"
what you want to say. Such words are likely to be vivid and
to let you observe nuance.

4. Select a topic that you can handle adequately within the as-
signed length, so that you need neither to pad nor overgeneral-
ize. For critical essays you will focus on a specific and limited
aspect of the work; however, you should discuss it in such a
way that you can give some sense of the work as a whole as
you see it.

5. Give your essay a title that is as specific as your thesis and helps
establish your focus. Do not just use the name of the work, and
don't be too technical: "A Study of Imagery in *The Waste Land* as
Compared with the Imagery in *Finnegans Wake*." Your title
should attract interest. It should also start your reader's thinking process. The title is part of the essay.

6. If the basis of your essay is a comparison, do not divide the essay in two if you can help it but maintain a dual focus. And
keep clear the terms of your comparison: To say "A cow gives
milk, but a chicken has two legs" is not to make a comparison.

7. As a rule, let generalizations grow out of specifics. Let specifics
illustrate broader points. In using examples, be sure that you
explain their point. Qualify any suspicious generalizations or
bold claims that you cannot reasonably justify.

8. Check for common faults of rhetoric: faulty reference of pronouns, faulty parallelism, excessive coordination, preposition strings, choppy sentence movement, shifts in tense and point of view, faulty agreement, general awkwardness.

9. Avoid mechanical procedures and formulas: "Here is what the author says about. . . ." "Another sentence I found meaningful is. . . ." "Now I will discuss my next point." Do not settle for empty conclusions ("So we see that . . .") that repeat in summary what is already clear. Come to a natural resting place. At the end you should be somewhere you could not have been earlier.

10. Use the present tense in plot summary; the story is always happening now—except, of course, for flashbacks. Don't refer back to the time of reading: "I thought this image expressed . . ."

11. Indent prose quotations of more than four lines and poetry quotations of more than three lines, without using quotation marks. (Indentation for these should be one inch or ten spaces.) When quoting two or three lines of verse within a paragraph, use slashes to show the line breaks, spacing once on each side of the slash. Preserve capitals at the start of lines, if they are in the original. You don't need ellipsis marks (. . .) at the beginning of quotations. Don't expect incomplete quotations to stand alone grammatically just because they are in quotation marks. Integrate them logically and grammatically into your sentences, as you express your line of thought. Before an indented quote, should you end your lead-in with a colon, a period, a comma, or no punctuation at all? In most cases whichever one you would use if the quote were not indented.

12. Remember that a character delivers speeches and makes statements but does not *speak quotations*—unless quoting someone else. A character may be said to do or say something in a situation or at a turn of action ("In her first exchange with Creon, Antigone says . . ." but not on a page ("Antigone says on page 41 that . . ."). Unless you have a clear reason for doing so, place a subject in its dramatic context ("When Romeo sees Juliet alone at her window . . .") rather than in act and scene or chapter number ("In act two, scene two, Romeo . . ."). After quoting from a play, you should give act, scene, and line number, in parentheses (either IV,ii,2 or 4.2.2).

Continued

13. Many people automatically "stick in" a comma before *and* when it is followed by a verb: "He read the poem, and eagerly composed his essay about it." A principle is being half-remembered: A comma separates two independent clauses joined with *and, but,* or another of the coordinating conjunctions. When no subject appears after the conjunction, however, there is no second independent clause. Hence, no comma. "He read the poem and eagerly composed. . . ." There is one subject here and two verbs relying on it: He *read* and *composed.* For very short independent clauses, the comma may also be left out: "He came and he saw and he conquered."

14. Similarly, don't let a comma split a pair of *correlatives: both . . . and, either . . . or, this . . . rather than that, not only . . . but.* In each case, the contrast makes up one thought.

15. Use italics or underlining for titles of plays, novels, and periodicals (complete publications); use quotation marks for titles of poems, stories, essays, and chapters (parts of publications).

16. Observe plurals derived from Greek and Latin, remembering that they *are* plurals: *media, criteria, phenomena.*

17. Avoid (1) the influence of casual spoken usage, as in "should of" (for "should have"), "suppose to" (for "supposed to"), and "as good of a poem" (for "as good a poem"); (2) the colloquial second person when you are not speaking directly to your reader: "This poem is about what you do with your life"; (3) "like" for "as" or "as though"; (4) "etc." when you are not actually making a list: "He was excited, happy, etc."; (4) "vs." or "versus" in ordinary prose style ("His choice was school vs. a job"); (5) the unnecessarily abstract passive. Remember the elegant subjunctive voice for wishes ("I wish I *were* going . . ." and for statements contrary to fact ("If I *were* going . . ."). Please don't use *fun* as an adjective. A usage that is fast becoming acceptable is the plural pronoun referring back to singular nouns or pronouns: "Everybody finds *their* own solution." "Neither Jack nor Jill knew what *they* were doing." Most English teachers remain wary of it, though. Avoid the superfluous *end* result, often times. A reason is *that,* not because.

18. Do not identify your pronouns parenthetically: "When he (Jim) was about to leave. . . ." Do not let pronouns refer back to the previous paragraph. Don't let a pronoun refer to a possessive. The possessive is weaker than the subject of a clause (some regard it as an adjective), so such a reference is somewhat awkward. Thus, instead of "In Shakespeare's play *Hamlet*, he . . . ," write "In his play *Hamlet*, Shakespeare . . . ," which is a little more dramatic. Don't talk about characters without letting us know who they are, unless they are as well-known as Hamlet or Macbeth.

19. Keep a list of your favorite spelling mistakes. Remember these old stinkers: *dilemma, occurring, lonely, villain, desperate, (in)dependent, definite, fulfill, tendency, (pre)dominant; already, all ready, all right; proceed, precede; discrete, discreet; except, accept; playwright, playwriting; effect, affect; on to, onto.*

20. Avoid short and punchy journalistic paragraphs. Try for smooth transitions from one paragraph to another. Don't let a new paragraph sound as though you are starting all over again.

21. To avoid the impression of sexism, you may want to say "he or she," but avoid the awkwardness of "he/she" and the unpronounceable "[s]he." The problem can usually be prevented by using the plural. This is a situation in which discreet use of the passive can be worthwhile. The pronoun "one" can help.

22. Don't trust spell-check. It will not catch names, missing words, and homonyms (*discreet-discrete, their-there*). Or faulty grammar! It is certainly no substitute for judicious revision. It tempts you to abandon control over your text.

Appendix I

Contemporary Approaches to Criticism

In recent decades, many academic critics have specialized in particular ways of interpreting literature, depending upon their philosophic convictions. I have chosen not to call these approaches "theories" because I have not noticed that practitioners (including myself) regard their rationales as particularly theoretical. Some of these approaches overlap and can be combined. There are other ways of studying literature, of course, the most important being literary history, which includes the study of influences, and biographical criticism, which shows how a work may reflect its author's life and personality. Critics still interpret literature as an element in the "history of ideas" and as a means of exploring religious or ethical themes. One need not belong to a "school of thought," of course, to interpret (or enjoy) what one reads. In this Appendix, I have suggested ways in which adherents of various contemporary approaches might (not necessarily the ways that they *would*) interpret Grace Paley's short story "Debts."

DEBTS

Grace Paley

A lady called me up today. She said she was in possession of her family archives. She had heard I was a writer. She wondered if I would help her write about her grandfather, a famous innovator and dreamer of the Yiddish theater. I said I had already used every single thing I knew about the Yiddish theater to write one story, and I didn't have time to learn any more, then write about it. There is a long time in me between knowing and telling. She offered a share of the profits, but that is something too inorganic. It would never rush her grandfather's life into any literature I could make.

The next day, my friend Lucia and I had coffee and we talked about this woman. Lucia explained to me that it was probably hard to have family archives or even only stories about outstanding grandparents or uncles when one was sixty or seventy and there was no writer in the family and the children were in the middle of their own lives. She said it was a pity to lose all this inheritance just because of one's own mortality. I said yes, I did understand. We drank more coffee. Then I went home.

I thought about our conversation. Actually, I owed nothing to the lady who'd called. It was possible that I did owe something to my own family and the families of my friends. That is, to tell their stories as simply as possible, in order, you might say, to save a few lives.

Because it was her idea, the first story is Lucia's. I tell it so that some people will remember Lucia's grandmother, also her mother, who in this story is eight or nine.

The grandmother's name was Maria. The mother's name was Anna. They lived on Mott Street in Manhattan in the early 1900s. Maria was married to a man named Michael. He had worked hard, but bad luck and awful memories had driven him to the Hospital for the Insane on Welfare Island.

Every morning Anna took the long trip by trolley and train and trolley again to bring him his hot dinner. He could not eat the meals at the hospital. When Anna rode out of the stone streets of Manhattan over the bridge to the countryside of Welfare Island, she was always surprised. She played for a long time on the green banks of the river. She picked wildflowers in the fields, and then she went up to the men's ward.

One afternoon, she arrived as usual. Michael felt very weak and asked her to lean on his back and support him while he sat at the edge of the bed eating dinner. She did so, and that is how come, when he fell back and died, it was in her thin little arms that he lay. He was very heavy. She held him so, just for a minute or two, then let him fall to the bed. She told an orderly and went home. She didn't cry because she didn't like him. She spoke first to a neighbor, and then together they told her mother.

Now this is the main part of the story:

The man Michael was not her father. Her father had died when she was little. Maria, with the other small children, had tried to live through the hard times in the best way. She moved in with different, nearly related families in the neighborhood and worked hard helping out in their houses. She worked well, and it happened that she was also known for the fine bread she baked. She would live in a good friend's house for a while baking magnificent bread. But soon, the husband of the house would say, "Maria bakes wonderful bread. Why can't you learn to bake bread like that?" He would probably then seem to admire her in other ways. Wisely, the wife would ask Maria to please find another home.

One day at the spring street festival, she met a man named Michael, a relative of friends. They couldn't marry because Michael had a wife in Italy. In order to live with him, Maria explained the following truths to her reasonable head:

1. This man Michael was tall with a peculiar scar on his shoulder. Her husband had been unusually tall and had had a scar on his shoulder.
2. This man was redheaded. Her dead husband had been redheaded.
3. This man was a tailor. Her husband had been a tailor.
4. His name was Michael. Her husband had been called Michael.

In this way, persuading her own understanding, Maria was able to not live alone at an important time in her life, to have a father for the good of her children's character, a man in her bed for comfort, a husband to serve. Still and all, though he died in her arms, Anna, the child, didn't like him at all. It was a pity, because he had always called her "my little one." Every day she had visited him, she had found him in the hallway waiting, or at the edge of his white bed, and she had called out, "Hey, Zio, here's your dinner. Mama sent it. I have to go now."

Textual Criticism

These approaches all look to the work itself as a written text and interpret it in its own term. They differ radically, however, in what they take its terms to be.

Formalism

Formerly called the "New Criticism," and sometimes known as "rhetorical criticism," formalism interprets literature primarily by explication, paying close attention to matters of style, figures of speech, symbolism, irony, and structure. The meaning of each work is seen in its imaginative use of techniques, the particular ways in which it uses language. The critic will consider the work as a product composed of words and images, existing in itself as a unified whole, without needing outside information to be understood.

The most obvious feature of Paley's style is its apparent lack of style. The story avoids eloquence, metaphor, the evolution of plot, and the usual procedures of character development. This studied lack of technique is, of course, a technique in itself, consistent and effective. It can be described as minimalist. The sentence structure is simplistic, even childish, yet it contributes to an ironically sophisticated view of life. Events that would ordinarily be considered tragic are reported casually in a brash, irreverent manner, depriving them of any special importance, but we feel that importance anyway. Life struggles that might have been explored in sympathetic detail are summarized in a couple of lines, barely acknowledging (it would seem) the characters' inner lives. We are given bare glimpses only of where the characters are right now, but those glimpses see deeply into a sense of lives lived. The order of events is peculiar: We are told first the brief story of Anna and Michael, then we are given the "main" story of her mother, Maria, then at the end we are given a brief exchange of dialogue between Michael and Maria that gives the whole triad of relationships their meaning. When the author-narrator explains Maria's reason for living with Michael, we are given a list. The narration has a gum-chewing sense of no-nonsense toughness, yet all this avoidance is clearly a technique of ironical understatement. Paley's characters are caught up in mute feelings, but the feelings are apparent, paradoxically, even intensified, through their avoidance. The restraint of the author's style bespeaks the restraint with which her characters must live. Her observation of their lives takes in their bewilderment and pain; she expresses it in a tone of tactful respect.

Although the style is not figurative, two metaphors dominate the story. The first is the notion of debts itself. The author writes out of a sense of debt; the character Anna must live indebted to the stepfather she failed to appreciate; we are all indebted to our immigrant forebears; readers and writers are also all indebted to each other; perhaps all human relationships are a form of debt, all life a way of paying debts. In the second part of the story, the name of Welfare Island echoes ironically over the character Michael's lack of welfare. This island suggests Ellis Island, the first stopping place for immigrants who arrived for their welfare only to find much hardship awaiting them. In a broader sense and with sharper irony, Manhattan itself is a "welfare island," where people live dependent upon public charity because well-being is so scarce in their lives. Anna's story culminates in the powerful symbolic image of Michael falling dead in the girl's unwilling arms, expressing the true intimacy that had always been there between them. Early in "Debts," the author-narrator tells us she will write "you might say, to save a few lives." The theme that literature perpetuates lives is at least as old as Shakespeare's sonnets, but here an off-handed pun gives it a fresh poignance. Telling the stories is life-saving because it preserves not just the memory but the value of lives; though the lives are gone, they can still be given meaning through the compassion of repayment. Although Paley's tone is superficially casual, therefore, it reflects an urgent pathos about the writer's task.

Structuralism

The structuralist passes by stylistics and characterization to disclose underlying patterns of signs, particularly in key words, expressions, or images that reflect significant values, interests, or intentions. These patterns carry the text's meaning in their relationships. The patterns recur in stories of a set type (such as fairy tales or detective stories), with variations in each instance. Commonly, a story or poem is shown to present conflicting signs which it must reconcile, perhaps in a further sign or sign group.

At the beginning of "Debts," the author turns her back on an old woman who wishes to memorialize her dead grandfather. At the end of the story, Anna turns away from her step-father and his offer of affection. The opening sets up a structure, therefore, that suggests a theme about the limits of human communion, a limit reaching perhaps to a kind of betrayal. In the middle part of the story, Maria's friends dismiss her when their husbands show too much appreciation. Thus we have a sequence of characters who are alone because of rejecting others or because of being rejected. How does the story interpret this asocial predicament?

First of all, by the act of storytelling. This provides a kind of sharing, although in literature it is still a sharing among solitaries, writers and readers far from each other. The old woman at the beginning says her theatrical grandfather was both an "innovator and a dreamer." The innovator is creative in practical ways, changing old things to new. The dreamer, on the other hand, lives in memory and in fantasy, dissolving time. Thus, the artist integrates opposing functions. Grace Paley will remember by telling (what was) and by imagining (what might have been); and she will negotiate in the world to produce her story in her own original way.

Later in the story, we have several significant images. Maria is the familiarly humble, naive serving maid, but she is not rewarded for her good faith, implying by contrast a vision of social justice that is not to be. She is also the traditional wife loyal to her husband after his death, but she shows her loyalty by taking another man because he repeats the most superficial qualities of the first. She recreates her husband through his signs: name, red hair, and so forth.

The main part of the story sets images of food (bread baking and Michael's dinners) against the river bank, wildflowers, and a sense of latent sexuality. We have the conscious efforts of civilization opposing the given reality of nature. The images of food and flowers also denote two kinds of sensual experience: physical nurture and spiritual. The food is prepared for need and it is consumed; the flowers are enjoyed and left, giving life value. To integrate these two sides of life, we require a third sign, which would be some image of love. What we get is the dead Michael in Anna's arms, an image of tensions that cannot be resolved, remaining in the realm of "debt." Anna does not bring Maria's dinner with love. The husbands' response to Maria's bread leads only to jealousy. The flowers emphasize what Anna cannot have. Only in the author's acceptance of responsibility can the frustration be assuaged. As she turns her back, she faces us, letting us pay our own debts to the past as we read.

Deconstruction

Deconstruction (often identified with "poststructuralism") challenges the surface meaning of language and the impression that literary forms have given values. It opposes in particular the formalist pursuit of unity in a work's structure and meaning—or any definitive coherence, or "closure." Structures, seen as artificial, are dismantled so that the basic instability of existence can be revealed. Specific words and images are shown to contradict the author's presumed intention. Through analysis of characters and narrators, the unity of personality itself is shown to be an illusion. Attention is paid to works that themselves "deconstruct" the familiar conventions of literature and the ordinary sense of what truth is. As in most approaches that have opposed formalism, deconstruction rejects the "privileged" authority of any particular meanings, intentions, or values in the work.

This story demonstrates that the technique of narrative can only produce an illusion of dealing with a presumably real world. The indeterminate author (Grace Paley or a fictional narrator or Grace Paley playing author?) begins by telling us *about* a story she is not going to tell us, leaving us with the void of lost life. She then proceeds to pay a "debt" by remembering someone else. Repayment should suggest a satisfaction achieved, but remembering others' pain prolongs the pain, so we may wonder whether the concept of debts is only the pretense of a solution. The author repays the debt for another person by calling upon us, as readers, to "remember" people we have never known—that even the author has never known. Undoubtedly, the friend's memory—like all memory—is as much her own creation as it is knowledge. Thus the author is paying a serious debt and preserving a real life through means that deny either that there is any coherent reality to be preserved or any valid means to preserve it.

The text that follows deconstructs the myth of literary reality by refusing to follow the conventions of fiction—in style, characterization, or plotting. We are simply given bare facts and are left to make our own story out of them. The "facts" may even be contradictory: We are first told Maria is married to Michael, then we are told she is not. The ordering of events is haphazard, as though we get them as they happen to occur to the author's mind: We are given first the later story of the child, then her mother's; we are told this is the main story but have no idea why we should think so. Maria's list of reasons for living with Michael deprives both feeling and logic of any substance. It is, of course, a joke that she is speaking to "her reasonable head."

Thus we may wonder whether there *is* such a thing as a story to be told—or whether there are only confused impulses without any clear relation to each other. All three characters are unknowable. We build readily upon the "facts," but we must realize how eager we are to think we *know.* Michael is hospitalized for insanity, but he behaves reasonably and even affectionately toward Anna, who responds toward him as though he were not there. Maria is strangely loyal to her first husband by taking, out of marriage, another man who is supposedly just like him. (Did the first Michael also die insane?) When Anna gives Michael his food, she sounds curt but she may be speaking in a friendly way. She may even be speaking provocatively towards him. At the end, she may be responsible for his death and she may not be. We may believe that she should feel guilty, but we have no reason to believe she does. We are left with our inability to know the truth of people's lives, our inability to know if there is any truth to know. The picture of Michael falling dead in Anna's arms is a grim joke and an ambiguous sign: an image of love where there is no love, suggesting knowledge where there is none. The story itself suggests that both writing and living are performed in guilt, to repay "debts," but we do not know if these debts are real or if they are themselves fictions by which we motivate ourselves.

Contextual Criticism

This broad term covers several types of interpretation that see literature as the inevitable expression of social forces, forces that may be depicted overtly in the work or that may be unspoken but implicit. Such critics look for factors that determine how the author portrays life, including cultural limitations and prejudices.

Historical Criticism

Historical critics investigate the cultural context of the work, including social institutions and political events. They interpret the work according to knowledge about what was going on in the world at the time it was written or the time it is taking place.

> "Mott Street in Manhattan in the early 1900s" was at the heart of the crowded immigrant community of lower New York, where Italian, Jewish, and other newcomers struggled side by side and often in conflict. The prelude to the story refers to the author's own background as the daughter of Jewish immigrants (a fact reflected in many of Paley's other stories); however, here she reaches out to her Italian-American friend to tell the story of *her* mother and immigrant grandmother, bridging the gap between Americans of different origin. The story reflects the hard lives of most of the immigrants, their struggles to earn a living, to raise children born in a world very unlike their own in a family split apart, so that ways of living have to be reinvented. We see Maria forced to work for one family after another, in spite of or, to her confusion, because of her household skills. We see Michael's failure to adjust to the new life. We see Anna growing up with an independence she is not ready to handle. When Michael dies insane and falls upon her, we see the old world giving way to the new but wonder whether, in this next generation at least, the new will succeed in making the transition.

The New Historicism

This approach brings to the text specialized knowledge about political and other social circumstances of the period when the work was written, information usually from popular arts, legal documents, business records, or other sources likely to be overlooked by the history books. It challenges the traditional view of history as events of state, large-scale movements, and the careers of major figures. For "Debts," this critic might do some research into marriage conventions among immigrants of this community and may turn up something interesting about conditions at Welfare Island, such as the nature of mental illnesses that were treated or perhaps what the food was like.

Marxist Criticism

Marxist critics emphasize the economic factors underlying the society depicted and its class structure, showing how they affect the portrayal of characters and events and the expression of values. They study authors who them-selves attack social injustice, but also they argue that the power structure of capitalist society implies an ideology that influences traditional writers unconsciously.

The Italian immigrants arrive (probably) from a peasant or village life in Europe, where they lived in poverty of a predictable kind, trapped in the traditional lifestyle dominated by an aristocracy. America prom-ises mobility, but requires competition that is often devastating—to fam-ily life as well as to the individual. Like the old-world order, the capitalist system concentrates money and power in the few at the top, but in the capitalist system, the few have risen at the expense of the multitude. Maria struggles desperately to understand the new life as well as to survive in it and provide a decent existence for her daughter. Her family life is impossible, however, her personal satisfaction not to be thought of. She cannot even begin to understand the larger forces she is caught up in—forces that prevail only because of the blindness in its mass of victims like herself. Maria's daughter, Anna, may have the New World in front of her, but she is a broken child, unable to return affec-tion and scarred by poverty. When she goes to feed Michael at his hospi-tal, she glimpses a world of flowers and fields that should be humanly satisfying, but it is not for her: She must return to the reality of the oppressive slums. As we see her briefly holding the dead Michael, we understand how poverty has deprived her of childhood and forced her into a dreadfully serious world alone and unprepared.

Feminist Criticism

Feminist critics study literature with special attention to the roles of women in society and in literary creations. On a basic level, they will focus upon the way a work characterizes girls and women, often exposing the prej-udices of male authors and male-dominated society. They emphasize the con-tributions of women writers, especially those who may have been underrated in the past, and advance works that portray female characters with sympathy and understanding.

Deprived of education, Maria must survive by doing for others the housework that has been her lot since she was a child. Although she excels in this, especially in providing the bread that should be the center of a family's well-being, she is continually rejected when men who can-not relate positively to their own wives put her in a position where she must compete with them. The men degrade their wives by praising Ma-ria's baking, and the women sense they are caught in a sexual rivalry as well. Paley claims they "wisely" ask her to leave: The word expresses just the right tension between their self-protection, their discretion, and their awareness of the masculine innuendo. In spite of her rejections, Maria's natural goodness and strength carry her through hardships that neither her husband nor Michael survive. Still, alone with her daughter in this difficult and vulnerable state, she assumes that she needs a man in her life. Knowing society does not recognize the kind of relationship available to her, she must resort to self-deceptive logic that makes something natural enough seem very strange. It is the woman who must rationalize, of course, not the man. When Michael is hospitalized, he cannot adapt to American food, and she must maintain what link he still has to the Old World by sending him dinners. When her daughter Anna takes the food to him, the child shows a natural response to nature that suggests the sensitive person she might become, but she too must live in service. Michael offers her affection, but he does so only out of his own need; this can only increase the confusion she feels about her mother's relationship with him. When he dies, she will be left feeling guilty although her own needs have never been addressed. He has fallen dead upon her, his unwanted weight a burden she will always remember. Supporting his lifeless body, she is forced into a womanly position beyond her years.

Cultural History

Critics following this general approach explain a work in terms of the values and interests of the day and the literary and social movements to which the author responded.

"Debts" reflects four movements of the later twentieth century that have influenced American literature: multiculturalism, feminism, political activism, and postmodernism. The daughter of Russian-Jewish immigrant parents, Paley has retained a strong interest in her own roots and those of other ethnicities as well, focusing closely upon the lives of immigrants and the lives of their children. In this story she reaches out to an Italian-American friend to help preserve through literature her family's past in the process of their Americanization. "Debts" is, therefore, an image of America—its diversity but also its unity in the common experience of living alongside one another during the difficult phase of cultural transition.

The story brings special attention to the plight of women living in hardship and to the line of heritage from mother to daughter. The author writes the story to help her friend pay a debt to her own mother and grandmother. She shows how they struggled to survive in a strange and overwhelming world. In the process, the author is confirming a bond among women and a commitment to literature as a means of exploring and commemorating women's lives. The deep concern for women's roles in American life is part of a broader concern for problems of social inequality. Paley has balanced her life as a writer with an energetic personal commitment to political activism, participating in the civil rights and antiwar movements as well as the struggle for women's rights. It is not surprising, therefore, that her stories reflect the values of social justice and sympathy for cultural minorities.

The style of writing Paley has developed to express her social and political values adopts many of the characteristics of postmodernism. This artistic movement has side-stepped or reversed many of the traits of traditional literary form, which expressed social, religious, political, and even technological assumptions that can no longer be taken for granted. These assumptions have included the dominance of European culture (Eurocentrism) and of masculine authority. Postmodern style has given writers such as Grace Paley, therefore, a sense of liberation, a freedom to find forms of expression true to their own experience. In conventional fiction we expect a coherent development of character and event. In such incidents as Michael's death, Paley casts events abruptly before us in an almost off-handed manner, as if to say they are trivial and important at the same time and beyond people's comprehension anyway. Michael's death also shows the masculine order, now old and helpless, its rationality gone, yielding to the young spirit of female potentiality.

Psychological Criticism

Most often, this means a focus on the psyche of characters, but psychologically oriented critics may also discuss an author's personality or symbolic aspects of the work itself. I am including under this heading "reader-response criticism," which studies the psychology of reading. Psychological critics may apply to literature the theories of any psychologist, but Sigmund Freud and C. G. Jung have been most influential. This type of criticism elicits unconscious factors motivating people and coloring their lives. It may reveal unresolved tensions that are worked out in the characters' story or in the author's process of writing. Seeing beneath the surface may give the reader insights unavailable to the characters themselves or their creators.

Psychoanalytic Criticism

Psychoanalytic (or Freudian) critics explain character motivation by unconscious family rivalries and/or repressed erotic fantasies. They often speak of the Oedipus complex, in which one wishes to replace the same-sex parent (perhaps by death) in order to fully enjoy the other parent's love. A story or poem may express psychological tensions unresolved in the author's unconscious mind, projecting perhaps the author's own "family drama."

Maria is an unconscious temptress, entering other households to "bake bread" (read "make children") and coming between the two parent figures until she is rejected by the wife because of her sexuality. For self-preservation, she chooses a man who will mirror her dead husband (symbolically, her father) but cannot marry him because he has a wife in distant Italy (her dead mother). Her insecurity masks aggression toward the men she is dependent upon, but she must feel that she cannot afford to recognize it. Her unconsciousness is emphasized by her transparent rationalization of the relationship. As a result of this neurosis, the relationship is, of course, impossible. Michael, her lover, is impotent in it and dies mentally ill. Maria's young daughter Anna is attracted to Michael, but is repelled by him because of her inevitable guilt. Aside from being her mother's lover, he has replaced Anna's father. When he is hospitalized, Maria cannot deal with his need and steps aside, allowing Anna to stand in for her. It is not surprising, therefore, that Michael offers Anna love, however he intends it to be taken. After plucking flowers in sexual fantasy, Anna goes to his bed, entering the realm of madness. In spite of her conscious resistance, she gives him sustenance. He dies "in her arms." This expresses sexual satisfaction and sterility at the same time. Through her fantasy, she can be said to kill him, out of the guilt she feels for replacing her mother. Anna's sexual awakening in adolescence is painfully thwarted, and she will probably relate to men out of guilt for the rest of her life.

Archetypal Criticism

Archetypal critics, who are often followers of Carl Jung (see footnote on p. 140), identify and interpret underlying patterns or rhythms of experience or categories of symbolism (the *archetypes*) that suggest universal dimensions of human nature. One aspect of archetypal criticism should be known as *mythography:* It compares a story to specific traditional myths or folktales, seeing the work at hand as a variation on some recurrent theme or motif inherent in the unconscious mind.

At the start of the story, the author presents herself in the position of a priestess, to whom supplicants come. They may not exactly wish to placate their ancestors, but they do seek relief from a responsibility they feel for their dead. We can even note that it is quite literally redemption, a paying of debts, that they are looking for. The author defines her role ambiguously as "saving lives." Writing for her is a healing ritual, and she performs it by reciting, in ritual fashion, unelaborated main points of the family's myth. In the story a young girl, Anna, takes a daily journey across water to an island, to bring sustenance to an ailing stepfather. One day, the routine is broken by the stepfather's sudden death at her side. The journey proves to be an initiation into the knowledge of mortality. Anna is like the children in folktales who journey into the woods, strange places dominated by dangerous figures: She *feels* threatened by Michael even though he speaks kindly to her. Anna is also like the Greek heroes who make passage over a river to the realm of the dead. "Welfare Island" is a place of insanity, illness, and death but also the fertility of flowering fields, where she loves to play. Away from the stifling world of the city, Anna experiences the conflicting pull between life and death, love and fear, childhood and maturity. Symbolically, the island suggests the unconscious mind, where dissolution and creation are integrated in each other. The Greek maiden Persephone is carried off to the Underworld by its overlord Hades, who claims her as his wife. He takes her from her mother's protection, and she comes back to her mother later with an adult knowledge of mortality. Persephone, in fact, is taken away while she is gathering wildflowers.

At the end of Anna's story, we see her as a failed Madonna holding the dead Christ in her arms: Michael has offered her love and has died in her indifference. Anna is left, however, with the possibility of what Jung calls *individuation,* or genuine emotional development, if she can integrate the guilt she feels about Michael and accept him as a father that she had refused to acknowledge. If we take this as an archetypal tale, we must note that it is a partly ironic one. If Anna is a version of Persephone, for example, her mother does not know she is lost (in emotional conflict) and does not search for her (as occurs in the Greek myth). This Persephone must find her own way back to the realm of daily life. She must await her incarnation in Grace Paley's story to be "saved."

Reader-Response Criticism

Reader-response critics argue that meaning lies not in the text but in the reader's experience of it. For some reader-response critics an appropriate response will depend upon identifiable features of the work, perhaps identifying with an "ideal reader" imagined by the author. For others, the text has no given meaning but will be understood variously according to the experience of each reader. In the process of reading, they argue, we all create the meaning for ourselves.

The story "Debts" reminds us how little we can know of other people's lives—how little, in fact, they can know of their own. Yet we experience in the story something that is touchingly there in the un-known realm. Paley leaves most of the story to our imagination. We fill in the characters' feelings, and therefore their personalities, with our own conjectures and our assumptions about human nature. We experi-ence, for example, a painful gulf between Anna and Michael. Although she is only a child, we can feel that she knows he is offering her affection that she would like to accept, yet she does cover up her feelings in a show of indifference and in procrastination among the flowers. We have been feeling sad for him, especially because he has had a breakdown from "bad luck and awful memories." Now we share the pain of his iso-lation. But she too is isolated. We understand her childish behavior—her sense of being stifled in a dreary world without play—and know she cannot afford to understand or appreciate him. But we are pained by her cruelty just the same. When he dies "in her arms," we are left with the knowledge she must now have a little more sharply in her own con-sciousness: she does love him after all. Their distance is bridged physi-cally only when it cannot be acknowledged personally. The story ends with a sense of "debts" that can never be paid, a desolate feeling that people are trapped in their own private needs, which leave them un-judgeable, unreachable, and unable to know how they can live.

Appendix 2

Sample Student Essays

A Comparison Between Poems

DYLAN THOMAS'S WOMB AND TOMB

Cynthia O'Neal

A versatile poet, Dylan Thomas wrote of love, death, the fears and joys of life, and the wonder and awe of childhood. In much of Thomas's poetry there is a profound sense of preoccupation with life and death and their relationship to each other, as well as their connection with the ever-present aspect of Time. Two poems that illustrate this are "Twenty-Four Years" and "Fern Hill."

"Twenty-Four Years" deals with a sense of doubleness found in Thomas' poetry—of womb and tomb as both life and death. It abounds with contradictory images of life in death and death in life. At the age of twenty-four, probably on his birthday, the speaker is moved by the fact that all life leads, ultimately, to death.

The womb/tomb idea is prevalent throughout, beginning with the parenthetical second line. The "grave" that the dead "walk" to could be the womb, and thus the womb as tomb. This idea is reinforced by the use of the word "labour," which could mean either hard work or the pains of childbirth.

The speaker "crouches" in the "natural doorway" (once again, the womb image) and, as embryo/tailor, sews a shroud (sack for baby within womb) for his journey, that is, life. These few lines are paradoxical in that they portray birth as the first step towards death, and this death is achieved only through life. We must live in order to die, and vice versa. "The light of the meat-eating sun" is Time, who leads us all in the "final direction" toward the "elementary town"—the basic, ultimate destination. The use of the verb "advance" in the last line shows courage and hope, as it implies a willingness to move forward toward destiny, rather than a sense of being pulled against the will.

The poem shows a deep concern for the self, and the "forever" of the last line has a positive, rather than negative, connotation. It could mean the "forever" of life after death, a very pleasant thought, or the "forever" of the human life cycle on Earth, which implies an acceptance of the life cycle of all humanity and an understanding of the fact that we all must die eventually. This latter idea is discouraging without the hopefulness of the former, which gives rise to the question: "What is the meaning of life?"

Similar to "Twenty-Four Years" but also a sharp contrast is the longer poem "Fern Hill." This poem, written about the summers spent as a boy on his aunt's farm, is a celebration of the delight of childhood as well as a realization of what it means to grow up and find that time "forever fled."

"Fern Hill" is not so much *about* childhood as it is about *what it was like* to be a child. It is also about what it is like to look back upon childhood as an adult. The language is not childlike, but rather reminiscent. It is clear from the biblical allusions in the second and fourth stanzas, as well as the revelatory sixth stanza, that the speaker is an adult, very well aware of the fact that time passes in the blink of an eye and our youth is gone before we know it.

The poem moves from a "young and easy" attitude in the first stanza, where the boy is oblivious to everything except his daily romps throughout the farm, to a realization in the last stanza of a paradise lost. Gone are the days when Time "let" him play. Gone also is the naiveté of youth that allows one to run his "heedless ways" and never even think about the passage of time.

The poem has a rhythmical quality that helps make it very different from "Twenty-Four Years." The tone is happy and light, and certain words are used to contain this tone: "happy," "lilting," "singing," "tunes," "tuneful," "songs," and "sang." The effect is a mixture of feelings evoking both the happy and carefree attitude of childhood and the sense of loss that one might feel as an adult looking back on his youth.

The colors in the poem also help to convey a youthful feeling. The two most prominent are green and gold, green suggesting youth, naiveté, inexperience, and finally (in the last stanza) a certain realization of the ignorance of death that accompanies youth ("Time held me green and dying"). The color gold in the poem is often associated with green ("green and golden"). Gold not only suggests youth, but also wealth, value, and pricelessness. Together these evoke an ironic sense of life—that we often go through life heedless of the passage of time and "wake" up later, "forever fled from the childless land."

The imagery of "Fern Hill" is strikingly different from that in "Twenty-Four Years." While the latter poem employs words like "shroud," "grave," "die," and "meat-eating" to conjure up images of gloom, the imagery of "Fern Hill" is much more pleasant. In this poem, the child is "young and easy" and "happy as the grass was green." He is "honored," "famous," royalty on this farm, his kingdom. He exists side by side with nature, living in harmony among pheasants, foxes, horses, and birds. He "lordly [has] the trees and leaves / Trail with daisies and barley / Down the rivers of the windfall light." He is captain of this warm, green place—this farm, this childhood. He exists in a place of perpetual summer, where it is always warm and where the sun is "born over and over."

Throughout the poem, something else exists alongside the boy in this warm, green, and golden childhood. This something else is Time, and the passage of Time. It appears in the very first stanza, where it "lets" the boy enjoy his youth. He is "golden" now, valuable, and lives in the "heydays of [Time's] eyes." In the second stanza, Time "let" him "play and be golden in the mercy of his means." In the fourth stanza, the child "awakes" and thinks of the farm as Eden, the "first, spinning place," and then in the fifth, the language points to the fact that time is a factor of the child's life. While running his "heedless ways," he realizes, but does not yet care, that "time allows . . . so few and such morning song / Before the children green and golden / Follow him out of grace." By the sixth stanza, the speaker is no longer a child, but a man who is painfully aware that time has taken him "up to the swallow thronged loft by the shadow of [his] hand." He realizes that, although the sun is "born over and over," the moon is simultaneously "always rising." He knows now that one lives in order to die ("Time held me green and dying") but that one also dies in order to live ("Though I sang in my chains like the sea"). It is a paradox, but one to which we are all subject. The speaker knows this now and is comforted by this knowledge. The final tone of the poem is not one of bitterness at this realization, but rather one of triumph because of it.

Imagery in a Poem

HAVE A NICE DAY?

Monica Libby

Surprisingly, "A Description of Morning" by Jonathan Swift does not describe a dewy, sun-kissed dawn but a grimy, guilt-ridden beginning to another day in a big city. As the people in the poem try to sweep away dirt and guilt, I picture a dark scene in a big city much like one from a novel by

Charles Dickens. Swift does not wish me a "Good Morning" and sees no good in any morning in the city.

There is no freshness in this dawn: The dust rises on the road as a coach approaches. The master's servants try to clean away the dirt around his house as the creditors gather around outside his gate. The water sprinkled on the floor by the careless apprentice takes the place of morning dew. One servant sweeps along the open sewer which runs through the road—even in the morning the air is not fresh.

The half-light which I associate with morning is a dimness used by the servant girl to sneak back to her own bed. After a night of stealing for their jailer, the inmates creep back to their cells. The light is not bright enough to pierce the dirt on the road and so the coach approaches "hardly here and there." There is a darkness in the souls of the master and jailer, and I suspect the schoolboys will use the darkness to slip by the bailiff and skip school.

The sound of birds singing often breaks the silence of the night. The people of this city must provide their own music—a four-part harmony sung by the small coal man, the chimney-sweep, the brick-dust seller, and the creditors. The rhythm is beat out by the sweepers and moppers. Perhaps the servant who "whirled her mop with dextrous airs" serves as their conductor.

Swift's concrete images of common people and things appeal to one's senses of sight, sound, touch and smell. He chooses words with strong connotations to set a dark tone for his poem. We can see and feel the dust swirl over the road as the coach appears to be "hardly here and there." The familiar names of Betty and Moll describe sturdy, uneducated girls working as servants in large houses. In the servant girl, the inmates, the bailiffs, and the schoolboys, I see guilty eyes darting back and forth as they try to hide their misdeeds. My favorite image is that of the sounds of the morning:

> The small-coal man was heard with cadence deep,
> Till drowned in shriller notes of chimney-sweep.
> Duns at his lordship's gate began to meet,
> And Brickdust Moll had screamed through half the street.

It is appropriate that the coal man would have a deep voice—the word "coal" suggests a deep place. The chimney-sweep and brick-dust seller should have shrill voices. The creditors must have deep voices, too—the word "duns" is formed deep in the throat. There are four voices here, suggesting a four-part harmony. The staging of this scene is easy to picture, with each character passing the others on the street as in a dance. But the scene is not a gay one: These are sullen, plodding people intent upon their business. As the servants clean the front of the house, also intent, I can smell the damp dust smell of the sprinkled walk and the pungent odors of the sewer. The feeling of grittiness covers everything in the poem.

Morning should be a time of hope and renewal, but no hope is present here. Swift's view of man and the city is pervaded by dirt and guilt. The master is corrupt and has corrupted the servant-girl. The creditors wait outside his gate for payment they may never receive. The servants and workers try unsuccessfully to keep up with all the dirt created by the city. The apprentice can only pare the dirt from the house and sprinkle the dust to keep it down for a little while. The youth has worn his broom to stumps with sweeping. If the jailer sends the inmates out to steal and the bailiff remains silent, then what has become of justice? Schoolboys go to school to gain the benefit of knowledge accumulated by generations of scholars. Swift sympathizes with their reluctance to go to classes. After all, the great wisdom of the ages has not given us the knowledge with which to cleanse the city of its dirt or human beings of their corruption.

There is a sense of renewal in the poem, but not the kind associated with hope. The coaches keep coming into the city, bringing more people. More people will create more dirt. As the master corrupts the servant, so the upper classes pass their blight down through the class structure. The meetings in the night between the master and the girl may very well produce a child, who will be tainted with their guilt from his very conception. The coal man's wares create work for the chimney-sweep, who creates a need for the wares of the brick-dust seller. The continued thieving of the inmates creates more work for the jailer and the bailiff. (And the jailer creates more work for the inmates.) The schoolboys, who should represent the hopefulness of youth, will only learn to perpetuate the society which educates them.

Such a dark vision of a common morning scene was not what I expected from the title of the poem. After experiencing Swift's pessimism, I checked the spelling of the word "morning" to see if I had made a mistake in reading the word "mourning." In a scene so devoid of hope, mourning seems appropriate. The servant girl might mourn the loss of her virtue. The creditors certainly miss their money. I believe Swift feels most strongly for the schoolboys who, representing the next generation, are doomed to renew the process.

Character and Theme in Fiction

MRS. MAY, THE VICTIM

Don Mason

In Flannery O'Connor's short story "Greenleaf," Mrs. May, a widow with a dairy farm and two unloving sons, struggles against an array of forces that she feels are united against her—the land, the weather, the hired help.

The blessings in her life are, ironically, her enemies, which she fears will make her their victim if she does not control them. In contrast to Mrs. May are the Greenleafs, the tenant family on her farm, who embrace life, its good and its bad, and flourish in body and spirit, living, she feels, off the "fat" of her land. This interaction between the worry-laden existence of Mrs. May and the vigorous lives of the Greenleafs generates the story's tension and culminates in Mrs. May's realization, which comes too late and too force-fully, that life must be accepted with its full range of energies.

The very names of the families Greenleaf and May suggest their quali-ties. The name "Greenleaf" conjures up a burgeoning growth that is aptly associated with this fecund family. The Greenleafs are complete and grow even more complete, like a tree, living naturally and spontaneously. On the other hand, the name "May" suggests the potential or possibility of acting or doing, as well as the spring month. This is appropriate because the May fam-ily has potential but is yet unfulfilled; the sons do not have wives and Mrs. May has no peace of mind, worrying about losing what she has.

It is Mrs. May's belief that she is capable of controlling events in her life, but this is an illusion. We get one small clue to this when, after we see her get up in the middle of the night wearing hair curlers "sprouted neatly over her forehead," we see her the next morning with her grey hair rising "on top like the crest of some disturbed bird." Her hair, in these images, is a natural phenomenon, part of herself she thinks she manages but does not. Just as uncontrollable as her hair is her hired helper of fifteen years, Mr. Greenleaf:

> She had spent fifteen years coping with Mr. Greenleaf and, by now, han-dling him had become second nature with her. His disposition on any particular day was as much a factor in what she could and couldn't do as the weather was . . .

Mrs. May learns to adapt to Mr. Greenleaf's moods, just as she does the weather, but, ironically, she continues to imagine she is "handling" him. Mrs. May is deceiving herself grossly when she thinks she can control either Mr. Greenleaf or her own hair.

In contrast to Mrs. May, Mr. Greenleaf's wife, who is "large and loose" and allows her daughters to dip snuff, renounces control over anything. She is a religious zealot who, in an act symbolizing taking on the sins of the world, collects newspaper clippings about death, destruction, and various heinous actions, buries them, and rolls on the ground over them, crying and asking Jesus to stab "her in the heart." In this supplication, which can be seen as a foreshadowing of Mrs. May's fate, Mrs. Greenleaf gives up control completely and acknowledges her own guilt. Far from feeling any emotion like resentment, she feels linked with the woes and irrational behavior of others and offers herself sacrificially.

When Mrs. May witnesses one of Mrs. Greenleaf's "prayer healings," she is shocked at the impropriety. She feels religious practice should be treated solemnly, even if one does not believe it. The word "Jesus," she thought, "should be kept inside the church building like other words inside the bedroom." Her compartmentalized and sterile view of life extends beyond religion. It is reflected in the arrangement of her dairy farm with rye planted here, clover planted there, cows kept in this pasture, and the bull of the Greenleaf twins kept in its pen, lest it mingle with her herd.

Following its instincts, the bull strays from his pen, an image of the latent power of nature, dark and slowly moving. It roams where it wants, from pasture to pasture, ignoring the boundaries and, in fact, eating the boundaries when it eats the hedges. The bull is difficult to control, even for the Greenleaf twins who own it. But no one seems so keen on controlling it as Mrs. May. In what could be seen as an outlandishly bold action, the bull stands at night just outside her bedroom window, munching the hedgewreath that he is wearing around his horns, as if taunting her or inviting her to join him. It is an image suggestive of Dionysus, a deity associated with the cycle of death and rebirth of vegetation, who appears as a bull in some myths and wears a wreath in others. In Mrs. May's dreams, the bull consumes everything except the Greenleafs; this image, rising from Mrs. May's subconscious, is fitting, because the energies that link the Greenleafs with the Dionysian image of the bull are growth, fertility, and vitality.

According to Mrs. May, the bull, the embodiment of life's energy, must not be allowed to roam at will, either in or out of her dreams. Deciding that the Greenleafs' bull is to be killed and that Mr. Greenleaf is to kill it, she takes satisfaction from the feeling that she is regaining the control she needs in order to avoid being the victim of others. But in the final scene of the story, the bull instinctively attacks the truck Mrs. May is resting on and gores her in the heart. This violent and irrational accident is the kind of expression of life's energy that Mrs. May fears, but it comes, ironically, as a result of her efforts to control it.

The Method of Comic Drama

TROUBLE IS BRUIN

Kathleen Budros

When one reads Anton Chekhov's one-act play *The Bear*, the old joke about the incompatible lovers—he has income and she is "patible"—comes to mind. Although he is a gentleman and a landowner and she is a dimpled, delicate widow, it is at first hard to conceive of two characters less likely to fall in love than Smirnov and Mme. Popov. Their relationship begins with bickering, escalates to vehement arguing, and nearly concludes with a pistol duel. Each character overreacts to the other in such a hilariously exaggerated fashion, however, that the reader soon becomes aware (long before Smirnov and Popov do) that they were meant for each other. Chekhov invites his audience to laugh at the foibles and folly of this man and this woman and their futile efforts to thwart their own instincts for love. He reminds us, humorously, that love prevails. In this case, it conquers Smirnov's misogamy, Popov's devotion to her husband's memory, and their combined vows "never to love again."

Smirnov and Mme. Popov are not looking for love when they meet; quite the opposite. Both of them, for different reasons, have foresworn love. Mme. Popov is reveling in the role of the wronged yet faithful wife and plans to remain in seclusion and mourn her unfaithful husband for the rest of her life (partly so she can confront him with her moral superiority when they meet in the afterlife!). Smirnov, a former ladies' man ("I've jilted twelve women, nine have jilted me"), has not found his relationships with women at all satisfying. In fact, he has concluded that "all women . . . are affected clowns, gossips, hateful, consummate liars . . . , vain, trivial, ruthless," and so on. He has not been in love for five years, and he intends to avoid falling in love ever again.

When Smirnov comes to Mme. Popov to collect money that her husband owed him, he is tired and angry, because he has failed at all of his other collection attempts that day. When she puts him off about it, it is the last straw. We see him getting comically angrier and angrier as he talks to her and himself. He's so angry he feels sick! He's so angry he feels faint! He has goose pimples from being so angry! As for her, she is annoyed that he has intruded upon her solitude. She becomes upset because he is stubborn and rude to her. She feels furious when he asserts that men are more faithful and loving than women, since her experience has been quite the reverse.

In his agitation, Smirnov takes hold of the back of a chair which unexpectedly breaks in his hands. He pays no attention as he is in the middle of a tirade. A bit later the same thing happens again, and his only acknowledgement of it is, "Why the hell do you have such fragile furniture!" The reader can imagine the effect of this comic bit of business during the performance of the play on stage: It serves to accentuate his single-minded anger and the absurd point to which their battling has progressed.

Their verbal exchange reaches a crescendo of livid rage, but there is a sexual tension between them, apparent to the reader/audience, which the characters themselves mistake for animosity. Mme. Popov calls Smirnov "a bear, a monster!" We know he has taken leave of his senses when he responds to this name-calling by challenging her to a duel; gentlemen do not engage in duels with ladies! She is obviously equally demented by this time, for she accepts the challenge—and she does not even know how to fire a pistol: Smirnov must teach her to shoot. As she leaves to get the pistols, Smirnov decides that she is quite a woman: He admires her spunk. During the few moments she is gone, he concludes that he loves her. This sudden change is comical because it hits him like a bolt of lightning. All his fury has turned to love. He is willing to give his life for the woman he was moments before ready to kill; he will fire in the air. When he tells her, she is aghast, disbelieving, confused. She tells him to go—to wait—to go—to stay. The tension is released not with a gun shot but with a kiss.

We laugh at Smirnov and Popov because their emotions are all so exaggerated and overblown for the situation. We also laugh at them because they have failed to live up to their own illusions about themselves and have broken their unshakeable resolutions. We recognize our own weaknesses and prejudices in these people, but we also celebrate the joy of love with them and feel happy that that too is part of human nature.

Appendix 3

Sample Student Research Paper: MLA Format

Johanna Binneweg

Professor Birenbaum

English

April 12, 1996

The Poet as Jeweler: Elizabeth Bishop and Her Art

Elizabeth Bishop is among America's most honored modern poets. Although she published only four slim volumes of poetry during a writing career which spanned the forty years from 1935 until she died in 1979, she won a major literary prize for each one, including the Pulitzer. But Bishop is best remembered as a poet's poet. She is one of a handful of poets that poets themselves study to learn poetry. In the beautiful <u>Voices and Visions</u> video production "Elizabeth Bishop: One Art," a number of contemporary poets and writers talk about her life and work. She is obviously greatly admired. According to poet Mark Strand, "She never wrote a bad poem." Mexican poet Octavio Paz, a close friend, rhapsodizes over her highly-developed artist's eye and sense of color: "She had the eyes of a painter. She had a beautiful ear, but even better than that, eyes." Indeed, looking into the comparatively small body of her work is very like looking into a treasure chest or a jewel box--every poem glistens and sparkles like a priceless, exquisite piece of jewelry. Even the darker poems of her youth and about her youth in Nova Scotia ("The Moose," "The Waiting Room") have a gentle and sensuous sheen to them, like the dark velvet lining of a beautiful jewelry box.

The difficulty in writing about Elizabeth Bishop's poetry lies in having to choose only two poems--they are

all remarkable and lovely. Each is unique, but somehow,
mysteriously, they are all very much alike. Bishop did not
live a spectacular life; she did not go through any radical
emotional changes in her maturing process. She did not
espouse any causes, except a basic respect for all forms of
life, including the outcasts (as in "Pink Dog"); she was
opposed to "political thinking for writers" (Brown 293). She
did not follow any "schools" of art or poetry. She was just a
basic, decent human being who happened to be a poet; writing
poetry was all she ever really wanted to do. According to
poet James Merrill in the "Voices and Visions" video, she
"gave herself no airs." "She had the ability," he says, "to
impersonate an ordinary person." This down-to-earth quality,
springing from a great personal integrity, is not surprising,
considering the facts of her biography.

    The most salient fact of Bishop's life is that she was
an orphan. When she was six months old, her father died. Her
mother, unable to cope with the loss of a beloved spouse,
became permanently insane after several breakdowns and
was institutionalized. Bishop never saw her again. At the
age of three, she was taken from her home in Worcester,
Massachusetts, to live in Grand Village, Nova Scotia, with
her maternal grandparents. These simple facts affected
much of her writing. Being emotionally abandoned by both of
her parents at such an early age established a sense of
detachment and emotional alienation which colors most of her
poems, certainly the earlier ones like "The Weed" and "The
Man-Moth."

Being an orphan set up the grand paradox of her life.
That she loved to travel is highly evident in such poems as
"Questions of Travel" and in the fact that most of her poems
are set in faraway, exotic places (for her day!): Paris,
Mexico, Florida, and Brazil--her home base for most of
her adult life. But travel for her was more than simple
sightseeing; she was seeking a home. This strong feeling of
rootlessness and restlessness comes through in many of her
poems. She becomes, as Helen Vendler notes, "a foreigner
everywhere, and perhaps with everyone. [She acquired] the
optic clarity of the anthropologist, to whom the local gods
are not sacred, the local customs not second nature" (829).

With her grandparents in Nova Scotia she lived on a
farm; thus her formative years were spent close to nature.
Even when she moved to Boston, she would spend summers in
Grand Village for many years. Her strong feelings for and
closeness to animals and the rhythms of nature strongly
influenced her poetry; most of her poems are direct
observations of nature and natural phenomena, notably "The
Moose," "Shorebird," "The Fish," "Electrical Storm," and
"Cold Spring."

When Bishop was eight years old, she was taken by her
sister's family to live in Boston. This was not a happy move
for her, and she succumbed to a series of illnesses which
prevented her from attending school regularly for many years.
She spent these years mostly alone, being privately tutored
and beginning to write poetry. The earliest poem in Bishop's
collected works is "Behind Stowe," which she wrote when she

was sixteen. This is a light fantasy, only twelve short
lines, about an elf who whistles at night under a "windy tree
where glinted little insects' wings . . .", whose singing
"split the sky in two. / The halves fell either side of me /
and I stood straight, bright with moon-rings." Already her
love of nature is evident, as is its renewing effect upon
her. That Bishop flair for drama and surprise (the singing
"splitting" the sky and the "two halves falling") is also
beginning to emerge; and she has her jeweler's eyepiece out,
examining those insects' wings! All is expressed with the
simple, direct diction which would bring her so much praise
later on in her career.

Her poems seem to be of a piece, remarkable in their
interrelatedness, their integrity as a body. But this is not
to say that her poetry is dull. Quite the opposite. The range
of subjects presented in her work and the diversity of forms
she chose to express herself in, are impressive. Although
nature is her oracle and preferred avenue of expression
(natural creatures appear in all of her poems), she also
wrote about city scenes and people. She was fascinated with
the loner, as in "Crusoe in England" and "The House Guest,"
which describes an itinerant seamstress. Her two most widely
anthologized poems "The Fish" and "The Filling Station"
demonstrate the wide variety of life which attracted her
painterly eye. She writes mostly in free verse, her lines
arranged according to the flow of natural relaxed conversation. But her ventures into rhyme are just as smooth
as her free verse. She is a master of off-rhyme. In

"Squatters' Children," she describes the living conditions
of the poorest of the poor in Rio de Janeiro, the off-rhyme
accentuating the precariousness with which their shabby
homes--and lives--cling to the mountainsides. Bishop also
successfully used a number of fixed poetic forms: the
villanelle ("One Art"), the ballad ("The Burglar of
Babylon"), and the sestina ("Sestina").

   The poets who influenced her the most are, by her own
admission, the metaphysicals. She especially admired George
Herbert for his "absolute naturalness of tone" (Brown 294).
According to Thomas J. Travisano in his recent book Elizabeth
Bishop: Her Artistic Development:

>   Bishop's lifelong affinity with Herbert was a natural
>   one. She shared with him a sense of the emblematic
>   significance of common things; for either poet, a
>   crumb, a flower, or a church window had a message
>   that would yield itself only to humble observation
>   and disciplined meditation. Meditation must be
>   disciplined to sort out nature's inherently
>   paradoxical implications. Despite their devotion to
>   paradox, each favored a clear, direct style--the
>   sense of the poet speaking. Each was, in this way, a
>   democrat of literature. (33)

Helen Vendler notes in her article that, "as any quotation
from Bishop will suggest, one of her formal aims was to write
in monosyllables for a substantial amount of the time . . .
imitating Herbert's great success in this mode" (830).

On the basis of the jewel-box metaphor, I have selected
from the body of Bishop's work two lovely "brooches," each of
which contains an opal, a stone noted for its soft, creamy
iridescence. In the first one, the opal is set off by flat
black onyx and glistening black jet; in the second, the opal
is set in silver and surrounded by beautiful, soft, light
gemstones: amethyst, aquamarine, pearls. These poems, though
quite similar in their dramatic use of color, are quite
different in tone, form, and setting.

The first "brooch," or poem, is "The Man-Moth," a dark,
surrealistic fantasy. This is one of Bishop's first major
poems, written while she was living in New York City right
after graduation from Vassar, when she was very much
interested in surrealism. This poem, one of a group of poems
published in Trial Balances with an introduction by her
friend and mentor Marianne Moore, won her instant critical
acclaim. It is complicated and surrealistic--a dream/fable
based on life in the Big City. Because of its central
character, a "Man-Moth," and its theme of thwarted
metamorphosis, Bishop was compared to Kafka; because of its
focus on the city and the subway as dehumanizing forces of
the modern world, Bishop was placed in the same school as
T. S. Eliot.

In six well-ordered stanzas, Bishop creates a world
which is both prison and womb--perhaps "cocoon" is a better
word. In this suffocating world, the Man-Moth "emerges from
an opening under the edge of . . . the sidewalk and nervously
begins to scale the faces of the buildings." In the next

line, Bishop surprises us, turning our familiar world on its
edge: the Man-Moth "thinks the moon is a small hole at the top
of the sky. . . ." The moon--that benign, giant opal set so
securely in the firmament of our imaginations--becomes,
through a flick of perceptivity, a hole, an escape route out
of the dull, dark, unwholesome cocoon of Bishop's devising.
Very weird, but brilliant.

   Although the poem is set in the dark, at night, in
the city, the tone is not dark or threatening. The narrator
tells the story in a natural conversational tone, as if she
were speaking of the most normal events; she does not
sensationalize. Both characters, man and the Man-Moth, are
treated with respect. Man is ordinary, pragmatic; he has
come to terms with the city; he perceives no magic in the
moonlight, he does not dream of escape, as does the Man-Moth:
"Man, standing below him, has no . . . illusions." But the
poet does not scold man for his resignation and indifference;
she treats him with a quiet and deliberate compassion. She
merely observes: "He does not see the moon; he observes only
her vast properties, / feeling the queer light on his hands,
neither warm nor cold. . . ."

   After bathing the first stanza in "battered moonlight,"
she introduces the Man-Moth as a creature driven to seek the
light: "He trembles, but must investigate as high as he can
climb / . . . what the Man-Moth fears most he must do. . . ."
One critic refers to "The Man-Moth" as a "despairing, dead-
end poem of the night" (Mills 93), but perhaps the focus here
is only on the Man-Moth's failures to escape, on his being

ill-suited to his environment ("he always seats himself
facing the wrong way" on the subway train). It is important
to the understanding of Bishop's work to consider the possibility that he also seeks communion or would at least be
happy if someone drew him out, asked for communion. Viewed
in this light, the last stanza is hopeful, with its promise
of the gift of "his only possession . . . a tear . . . cool
as from underground springs and pure enough to drink"--for
the person patient and attentive enough to wait for it.

The early critics of Bishop's work saw "The Man-Moth" as
highly symbolic--a fable in which the Man-Moth stands for the
artist seeking his place in society. Contemporary critics,
more in tune with Jungian psychology, view this dark poem as
representing the psychic journey--the Man-Moth is the soul
longing to emerge from the "womb" of the subconscious. Both
interpretations have merit; neither excludes the other,
demonstrating what Bishop felt about the impact of her work.
She deliberately left the theses of her poems unstated
because she felt that the reader must share the process of
observation and discovery (Travisano 13).

Bishop uses a few simple devices of sound to augment
the conversational flow of words in this poem. Soft, liquid
sounds predominate: m's, n's, l's and r's, plus soft
vowel sounds--lots of "oo"'s sustain the air of mystery,
while "s" sounds remind us of the swishing of the subway
trains far below. The words just roll along, almost
hypnotically. Everything is soft, like moonlight, smooth
like the highly polished surface of the opals.

In "The Man-Moth" the subject matter is fantasy, the
theme one of inner struggle, of an emotional journey towards
the light. The jewel--the opal--is the moon, set against the
darkness, imparting its glow to a mythic world starving for
light. In the poem "Sandpiper," Bishop the jeweler sets her
opal not against the other precious stones, but in among
them, to supplement the glow of the others. The setting of
"Sandpiper" is the real world, the natural world. In this
simple set of five quatrains, Bishop gives us a shore bird's
view of its world so accurately, so minutely, that we are
there. In his short essay "On Elizabeth Bishop," Frank Bidart
says: "The world in Miss Bishop's work seems almost to demand
that someone observe, describe, bear it; the great triumph in
her descriptions . . . is the drama of perception lying
beneath them and enacted by them, her sense of the . . .
pleasures of such observing" (214).

In this simple descriptive poem, everything is light and
bright and fresh and clear, like the ocean water itself and
indeed everything about the ocean. The form of the poem is
itself a metaphor for the action of the ocean waves. The
lines end with alternating rhymes and alternately rising and
falling syllables which suggest the crashing and receding of
the surf. The meter is irregular, varied to suggest the play
of the wavelets and foam upon the shore. "Sandpiper" appeals
directly to the senses. The reader can hear the ocean ("The
roaring alongside"; "The beach hisses like fat"), can feel
its weight and power (". . . every so often the world is
bound to shake"). But mostly we can see it, opalescent,

sometimes in a mist, sometimes as a "sheet of water." Unlike
the darkness of "The Man-Moth," the mood in this poem is
governed by shimmering light and vast open spaces, not
darkness and enclosure.

Both of these poems are good examples of what has come
over the years to be known as "the Bishop style"--a "new sort
of lyric . . . a clarity of expression, simplicity of effect,
and naiveté of tone while making the matter of her poetry the
opacity and inexplicability of being" (Vendler 838). Her
poems are deceptive. On the surface they are simple and
clear. But they resist easy explication; the themes are
multilayered.

In "Sandpiper" we feel the same compassion for the
"main character" as we feel for the Man-Moth and his blind
instincts, which challenge him to constantly try--and fail--
to escape his enclosure. For the "finical, awkward" sandpiper, the challenge is to live in harmony with all that
unruly water--a tall order for such a tiny creature. We
sense the urgency with which he runs to and fro, "looking
for something, something, something . . . in a state of
controlled panic." (In another witty fillip of perceptivity,
Bishop compares this harried little creature to "a student of
Blake.") The sandpiper is the symbol of modern man, who has
forsaken his soul (the ocean) and consequently is condemned
to a life focused entirely on the moment, on the tiny details
of day-to-day existence. Oddly, the sandpiper does not look
for food; as for modern man, food is a "given"--abundantly
supplied and readily obtainable. Instead, he seems

preoccupied with delighting and entertaining himself--with those beautiful grains of sand, those marvelous "sheets" of water--while frantically side-stepping the intrusions and demands of the ocean. Like modern man, this frail creature never quite succeeds in making himself happy; everything is constantly shifting beneath his feet and slipping away.

Bishop wisely does not draw any conclusions about the sandpiper or the Man-Moth; understatement is one of the hallmarks of her work. She simply describes their worlds-- minutely and intimately. Magnifying glass in hand and with her jeweler's eye, she shows us the imaginary beauty in the very grains of sand in the last two lines of "Sandpiper": "The millions of grains of sand are black, white, tan, and gray, / mixed with quartz grains, rose, and amethyst." Elizabeth Bishop is best known for these vivid visual images and for responding with wit and gentle irony to some of the problems of contemporary life--alienation, rootlessness, and emotional loss. In every poem, she captures some slice of the world and, with her "painterly eye" and jeweler's touch, fashions it into a highly polished and unique creation. "The Man-Moth" and "Sandpiper" are only two exquisite examples of her jeweler's art. A whole treasure trove awaits the seeker of more.

Works Cited

Bidart, Frank. "On Elizabeth Bishop." World Literature Today
    I (1977). Rpt. in Elizabeth Bishop and Her Art. Ed.
    Lloyd Schwartz and Sybil P. Estess. Ann Arbor: U of
    Michigan P, 1983. 214-15.

Brown, Ashley. "Interview with Elizabeth Bishop." Shenandoah
    17 (1966). Rpt. in Elizabeth Bishop and Her Art. Ed.
    Lloyd Schwartz and Sybil P. Estess. Ann Arbor: U of
    Michigan P, 1983. 289-302.

"Elizabeth Bishop: One Art." Voices and Visions.
    Videocassette. PBS.

Mills, Ralph J., Jr. Cry of the Human. Urbana: U of Illinois
    P, 1975. PBS 19XX.

Travisano, Thomas J. Elizabeth Bishop: Her Artistic
    Development. Charlottesville: UP of Virginia, 1988.

Vendler, Helen. "The Poems of Elizabeth Bishop." Critical
    Inquiry 13 (1987): 825-38.

TEXT CREDITS

W. H. AUDEN, "Lullaby," from *Collected Poems* by W. H. Auden. Copyright © 1940 and renewed 1968 by W. H. Auden. Reprinted by permission of Random House, Inc.

ROBERT FROST, "The Silken Tent" and "Acquainted With The Night" from *The Poetry of Robert Frost*, edited by Edward Connery Lathem. "The Silken Tent": Copyright © 1942 by Robert Frost. Copyright © 1970 by Lesley Frost Ballantine. Copyright © 1969 by Henry Holt and Co., Inc. "Acquainted With the Night": Copyright © 1956 Robert Frost © 1928, 1969 Henry Holt and Co., Inc. Reprinted by permission of Henry Holt and Co., Inc.

LANGSTON HUGHES, "Children's Rhymes," from *Collected Poems* by Langston Hughes. Copyright © 1994 by the Estate of Langston Hughes. Reprinted by permission of Alfred A. Knopf, Inc.

OKITO JUNKO, "My Mother's Breast" by Okito Junko appeared in *There Are Two Lives: Poems by Children of Japan*, edited by Richard Lewis and translated by Haruna Kimura. Copyright © 1970 by Richard Lewis and Haruna Kimura.

DONALD JUSTICE, "Counting the Mad" from *Summer Anniversaries*. Copyright © 1981 by Donald Justice, Wesleyan University Press. Reprinted by permission of University Press of New England.

GRACE PALEY, "Debts" from *Enormous Changes At The Last Minute* by Grace Paley. Copyright © 1974 by Grace Paley. Reprinted by permission of Farrar, Straus & Giroux, Inc.

JOHN CROWE RANSOM, "Bells for John Whiteside's Daughter," from *Selected Poems* by John Crowe Ransom. Copyright © 1991 by John Crowe Ransom. Reprinted by permission of Random House, Inc.

LOU SALOME, "Nietzsche," translated by Siegfried Mandel, Redding Ridge, CT: Black Swan Books, 1988, pp. 77ff. Reprinted by permission.

WILLIAM CARLOS WILLIAMS, "This is Just to Say" by William Carlos Williams, from *Collected Poems: 1909–1939*, Volume I. Copyright © 1938 by New Directions Corporation. Reprinted by permission of New Directions Publishing Corporation.

INDEX